Metaphysical Media

Metaphysical Media

The Occult
Experience in
Popular Culture

Emily D. Edwards

Southern Illinois University Press / *Carbondale*

Copyright © 2005 by the Board of Trustees,
Southern Illinois University
All rights reserved
Printed in the United States of America
08 07 06 05   4 3 2 1

Library of Congress Cataloging-in-Publication Data
Edwards, Emily D.
Metaphysical media : the occult experience in
popular culture / Emily D. Edwards.
     p. cm.
Includes filmographies.
Includes bibliographical references and index.
1. Occultism in motion pictures. 2. Occultism on tele-
vision.
     I. Title.
PN1995.9.O28E38 2005
791.43'67—dc22
ISBN 0-8093-2647-7 (cloth : alk. paper)
ISBN 0-8093-2648-5 (pbk. : alk. paper)   2005005645

01705

Contents

List of Illustrations vii
Preface ix
Acknowledgments xiii

Part One: Magic in the Medium

1. Possessed and Dispossessed by Mass Media 3
2. Out of Body
   Transmission and Transcendence Through Popular Culture 18
3. Creating Worlds
   The Cult Value of Media Production 48

Part Two: Magic in the Message

4. Evil, Enchanting, Divine, and Ecstatic
   A Century of Witches in Moving Images 73
   Filmography
   A Century of Witches in Film and Television 131
5. The Divine Animal
   Evolution and Atavism in Popular Media 139
   Filmography
   Atavistic Media 162
6. The Recycled Soul
   What Movies and Television Tell Us about Reincarnation 165
   Filmography
   Recycled Souls 189

Conclusion: Marketing the Metaphysical 195

Notes 217
Bibliography 231
Index 241

Illustrations

Figures

1.1. Linda Blair in *The Exorcist* 4
1.2. Harry Potter merchandise 12
2.1. Television on a neopagan altar 25
3.1. Preparing to record room tone 62
3.2. Cinematographer Michael Corbett 63
4.1. Historical witch in *Häxan* 84
4.2. Historical witch in *Witchfinder General* 91
4.3. Dubious witch in *The Seventh Seal* 93
4.4. Satanic witch in *Rosemary's Baby* 96
4.5. Fairy-tale witch in *The Wizard of Oz* 103
4.6. Shamanic witch in *Medea* 106
4.7. Ingenue witches in *The Craft* 116
4.8. Enchantress in *She* 118
4.9. New Age witch in the television series *Farscape* 123
5.1. Animals turned into human beings in *The Island of
      Dr. Moreau* 147
6.1. American housewife under hypnotic regression in
      The Search for Bridey Murphy 175
7.1. Ghost walk brochures 199
7.2. Cemetery in Charleston, South Carolina 202
7.3. Modern witch paraphernalia 206

Tables

4.1. Number of Films and Television Programs
      Containing Witch Characters 81
4.2. Witch Films Categorized by Type 83

Preface

$\mathcal{M}$etaphysics is that discipline of philosophy that deals with things that cannot be explained by our senses; this includes ontology, the science of being, and cosmology, the science of the fundamental causes and processes in things. For some, metaphysics is the science of the soul; for others, it is the science of the conditions of knowledge. In a liberal sense, metaphysics is all of the more profound philosophical disciplines.

Critics of popular media will be quick to argue that film and television are hardly deeply profound or philosophical. Yet, popular media provide audiences with an array of explanations for the human condition in an unsystematic study of being that assuredly contributes to our understanding of human nature and the nature of our reality. This discourse about our "being" comes delivered through technologies that expand human senses beyond their biological limits, providing experiences that are transpersonal. Instead of identifying with their own bodies and egos, audiences participating in the mediated experience might feel omniscient. Media viewing places audiences out of the usual state of consciousness, allowing us to vicariously visit distant places and become sympathetically involved in the lives of people we cannot personally know. There are aspects of popular media that seem innately metaphysical, implying that our physical existence is not the only or most valid reality. The ability to engage in mediated experience is a remarkable shift in human evolutionary development, but it has become so commonplace in contemporary American life that we no longer consider media use as intense, personal phenomena requiring unusual conditions of consciousness. For Americans, the media experience has become unremarkable. Yet, there is no denying the excitement many American audiences still find in having vicarious adventures through shadowy legends, particularly those about the supernatural that become replayed, altered, and extended by our media culture.

Occult traditions are that legacy of supernatural beliefs, spurned rituals, and old stories disparaged by many Americans as silly or superstitious. The occult encompasses a faith in the paranormal and the idea that supernatural forces can be manipulated by trained or chosen practitioners in the occult arts. The Western heritage of reason regards these occult traditions as sinister, amusing, or neurotic. Those who believe in them too deeply may be considered weird, disturbed, or dangerous. Yet, paranormal belief is one category of human behavior that is tyrannically universal. Cultural anthropologists have not discovered any culture where there is not a system of paranormal belief that embellishes the reality of the human condition. Polls and surveys reveal that contemporary belief in the paranormal remains substantial. In *Wings of Illusion*, John Schumaker asserts that paranormal belief

> is so obvious and all-pervasive that it is hard to see. It shows itself everywhere, which makes it as difficult to grasp as if it were to be seen nowhere at all. It is the canvas against which all other facets of human consciousness and human endeavor are painted. (5)

Paranormal belief is a ubiquitous secret, and our conceptions of it haunt popular media with diligence.

There is some dispute about the relationships among paranormal belief, occult ritual, and orthodox religious practice. Some people recognize no real distinction between religious and occult positions; both share the assumption that our physical reality is not the limit of our existence. However, others do see a distinction. For example, Sparks's survey could not find substantial consistency between items defined as paranormal belief and those defined as religious belief ("Relationship"). One prime distinction between occult belief and orthodox religion may be that the orthodox will be supported or endorsed by mainstream culture, while the occult will not. Another prime distinction concerns the difference between supplication and application: the orthodox believer prays to the supernatural, the occult practitioner attempts to manipulate it.

Occult traditions are supposed to be that arcane, concealed, carefully hidden knowledge about the supernatural possessed by the wizard or shaman and revealed only to the acolyte in training. Occult beliefs and practices, though they are presumed to be spurned and esoteric, are exposed through popular culture. Popular art has always had a close association with both paranormal and religious beliefs; sometimes in illustration of an ideology, sometimes in ridicule of it, sometimes as invocation itself. There is no doubt that popular culture—specifically moving-image media—perpetuates, criticizes, and negotiates occult traditions. Occult legacies have an oral heritage that makes them easily adaptable to moving-image media, where they are persistent denizens. Sandwiched between commercial messages, promotions, political announcements, jests, and tragedies—perhaps embedded in the very celluloid or bare silicon of electronic technologies—are the sometimes contradictory frameworks of occult beliefs. There is an energy in seemingly irrational occult themes, which supply popular media with an endless transfer of patterns from audience to media and back again.

My dominant concern in this book is with the function of popular media—particularly film and television—in helping us to achieve, maintain, or contradict that magical thinking that is the heritage of occult belief. This book is an exploration of what media treatment of supernatural subjects reveals about the obstinacy and ubiquity of the occult in popular culture. The focus of my interest is the relationship of media to magical thinking, that legacy of occult belief that allows people to deny the physical limits of human existence even when that denial may be counterproductive to modern life. Magical thinking is related to the way people look for the causes of events, how they find and categorize patterns. Recognized patterns can reveal the source of either fact or superstition, but magical thinking prefers miraculous explanations for events over physical ones. Through magical thinking, patterns and events become invested with spiritual certainty and existential purpose.

This book is divided into two parts. The first part, "Magic in the Medium," examines what might be considered the "supernatural experience" of media use and the "cult value" of media as art. It investigates how media technologies take us beyond physical limitations and explores ideas about the effects of such "metaphysical" experience. I also consider the "wizardry" associated with the creation of media narratives and the process of production, which perhaps retains some of the cult value of the art once produced to persuade or please a god.

Part two of this book, "Magic in the Message," examines the media discourse about topics such as magic and witchcraft, atavism and the divine animal, reincarnation and the afterlife. Chapter 4 makes an attempt to be as comprehensive as possible in looking at media portraits of witches, developing a census of films and television programs with themes of witchcraft that have been distributed in the United States, themes that may be associated with the occult themes of subsequent chapters. The filmographies at the end of chapters 4, 5, and 6 are selective rather than comprehensive in order to save space in this book. The listed items are ones that have been cited or that may be of special interest to readers.

Ideally, interpretative research doesn't rely on a single type of data but takes advantage of triangulation, "bringing more than one source of data to bear" on a question (Marshall and Rossman 146). The research methods I use are largely interpretative and historical, surveying and synthesizing an abundance of material. However, some chapters also include material drawn from participant observation and in-depth interviews as well as interviews completed for some of the documentary or narrative films I have produced. Regardless of methodology, my focus is always on moving-image media as devices that help to structure our understanding of supernatural worlds as well as provide us vicarious experiences of the worlds we all create.

Acknowledgments

I owe a superb debt to those who helped me with the research for this book, especially my undergraduate research assistant, John Lay, and the many students who watched and coded hundreds of hours of film and television programs. Thanks also to the University of North Carolina at Greensboro and the semester's research leave that allowed me time to put the manuscript together. I also need to acknowledge the many media artists who shared with me their insights regarding media production and the several Wiccans and wise women who allowed me to nose around and ask questions. Finally, thanks to my husband, Doug Mokaren, and my daughter, Marissa Mokaren, who put up with this "bizarre topic" over the course of several years.

Part One

Magic in the Medium

Possessed and Dispossessed by Mass Media

The world is all the richer for having a devil in it, so long as we keep our foot
upon his neck.
—William James, *The Varieties of Religious Experience* (1902)

The Devil in the Bullet

O ccult traditions are the heritage of enigmatic beliefs, the knowledge
and practices regarded as irrational and bizarre by mainstream society and largely discarded by it. Belief in demon possession is an example. Widespread until the end of the sixteenth century, it was no longer
acceptable by the twentieth century to suppose that a person's soul could
be suppressed or evicted from his or her body, allowing a discarnate
entity, spirit, or "devil" to take up residence. In 1972, a short while before
the release of the film *The Exorcist*, the Roman Catholic Church had abolished the practice of ousting a possessing devil. It had become an occult
practice. Yet, the following year, exorcism was no longer an esoteric and
forgotten ritual because of its display in a widely popular film. When *The
Exorcist* opened to packed cinemas in 1973, secret rituals that had been
known only to a few select members of the clergy and then abolished were
suddenly part of the popular vernacular. Interest in the occult practice
of exorcism grew. (See fig. 1.1.)

By 1999, the United Press International reported that the Vatican had
developed new guidelines for the process of exorcism, the first update of
the ritual since 1614. By the turn of the twenty-first century, it appeared that
the number of exorcism rituals were increasing, with hundreds of Protes-
tant evangelical rites occurring in the United States. Fordham University
sociologist Michael Cuneo believes popular books and movies provided
models for possession, which resulted in revising the once obscure oc-
cupation of the exorcist. Addictions, compulsions, and depressions were
no longer considered the psychological problems of modern times but

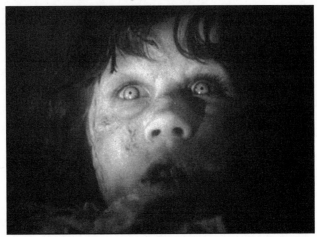

Fig. 1.1. Linda Blair as the demon-possessed Regan in *The Exorcist* (1973). Warner Brothers. Photo courtesy of Photofest.

evidence of demon possession from earlier ones. The modern exorcism became a recovery program with a supernatural bent. Attending these exorcisms as part of his research, Cuneo even suggested that for some cases, the process of exorcism was therapeutically useful.

In 1973, I was working for a small NBC affiliate in Alabama when I began hearing about the odd effects of the motion picture *The Exorcist*. Some audience members watching the film vomited, left the theatre terrorized, or became convinced that they were possessed by demons. Although such effects were rare, occurring to only a handful of the many people that viewed the popular film, they were astonishing enough to become the topic of American news reports and for the British Board of Film Classification to ban the movie.[1] I was aware of no one in my community who suffered such an extreme effect of watching the film, yet its influence on some audience members in other communities became a featured news item on my station's local newscast. *The Exorcist* renewed old concerns about improper media influence.[2] Some parents, teacher groups, and concerned citizens believed that if a film produced hysteria in one audience member, it must—to some degree—have a similar effect on us all. This theory of direct media influence on a mass society is a vintage, much criticized, and yet enduring concept about the effects of media on audiences. The notion of direct media effects can be compared to possession itself. The "devil" media eject or suppress the audience's "mind," replacing it with the whims and will of those forces behind the media to which the possessed public responds helplessly. The theory proposes that mediated content triggers an immediate, predictable, and uniform response on defenseless people. Though the concerns underlying the concept of direct media influence are more often about the viability of democracy and the media's responsibility to ensure an informed electorate, or about whether media violence directly impacts social violence, there is a lesser but parallel worry for the healthy psyches of a media-influenced population. The anxiety about audience reaction to *The Exorcist* in 1973 was based on parallel assumptions about the direct impact of mediated messages.

Because human beings are biologically similar, the reasoning goes, we must be emotionally similar as well. The idea of direct media effects assumes that there is very little negotiation or discussion among audiences about the messages in popular culture. The social changes during the last century detached some people from traditional ties to church and family, a type of isolation that several critics believe left young people particularly vulnerable to media influence. This perceived vulnerability promoted a general discussion about the direct influence of popular media on socialization and a coincident discussion about the influence of media stories like *The Exorcist* on the religious imagination. When individuals are separated from one another, confused about their role or purpose in life, this theory suggests, dominant and authoritative media messages can easily induce audiences' beliefs and inspire audiences' behavior.[3]

When it opened in 1973, *The Exorcist* shocked some audiences with its sensory onslaught of avant-garde imagery. Author and producer of the film William Peter Blatty intended *The Exorcist* to be an uplifting work, reassuring a skeptical modern public about the absolute existence of God by rendering a portrait of the Devil (Kermode, "Exorcist" 43).[4] Never mind that the movie's message ultimately restated a fundamentalist religious position, some religious groups condemned *The Exorcist* and similar movies as vectors of spiritual pollution. As Drury observes of the period, the motto of those who denounced *The Exorcist* appeared to be "mention the devil and he will appear" (97). With their criticisms based on the assumptions of direct media influence, those who denounced the film for glorifying the Devil were themselves proof that audiences actively interpret and form opinions about the meaning and impact of a movie, at times without even watching it. Plenty of people did watch *The Exorcist*, however, waiting in long lines for tickets. This became another concern for critics, because the "bullet theory," or concept of direct media effects, also gauges media success by numerical superiority: the bigger the audience, the larger the influence. A successful movie must have a large box office draw. This was certainly true of *The Exorcist*, which brought in unprecedented crowds with its combination of violence, magic, and nasty visuals. The film placed "cheap thrills in the context of serious work," producing an enduring cultural image of a possessed preteen vomiting in a priest's face (Paul 84). The movie received ten Academy Award nominations following the original 1973 release and won an Oscar for best adapted screenplay. The undeniable critical and economic success of *The Exorcist* inspired sequels, books, television programs, additional movies with related themes, and a twenty-fifth anniversary re-release.[5] Clearly, the movie touched a responsive nerve in audiences and a corresponding fiscal nerve in producers.

Noticing the popularity of this film, critics who longed for a more paternalistic media system reiterated the dilemma of our capitalistic scheme: the economically successful media product might not be socially healthy for most or even aesthetically bearable for others. The commercial structure of the American media system means an audience can choose what it finds interesting and affordable. Rather than watch programs a government committee selects for the public good (or because of the influence of a lobby), audiences consume what they like. The result, say critics, is a gluttonous public feeding on the "mind candy" of a frenzied cultural diet rather than reasoned consumption of balanced and enriching fare. Critics believed impressionable young children and teens, just beginning to form their ideas about the world and how it works, were particularly vulnerable to disturbing films like *The Exorcist*. Other popular horror movies of the era helped to reprise discussion similar to the great comic-book scare of the late 1940s and early 1950s, in which fear of a government-controlled media contended with the fear of media-warped children (Muhlen; Thrasher; Wertham; Warshow).

Though the concept of direct media influence has fallen out of favor with most scholars, the outmoded concept continues to fuel the anxiety of ordinary people, particularly as it relates to popular media and stories about the occult. Observers remain troubled that popular culture, especially movies and television, are the major spiritual force and ethical guide in children's lives (Rust and Wagner).

In addition to concern about the stories in popular media, some anxieties centered on media technologies themselves as the primary risk. This concern is that not only are the messages dangerous but the technology that transmits them is itself a powerful, dark force that can overtake individuals. Technology, like tarot cards and Ouija boards, becomes the very instrument that lets the Devil in.[6] Like the "magic bullet" theory, which asserts a direct link between media and their effect on audiences, the idea of media as evil presents human beings as defenseless in the path of powerful technology. In this instance, the "bullet" is not simply a mediated message but the system that delivers it. Some have taken the idea of technology as evil to the extreme. For example, one story in online version of the supermarket tabloid *Weekly World News* reported the fears of a Savannah clergyman who believed the personal computer is yet another device through which Lucifer and his minions can poison human souls. According to this thinking, the more powerful computers become, the more dangerous they are to the spiritual well-being of ordinary people who use them. Reverend Jim Peasboro suggested that any PC built after 1985 has the storage capacity to accommodate evil intelligence and disclosed cases from his own congregation where people "became in touch with a dark force whenever they used their computers. . . . One woman wept as she confessed to me, 'I feel when I'm on the computer as if someone else or something else just takes over'" ("Is Your Computer"). The idea here is clearly a fear of being "directly possessed" through media technology. Upon the initial release of *The Exorcist*, the Reverend Billy Graham suggested ominously that there was a dark power in the film that went beyond its story, hinting that the spirit of the Devil resides within the celluloid. Blatty responded to Graham's alarm that the film had uncanny power: "There is a power to move you and have a disturbing effect on the viewer, which is greater than the sum of its parts. It's enormous and mysterious but, my God, it's not the power of evil."[7]

The Occult and the Obstinate Audience

In contradiction to the idea of direct media influence is a concept of audience members as complex negotiators between media and effects. Media scholars first noticed a limited media influence as it concerned the effect of radio and newspaper endorsements on voting behavior. But there were other areas in which media influence was also less powerful than might be presumed. Bishop Fulton J. Sheen's prime-time preaching during the 1950s and 1960s might be considered successful by some accounts but didn't convert all viewers. The Reverend Robert Schuller's ministry, begun in 1955 in a drive-in movie theater, would discover its congregation through the airwaves and become a highly rated religious program by 1998. Yet even Reverend Schuller's charismatic television presence on the *Hour of Power* (1955–) doesn't persuade every audience member to accept his message.[8] Advertisers had realized long ago that not every viewing of a commercial resulted in a purchase. The observation that many media attempts to persuade audiences often fail caused scholars to reconsider the notion of the media's ability to have a direct impact on a mass society.

Many scholars will agree that media communication is more complicated than a simple linear model would suggest. An unambiguous message rarely rolls effortlessly and unabated from sender to receiver, where it gets the intended response. Media writers and producers may be oblivious to the latent messages they send. Some messages may be incomplete or obtuse. Audiences may be unaware of the messages they've received or miss their intent altogether. The narratives of mass consumption, the stories told through movies and television, are the result of many layers of the communication process: human involvement, human response, understanding, and misunderstanding. Confusion, misinterpretation, and negotiation are possible at every juncture. Audiences may be as active and inventive as media writers and producers in the process of creating meaning for media messages. For example, Callie Khouri, screenwriter for the popular film *Thelma and Louise* (1991), observes that audiences don't always react to a movie in the expected way. She was troubled by the response of an audience to a scene in her movie where the character Louise, a world-weary waitress, shoots and kills a man who only moments before had attempted to force himself on her friend. "When I first viewed my own movie with an audience and the shooting occurred, the audience cheered," Khouri explained,

> and I was stunned because I had expected—hoped for—a completely different reaction from the audience—[one] of realization that this character had just sealed her fate in a very horrible way, but instead they burst into applause. I was terrified. I realized I can't control how my work is perceived—that people bring to it what it is they come from.[9]

Even when audiences fully understand the communication intentions behind a media message, they may still refuse to accept, believe, endorse, or act upon it. If the process of watching film or television is a creative one, some audiences may be creating alternate scenarios from the images they see, "writing" entirely new scripts in their imaginations. Raymond Bauer noticed the many defeats of media attempts at persuasion and referred to this phenomenon as "the obstinate audience." It seems that audience members do indeed filter the meanings of messages through a shield of personal experiences and beliefs. Some audience members may belong to groups with opinion leaders or have influential friends who can alter the intended effects of mass media. The idea of an obstinate audience denies the notion that media influence is as immediate and as verbatim as a writer or producer might intend. This newer concept suggested that there are many variables involved in audiences' responses to what they hear and see. Audiences may selectively edit, reinvent, or mentally argue with media messages. They may choose to turn away from them altogether, never exposing themselves to the messages. This was a reassuring concept. If the audience is obstinate, not only is democracy safer, but critics need not be so concerned about the direct influence of media violence or other potentially harmful messages. Similarly, if families and friends help audience members interpret and filter what they see, occult material disbursed through popular media should be much less of a threat. Contemporary audiences more savvy about the methods of media production may have an additional "filter" allowing them to be less persuaded by media contents. The "bad aesthetic" film is a case in point. Low-budget horror movies originally produced with the intention to terrify often have the opposite effect, empowering adolescents to laugh at what was meant to be scary. Clumsy film and television treatments of occult themes establish a following among audiences who enjoyed feeling superior to both the film's poor aesthetic as well as its occult message. Some within these audiences have indeed become "aesthetic skeptics," unwilling to suspend disbelief even for mainstream films because they like the position of domination over the media experience that the critical outsider enjoys.

Yet, American media critics were still concerned. Lonely young people, curious about the taboo, seeking out media messages about magic and the supernatural, might still be vulnerable audiences. Believing that many audience members are without strong interpersonal filters and not stubborn enough to resist compelling media narratives, some feared the obstinacy of a media system that distorts religious people, making the heretics the heroes (Gahr). Others noticed the tendency for Hollywood to tell stories predicated on the "reality" of the supernatural (Hess), even within a "culture of disbelief" (Carter).

The Uses and Gratifications for Occult Narrative

Some people began to see the expansion of cable and alternative media in the 1970s and 1980s as a healthy indication that a stronger diversity of messages and audience options would mean a less powerful, more diluted media influence. Though the questions of why audiences make the choices in media content that they do and how audiences are gratified by those choices had been studied earlier, the 1970s and 1980s brought new interest in the ways audiences select and employ media. This "uses and gratifi-cations" approach argues that audiences actively select media content to satisfy their own needs, an essential factor determining media effects (Palmgreen, Wenner, and Rosengren). Uses and gratifications research examined relationships between individual audience members' person-ality traits and media choices. Studies found that audiences experienc-ing social or psychological problems used media to resolve those prob-lems. Often the research was concerned with social isolation and the ways lonely individuals found gratification in media use. The research sug-gested that an audience member's psychological disposition and social circumstances influence habits of media use. These factors, along with judgments about past media experience, shape expectations about me-dia content, which continue to determine an audience member's choices (Rubin). For example, curiosity about the taboo, a need for magic and ritual, a quest for meaning in a disposable culture, or simple boredom might be factors leading audiences to media messages about the occult and the supernatural. Because occult themes are more often the depart-ment of popular culture than high culture and are rejected by authori-tative critics, adolescent audiences may consider these taboo topics more intriguing and glamorous. Occult themes are not frequent topics of dis-cussion among parents, teachers, and their charges. With no appointed intermediaries to guide young audiences' understanding of what they consume, many critics regard popular culture as not only aesthetically inferior and escapist but dangerous.

Even with an expanding number of media outlets, more variety of media content, and audiences that might be considered more active con-sumers, critics held out even less hope for "highbrow" or superior content as the 1980s progressed, expecting a continuing deterioration of aesthetic tastes and cultural standards as programmers looked to schedule what-ever content was cheapest and appealed to the largest audience (Winston 480). Though most of the concern about media influence concentrated on the effects of media violence and the atrophy of cultural ideals, a par-allel concern pondered the effects of media on faith and the spiritual life of audiences. Some critics worried that media or "electronic churches" were replacing traditional worship. Others believed more channels might lead to wider exposure for cults. Relaxed, rested, and comfortable in front of their home televisions, individuals might be more receptive to cult mes-sages than they would be if accosted on the street by a smiling cult mem-ber (Dobson). Most vigorously criticized on its debut in 1980 was MTV (Music Television) for its violent, erotic, and dreamlike imagery. Conservative groups felt that heavy metal music and the diabolic imagery exhibited on MTV were serious threats to the spiritual well-being of general audiences. During the 1970s and 1980s, devil hunters found Satan everywhere in popular culture: in movies, books, comics, and the lyrics of rock music played backward. If producers of popular culture looked to attract audiences, then the abundance of paranormal subjects in popular culture must be in response to some perceived audience need or desire. Research on effects of paranormal themes in media indicated physiological arousal in audiences and a postviewing anxiety for some (Cantor; Cantor and Sparks; Sparks, Nelson, and Campbell), arousal effects that some audiences might actually seek out (E. Edwards, "Ecstasy").

As the new millennium neared, critics continued to voice concerns that certain media contents threaten the well-being of audiences. Such items of popular culture as Pokemon[10] and the Harry Potter trilogy[11] excited sentiments to boycott the movies or ban the books and subsequent movies the books would instigate. (See fig. 1.2.) This fear was articulated primarily by Christian conservatives distraught with the notion that the Pokemon media and Potter novels glorify "dangerous" alternative religions and witchcraft. For example, one woman wrote the editor of a North Carolina newspaper warning that Eastern mysticism inspired the Pokemon phenomenon: "There is occult energy involved, tapping into water, fire, leaf and wind energy. You can supposedly achieve enlightenment and success from Pokemon and the demonic realm" (Pulliam). For the monist who cherishes the one Bible-revealed truth, Pokemon, Harry Potter, and movies like *The Exorcist* served to remind the orthodox that there was a spiritual war to be waged. Some critics felt that this repetition of narratives about the supernatural might combine to create a cultural insistence on the authenticity of the occult, helping to break down the obstinacy of audience belief (Sparks, "Paranormal Depictions"). Through repetition, the stories of popular culture tend to validate a certain perception of the world rather than improve it, reiterate old stories rather than initiate new ones, and help to cultivate audiences' perceptions of the world in which they live.[12] Media discourse is one process in the cultural negotiation of ideology, that "articulated system of meanings, values and beliefs that can be abstracted as a world-view or class outlook" (Williams 109). Some media scholars believe that widespread and frequent repetition of similar media texts can have a forceful impact on social consensus (Gerbner) as well as a powerful effect on individual conviction (Noelle-Neumann). When media narratives feature ghosts, angels, witches, demons, and other supernatural events, they comment

11

on the metaphysical, the nature of a world we cannot directly know. If media narratives repeat similar concepts, these concepts are likely to become part of the predominant worldview. In an era in which knowledge of an experience substitutes for experience itself, moving-image media can have a powerful influence on what audiences think they know. The assumption is that if audiences consistently hear other people describe supernatural experiences in documentaries and frequently see fictional characters interact with magic in the movies, the repetitions combine to shape a cultural insistence on their authenticity.

Fig. 1.2. Harry Potter merchandise based on the popular children's series, a demonstration of media marketing. Photo by E. D. Edwards.

David Hess (120–41) believes that Hollywood is primarily a defender of the paranormal. He argues that American movie narratives frequently reject skeptical interpretations and ask audiences to accept a paranormal reading for events within the narrative. Particularly when the paranormal appears in the horror genre, skeptical characters are depicted as foolish when they cling to their skepticism. This reading of horror movies has some validity. During the course of a typical horror tale, the paranormal, which makes its existence known and "real" in the story, causes the authoritative forces of science and society to appear helpless, even silly. The skeptic in the narrative must convert to belief or be defeated.

However, Hollywood narratives about supernatural events are not always one-sided in support of paranormal explanations. Within the broader scope of American media, there is discourse in the dramas, contradictions for audiences to negotiate. Even though the idea of exorcism may have spread through media repetition of the theme, not all media stories endorse the idea of possession. For example, an episode of a 2002 television series, *Glory Days*, demonstrates the contradiction.[13] The television program paid homage to *The Exorcist* by revisiting the film's visual style in some scenes, rehashing its story of possession, and making overt references to the original movie and the case that inspired it. Yet, the plot supports skepticism over belief by revealing the possession as a hoax. Similarly, news reports about the increase in exorcism at the end of the twentieth century clearly blamed social tensions over supernatural ones as reasons for the seeming proliferation of exorcisms in the United States (Rotschild; Fountain). The public was reminded that *The Exorcist* is only a movie after all. While the practice of exorcism appears to have increased in America in the decades following the movie, it's still far from a widespread phenomenon. The percentage of the population requesting the ritual remains a tiny one.

Media as "Tribe"

For modern audiences, the consumption of media has become one ritual central to socialization and the dissemination of sacred and secular myth. Even so, sacramental needs may not always be fulfilled by remaining a member of the audience and simply watching. There may also be a need to participate. By watching, audiences receive the myths but don't engage in the ceremonies that recognize individuals as members of a tribe. During the 1980s, 1990s, and into the new millennium, ordinary people seemed to have a desire for media fame, to become a recognized member of the media "tribe," to be revealed, recorded, and distinguished by the camera. Television began to respond to this need for participation in the media tribe with so-called reality programming. Public confession on television brought notoriety, and it substantiated and authenticated an ordinary individual, even if it meant that individual must show the most embarrassing and private moments to the nation. Modern life might seem pointless at times, but appearing on television even in the most trivialized way offered a wink at significance, acknowledgment as an initiate into that sacred clan of media personalities.

Audiences choosing to remain outside the screen also appeared to have developed a desire to hear others acknowledge guilt; to see the spontaneous, unscripted interactions of ordinary people dealing with challenging and wicked situations inside the public venue of media display. Seeing these "average" people exposed, members of the audience could have a moment of superiority. These twin desires for public notice and private arrogance accompanied the rise of reality media in the 1990s, as talk shows like *Jerry Springer* and programming like *Survivor* and *Real World* came into vogue.[14] The attention such programs gave to the "average" life was brief, arbitrary, and cheap, but some audiences seemed eager to watch, even to participate. People appearing on television could become famous for no other reason than the drama of that public appearance. Through exposure in the media, the ordinary individual would no longer be average but would become a celebrity. If traditional ties to interpersonal "tribes" of family and friends were weak or extinct, or if an individual felt socially isolated and confused about a purpose in life, that person might feel a greater need to belong to the mediated tribe. Eager for that fifteen minutes of validation in a culture that celebrates the individual, some audience members might become desperate for the media to notice them as unique and cherished; or if not cherished, at least noticed. In this sense, the media could unintentionally add to a powerful psychological problem.

Critics will often blame the exotic portraits of occult ritual found in film and television for the bizarre, even violent, behavior of some teens. When young people turn away from sanctioned values and beliefs to dabble in shockingly dramatic occult ritual or to dismay society with public violence, media fantasies often get the blame. Yet, more than inspiration from any music, film, or television imagery, the need to participate, to be recognized and validated, may be the real inspirations for the violence of situations like the Columbine High School shootings and the copy-cat violence that followed at other schools. Even the suicide of the teenage pilot mimicking the September 11 terrorist attacks on the World Trade Center may have been the result of a desperate need for notice, regard, and purpose, though news coverage of September 11 inspired that specific violent behavior.[15]

If there is a devil in American media, it may be in the predilection to make us see ourselves as base and ordinary, unable to compare favorably with the glamour, talent, or beauty of media stars. Media personalities are noticed, remembered, adored, and sometimes respected. Removed from the bitterness of everyday frustrations, they seem smarter, more attractive, with more money, greater athletic prowess, more enriching experiences, and more interesting stories than most of us can hope for. Their lives end and begin again; they age, yet seem immortal. Ordinary men and women are no match; the standard is too high. The real devil may reside in the propensity of popular media to make poor and average citizens see themselves as repulsive and unimportant. Their resources may be too meager to purchase the corrective remedies commercials promise will cure their degraded condition and bring beauty, pleasure, or approval. American media let the "have-nots" know what they are missing, so that a have-not individual may eventually come to reject the possibility of personal happiness or acceptance in an idealized, media-defined world.

In a scene cut from the original release of *The Exorcist*, Father Lankester Merrin (Max von Sydow) and Father Damien Karras (Jason Miller) have a discussion during a lull in the exorcism ritual. Father Karras asks why an ordinary, sweet-faced young girl should be selected as the Devil's victim. "Why this girl?" Father Karras asks, "it makes no sense." After a moment, Father Merrin explains, "I think the point is to make us despair. To see ourselves as animal and ugly. To reject the possibility that God could love us."

Yet, media images may paradoxically suggest that the ordinary individual can accomplish a moment of media notoriety and even social power, and that the effortless way to achieve entry into the media world is to flaunt an embarrassing moment, expose personal failure, perhaps even adopt violence. By embracing the genuinely degraded condition, an unexceptional individual is guaranteed attention. People do not need to be beautiful, talented, or clever to drop their pants or wield a gun.

When ordinary lives can't compete with the media ideal, the hopeful initiate looks for alternative routes to validation.

The Occult and Social Anxiety

We define the occult as the remnants of *abandoned* religious beliefs. However, contemporary neopagan movements and similar alternative religious groups have reactivated various occult traditions that had once been abandoned. The result was an occult renaissance at the end of the twentieth century in America that mirrored the spiritualism of the late nineteenth century. New Age, Wiccan, neopagan, and new evangelical charismatic groups began to surface (Howard).[16] As American audiences searched for meaning in a bewildering era, alternate religious groups enriched the landscape with various hopes and spiritual visions. Many of these visions fueled the conflicting currents of mass media stories.

When change in society is rapid, people may be forced to reevaluate their choices, their roles, and their beliefs about established institutions, including religious institutions. This was certainly as true at the end of the twentieth century as it was at the end of the nineteenth. Rumors about the dangers of new technologies, scientific discoveries that altered old assumptions, advancements in medicine, changing social roles, and rapid shifts in the ethnicity of a population combine to create social anxiety. For example, when Darwin's concepts about the origins of the species emerged in the latter part of the nineteenth century, it laid suspicion on the existence of God as traditionally viewed. Having evolved along with the rest of the cosmos, humankind lost the status of a privileged creation cast in the divine image. This was a disturbing idea for the Victorian era, yet an idea still largely confined to discourse among the educated elite. Tensions that had only begun to crawl to the surface at the end of the nineteenth century were standing upright and walking by the end of the twentieth. As scientists began deciphering the three billion units that make up human DNA, the human body no longer seemed a sacred vessel of the soul, but territory on which biotech companies could stake a patent claim (Sagoff). By the start of the new millennium, people learned that humans share DNA with lettuce. Films and television programs about the supernatural provided a comforting space, where audiences could continue to indulge in a world propelled by a magic that held humanity at its center. Media stories allowed audiences to suspend time and become emerged in a miraculous world of personal gods and spiritual purpose, even if scientific findings cast doubt on such a world. Paradoxically, media narratives about the supernatural may also have functioned to weaken alternative ideologies and even some aspects of orthodox belief by reducing these to popular-culture myths.

The obstinacy of the occult to persist in modern media may be related in part to what Alper describes as the "God" part of the brain. Recognizing that every culture from the earliest records of humankind have believed in some sort of spiritual reality, Alper suggests that human spirituality must emanate from a congenital trait passed from parent to child. Human beings have an awareness of their own mortality. To counter the anxiety of this knowledge, Alper believes, the cognitive centers of the human brain are "wired" to perceive reality with spiritual determination, so that human spirituality has evolutionary origins. What creates social issues is the different ways that spirituality becomes articulated. Though some audiences may be shocked or disgusted by media narratives about the occult, others embrace the message that there are genuine supernatural forces in this world. The popularity of messages about the supernatural may reflect both audiences' and producers' dread of becoming dispossessed by the meaninglessness of a profane existence.

During times of social stress, audiences' reliance on media communication increases. Though recognizing that media are hardly "devils" dispossessing individuals of their reason, scholars have come to recognize the dominance of mass communication in satisfying the needs of audiences. Audiences depend on media to answer questions, to help shape attitudes, to decide what's important, to expand belief systems, and to clarify values.[17] Even in their entertainment function—perhaps especially in the entertainment function—media stories assist audience members in the quest for identity and inspire the meaning that audiences bring to their lives.[18] For example, when asked their religious affiliation on the 2001 census forms, many Britons wrote in "Jedi Knight." So many professed to believe in the "force" as depicted in the American *Stars Wars* films that the government had to create a category of "Jedi Knight" when compiling census results.[19] There's no denying that media have power. Indeed, after a movie is finished, it may for many years continue to launch new ideas, discussion, and misapprehension, just as the Warner Home Video re-release of *The Exorcist* inspired new deliberation and review of a twenty-five-year-old movie (Kermode, "Exorcist"; Hibbs). Film and television, as Walter Lippmann might say, put "pictures in our heads," and some of these pictures become enduring cultural icons.

C. Wright Mills observed that communication stands between human consciousness and existence, influencing what we know about our life and the meaning we bring to it (333). In the twentieth century, media communication became both the agent of human knowledge and the delegate of social consensus. In addition to making audiences think about certain things, powerful media messages tapped emotions and "other processes over which individuals have little voluntary control" (DeFleur and Ball-Rokeach 165). If emotions are the doorway to our spiritual life, media communication may stand alongside interpersonal rituals as a path to that door. Not only the valve between human emotional experience and human understanding, media communication might also be the agents that arouse our spiritual dispositions and shape our understanding of a metaphysical world. This would make media communication—moving-image media in particular—very powerful indeed.

Out of Body
Transmission and Transcendence Through Popular Culture

There are half hours that dilate to the importance of centuries.
—Mary Catherwood, *Lazarre* (1901)

The patron saint of television, Clare Offreduccio, was born into Italian nobility in 1194, centuries before television technology would be developed. She defied her parents and ran away from her family's palace to take the veil and follow St. Francis of Assisi. She would later become the founder of the oldest women's order, the Order of the Poor Ladies (Gibeau). At the end of her life, confined to her bed, too sick to attend mass, the dying nun saw a vision of the liturgy on the wall of her room. She could see and hear the service as if she were actually attending the mass. Although the thirteenth-century nun had been credited with many miracles, it was this "out of body" vision that caused Pope Pius XII to declare Clare Offreduccio the "patron saint of television" in 1958. The miraculous ability to have a vision of something happening in another place or time was wondrous in the thirteenth century, but it has become prevalent today through the use of communication technology. Though this technology surrounds contemporary life, moving-image and sound media still seem to retain a strange sense of mystery and connection to those things we can't explain. To the naive mind, media technologies are themselves miraculous.

I remember as a young girl having a discussion with my grandmother about her early film experiences, experiences that astonished and confounded her. Born in 1898 of immigrants from Norway, she had seen theatrical plays but was completely baffled when her parents took her to see a black-and-white silent film in 1912. The film bewildered her. She couldn't understand why the actors looked so "pasty" and was astounded by how quickly those sickly looking actors changed clothes and scenery.

18

When her parents tried to explain that she was seeing a film, she could only grasp the phenomenon as something wizardly. She had trouble understanding her early media experience because it didn't seem to be limited to the physical world as she knew it, by the natural decrees of time and space. The technology, as her parents attempted to describe it, made no sense to her, but magic, the kind that powered flying carpets or turned pumpkins into coaches, was something she understood. She decided that it was magic she had seen.

I knew how my grandmother felt because of my own early experiences with magical thinking and the new medium of my childhood: television. I was quite small when my family bought a television set, and I became a faithful viewer of *Captain Kangaroo*, which was already a well-established children's program when I began watching it.[1] The captain created a fanciful world where sock puppets seemed alive and invisible hands drew pictures on a magic drawing board. Occasionally, he would read aloud letters from viewers. I desperately wanted Captain Kangaroo to have a letter of mine to read aloud. I carefully wrote him a note and made a drawing, folded these together, stuffed them in an envelope addressed to "Captain Kangaroo," and slid the envelope under the television set, where I expected it would be wondrously whisked away to the captain's imaginary world. I was disappointed when program followed program and the captain never elected to read my letter or show my drawing to the viewing audience. Many years later, when my family moved the television set to replace it with a new one, I found the letter still under the set, yellowed with time. My childhood missive had never been magically spirited through the television set to the captain's mailbox, as my child's logic supposed it would be. I tell this story because it illustrates how a naive mind conceives the technology of television and motion pictures as wizardly devices. If they can transport our imaginations, which seem so real to us, surely they might transport material things.[2]

Because our communications technologies seem to be beyond the physical limitations of time, space, and physical substance, a child might easily assume the technology has supernatural capacities, not only to miraculously transport items of substance but to eclipse death. For example, on September 13, 2001, following the tragedy of the terrorist attacks on the World Trade Center and the Pentagon, Diane Sawyer reported on ABC News the plaintive account of a young child who lost her father to the attack and was confused by reports of victims who had used their cell phones to contact loved ones before they died. The child wondered why her mother couldn't just use a cell phone to contact her father in heaven.

Children aren't alone in thinking that communications technologies may have metaphysical connections. In the 1970s, Beth Bentley examined a collection of narratives from people who believed they had received telephone calls from deceased loved ones. Jeffrey Sconce's book *Haunted Media* provides numerous examples of belief in "electromagnetic mysteries," where mysterious new technologies are thought to open telegraph lines to supernatural worlds (21–44). Communications media that can empower an eerie form of bodied disembodiment seem nothing less than magical.

At the end of the nineteenth century, various predictions suggested that the world was about to enter a true period of enlightenment. People believed that as our technologies matured and human beings mastered various problems through science, we would come to reject our superstitions and fully embrace scientific reason. The expectation was that as we stepped into the twentieth century, humankind would advance, and—with scientific wisdom—divest our culture of childish magic and superstitious artifacts. Yet, one of the earliest uses for the newly developing technologies of photography and motion pictures in the late 1800s was to produce hoaxes in an attempt to reinvigorate and profit from ancient superstitions. In darkened rooms, "mediums" used the new film technology for faked seances, projecting images of deceased individuals on smoke columns or walls to create the illusion of contact with spirits. Through use of the new technology, magicians created the illusion of "real" magic (Barnouw). As the motion picture industry developed and understanding about the technology of motion picture photography matured, audiences abandoned these fraudulent seances, knowing the sorcery was counterfeit. However, movies continued to tell supernatural stories, relaying the folklore if not the belief.

Not long after people had abandoned faked seances, more scientific minds came to consider that if a supernatural world does exist, it might be revealed through "wondrous" communications technologies. In 1920, the man who invented the phonograph and the first motion pictures, Thomas Edison, related that he had started work on an "apparatus" so delicate that if personalities existed in another domain, they would have an opportunity to express themselves. "I cannot conceive of such a thing as a spirit. Imagine something which has no weight, no material form, no mass; in a word, imagine nothing," Edison was careful to add. Yet, Edison conceived the possibility of entities grouped together as a collective to form the human personality, just as cells cluster to form the organs of the body. If the grouped entities remained assembled after a person died, then the personality might survive death and might communicate with the living (Lescarboura 446). Edison believed his scientific apparatus would be a better means of communication than raps or tilting tables.[3] Though we know little about the success of Edison's supernatural communication apparatus, his other technological contributions have been highly successful—if not in contacting other dimensions—at least in replaying supernatural narratives. In this sense, Edison's inventions did connect living audiences with ghosts.

One consequence of occult themes in popular film was that some elements of the occult would no longer remain hidden. Some previously occult rituals became adapted and transmitted so frequently in media stories that they became clichés. Half a century later, supernatural themes would find new and bigger audiences in television, which created its own magical narratives, sometimes as weekly series, as well as through broadcasting older films. A full century later, supernatural narratives were more dominant than ever, continuing as subjects of film and television, but also becoming prevalent on computer media. Technopagans declared the true habitat for gods and spirits to be the newly discovered realm of cyberspace, and thousands of websites offered Internet users information, discussions, and personal stories about the supernatural.

The media tell us stories about the occult, about those wonders beyond human understanding, revealing secret knowledge that was formerly known only to the initiate. Yet, through the wonders of broadcast, cable, film, and the Internet, the secret knowledge of the initiate—even the master—becomes available to all. The media provide audiences with anecdotal knowledge of wondrous incidents concurrent with experiences that extend human senses.

Our media experiences are similar in some aspects to the folk belief that the human spirit can travel unfettered by the physical self through astral projection or out-of-body states. Through media use, individuals need not go on a "true" psychic voyage to know what it is like to suddenly be in another time and place. While watching a film or television narrative, audience members break free of the restrictions of the physical world to travel spiritually and emotionally wherever the media take them.

Media Technology, Immortality, and Extension of the Senses

Stories about the supernatural told in film and television may reflect human understanding of a metaphysical world, but moving-image media allow ordinary people to share in these extraordinary events. The images execute and project the fantasies, making them seem real, at least while audiences are engaged in the media-viewing process and the "suspension of disbelief" that allows them to become engrossed in storytelling and drama (Brockett). From early in the history of film, the ability to create double exposures told us how a detached spirit might look. Camera effects showed us how a wizard might appear and disappear. Green screens and special camera angles made the impossible seem possible. Digital video effects would later sharpen and magnify media capabilities to make supernatural visions more convincing. While moving-image media have never been hesitant to emphasize supernatural stories, the technology used to render the narratives and the very process of watching may be as important in shaping popular discourse about the supernatural as the stories themselves. For example, one prominent supposition about the nature of hauntings, which was not widely articulated until after the development of film and electronic media, was that ghosts were tragic emotions *recorded* on the damp electrical fields of an area where misfortune occurred (Lethbridge). Just as images can be recorded on videotape, some people came to believe passion could be recorded on the atmosphere, thus explaining apparitions. It seems reasonable that the very properties of recorded media inspired this idea about what causes hauntings, as movies and television narratives perpetuated the folklore. Another popular explanation for apparitions was that "ghosts" were alternate lives on a "channel" that had somehow slipped its frequency. Engineers even refer to signal interference or the weaker of competing broadcast signals as "ghosts." Clearly, some people have found in the properties of electronic media possible metaphors, if not explanations, for anomalous events.

Harold Adams Innis and Marshall McLuhan suggested that human beings may be more affected by physical characteristics of media technology than by media contents. McLuhan proposed that media characteristics create the conditions of human perception (*Understanding Media*). He believed it was the logical, left-to-right, linear constraints of print media that cause people to perceive their world in a logical, linear way. Film and television allow audiences to see a world of rapidly changing shifts of location, time, and perspective, influencing a less logical, more emotional perception. Popular media become extensions of human senses beyond our biological limitations. For example, in the film *The Serpent and the Rainbow* (1988), audiences cross the globe, one moment viewing a Haitian spirit ceremony and then in the next moment watching as pharmaceutical chemists sit down to a business dinner in New York. Even within a scene, the perspective can shift rapidly, from a wide shot of dancers to an emotional close-up of the spirit doctor's face. By extending the physical senses to impossible dimensions, media provide audiences a near-metaphysical adventure. Perhaps even more than as annexes to human senses, as expansions of human sight, hearing, and touch, but through engaging the imagination, media also engage human metaphysical faculties.

Media properties additionally allow human beings to transcend mortality, to continue speaking and acting after death through visual recordings. Interestingly, we define the word *medium* in English as the agent through which something is transmitted, in the way that newsprint, film, videotape, and satellite waves transmit ideas, but we also use the word to designate a person who claims occult power to communicate with the dead or with spirits. In this sense, film, television, and sound recordings become a "medium" both as an agency of transmission and as a channel of occult power. They can allow the living to feel as though they have had contact with those who have died. Through the manipulation of recordings, deceased talent can even achieve "new" performances.

An interesting case of postmortem performance occurs in the 1983 film *Brainstorm.* Actress Natalie Wood died before the filming of the movie had been completed. The film's director, Douglas Trumbull, used outtakes from scenes shot earlier, a stand-in, and reversed camera angles to produce a performance that Natalie Wood never created while she lived.

Not only does *Brainstorm* provide an example of deceased talent continuing to speak through the medium, but the movie's narrative comments on the supernatural aspirations of media technologies. The film tells the story of scientists who realize the full ambition of media to extend human senses through a virtual-reality system that reaches all the senses, not just sight and sound. This "wondrous technology" makes recordings of all the sensory input of an experience. When a spectator replays the recording, the virtual system sends sensory input directly into that person's brain, engaging the spectator in a mediated experience that has the full effect of reality.[4] With such a device, a physically handicapped person might enjoy the sensation of running, a blind person could relish any view, and a deaf person could enjoy sound and music. Interestingly, the movie ends up suggesting that the real ambition of such technology is not to fully experience life without limitations but to experience death in life. One of the scientists, Lillian Reynolds (Louise Fletcher), has a heart attack and dies while recording her death on the virtual-reality machine. This allows her co-worker, Michael Brace (Christopher Walken), to glimpse the afterlife through a playback of this recording. However, in order to do this, he must turn off some of the sensory input, because otherwise he would also experience a heart attack and die. By this, the film suggests that death is a sensory experience that only the aural and visual senses can survive. Of course, these two senses are the peculiar bias of moving-image media.

Computer gaming extends the senses in a manner similar to film and television but permits physical interaction with the narrative. In the video games *The 11th Hour* (1996) and *The 7th Guest* (1994), a player becomes an actor visiting a haunted house. The player is no longer a detached voyeur, but an active performer who can make changes in the events he or she witnesses. In the game *HEXX: Heresy of the Wizard* (1994), the player can learn to "use magic" and "cast spells" in an adventure to save the spirits of the four gods imprisoned by an evil wizard. It is imaginary, yet in this virtual world, the players' use of "magic" has consequences for the outcome of their individual narratives. The players know what it might feel like to cast a spell and see their sorcery have a measurable impact within the environment of the game.

The characteristics of media experience, which directly involve audiences through emotion, imagination, and intellect, are the very type of experiences the ancient wizards wished to control through magic. Media experience, like "psychic travel," is a disembodied state much like the astral body depicted in folklore. To achieve emotional travel through media, audiences learn to disengage the ego, to suspend disbelief, and to become connected with the mediated experience. As McLuhan noticed, "we have extended our central nervous system itself in a global embrace" (*Understanding Media* 3). This sensory expansion was the occult ambition of the ancient wizard. Through expansion, the wizard could become the sum of all things, absorbed in the universe.

The technopagan movement, a branch of the new paganism that surfaced in the latter part of the twentieth century, accepted and celebrated new technologies as tools for enlightenment or as instruments to be used in neopagan rituals. In the book *City Magick*, Christopher Penczak explains to modern pagans how the television set or office computer can become the focus of a neopagan altar, adding that entertainment centers are handy places to store magical items like candles and stones. The book provides diagrams for how the modern shaman or "CyberWitch" might set up such an altar. He also explains how the television might be used as a spiritual tool and includes in the book exercises for "TV scrying," a form of divination in which the practitioner gazes into some reflective surface like that of a crystal ball, a bowl of water, or a television screen. After gazing for a while, the practitioner's mind slips into a trance, supposedly opening up a psychic channel. Penczak strongly recommends substituting the television or computer screen for more traditional surfaces like the crystal ball. "A television makes an excellent surface for the modern practitioner. There is no better icon from the urban age than the magick of the TV." He writes: "The static on the TV can be used as your ritual tone to enter gnosis," meaning that intuitive state through which the neopagan intercepts knowledge. (See fig. 2.1.) Penczak goes on to explain that the television set can also be used as a conducting medium for ritual prayer:

Fig. 2.1. In a neopagan altar, the television set becomes an instrument for divination. Photo by E. D. Edwards.

I have found the TV to be a medium for magick traveling over distance, much like a photograph or voodoo doll used in traditional magick. In some ways the television can replace the crystal ball as a divining surface. On a mundane level it brings such terrible information to us about the world. Although we need to be aware of these atrocities, they often convey a feeling of helplessness. . . . When I see a tragedy, my immediate response is to help. . . . At other times my reasonable response is magick. When sending healing energy to a war-torn area or disaster zone, I go right up to the TV and send my intent through the image to the actual people and place needing it. It can work with any spell. . . . When doing money magick, watch or tape the stock market report. Then send your intention for increased property through the image. . . . Transform your TV from a tool of dis-information and hypnotism to a global healing device. (110–12)

More than sacred tools, for some technopagans, the frequencies of broadcast and the cyberspace of the Internet are endowed with metaphysical reality. Electromagnetic waves are not merely the conducting medium for broadcast messages; they are the interstate for angels. For the technopagan, cyberspace is more than a virtual environment; it exists as a spiritual paradigm.

Media Use and Archaic Time

McLuhan's "global village" is the reemergence of a communal space created by the properties of electronic media. McLuhan noticed that because of our media experience, modern people have returned to the sense of time enjoyed by archaic or tribal peoples, where time was always "present" time. When technological breakthroughs have become "so massive as to create one environment upon another . . . to give us instant access to all pasts," there is no history (McLuhan and Zingrone 325). We experience a present, cyclical time.

Audiences consume media stories, but the stories are never completely consumed, never quite history. By watching the cable network Nick at Nite's TV Land, we can instantly jump backward three or four decades to watch old television series. We might switch cable stations to American Movie Classics (AMC) or the History Channel and go back even further in time; and then just as easily switch to the Cable News Network (CNN) and watch a "live" or current event. We need not worry too much about missing something, because media narratives are reproduced and rebroadcast. News stories may be reincarnated as film narratives or docudramas; films become television series; television stories get retold as films; film narratives get remade as newer film versions. Through repetition, cliché becomes archetype. Through media experience, audiences have the opportunity to live in many cultures and many times all at once, contributing to what Pico Iyer calls the "global soul," a citizen adrift not in a "global village" but in a "global city, with all the problems of rootlessness and alienation and a violent, false denaturing that we associate with the word *urban*" (28). This global-media city is a place paradoxically afloat in time, yet relentlessly docked to clock and schedule.

In *The Myth of the Eternal Return*, Mircea Eliade distinguishes the Judeo-Christian "historical" time from the archaic or primitive conception of a cyclical time that was in harmony with cosmic rhythms. In the primitive conception, time is a continuing series of cosmic cycles. The primitive individual has an archetypal memory and doesn't record specific events or associate them with a particular date or hour. Like the moon, which waxes and wanes, all things are perpetually becoming and then reverting to an original state, only to "become" again. Upon death, the primitive individual loses personal memory to also become the archetypal ancestor (47). Personal memory has no value; time is mythical. This is time like that in Hazrat Inayat Khan's observation: "In reality there is no such thing as time; it is we who have made a certain conception of it. There is only existence . . . an eternal continuity of life" (182).

In contrast, the Judeo-Christian concept of "historical" time is one-way, or linear (Eliade, *Myth* 104). Individuals and their actions are considered unique and are valued as singular. History is acknowledged. Time is irreversible. It is a goal-oriented concept in which things are not continually becoming but are finished. The world is finite. In linear time, life's tasks are not an arrangement of repetitive rituals to be experienced but a progression of chores to be completed.

Characteristics of film and television media suspend the flow of historical time for audiences, removing them from linear time and projecting them into the mythic, archaic moment. More than the instant access to history, audiences experience media—beyond time—as disembodied observers. Spectators can journey backward into history through the technique of "flashback" or be projected into a distant future. Shooting and editing techniques can cause time to speed up, letting a character zip unnaturally across the screen; slow down, as in slow motion; or freeze a character's action altogether. A lifetime can be compressed into two hours; generations can be condensed into a miniseries. Through repeats and syndication, the lives of characters in television series are also cyclical, not ending with the season or even cancellation of the show. By using such a device as a videotape recorder, audiences can fast-forward and rewind, replaying an instant over and over. On film and in television, time is never irreversible; never quite gone. By their very properties, moving-image media return audiences to that tribal world of cosmic cycles and primordial archetypes, energizing the archaic conception of time. The ABC broadcast of the millennium celebration, a full day of replaying midnight revelries across the world, provides a prime example.

The year leading up to the new millennium was one filled with pessimistic and apocalyptic stories informed by a linear world concept. Under the linear model, the duration of the world is limited; its demise is foretold by a series of cosmic and historical calamities (Eliade, *Myth* 126–27). Concerns for the Y2K bug, a computer glitch that, it was feared, would render helpless most computer-governed systems, combined with a general end-of-the-millennium anxiety in the days before the century's end. For example, a January 1999 issue of *Time* reported the growing Y2K survivalist thinking in America as some families stockpiled canned goods and candles, waiting for the crumple of civilization, the collapse of public utilities, and the Four Horsemen of the Apocalypse to swoop down from the skies. Yet, even as ABC broadcast news stories about Y2K and reported the restless fears of some fundamentalist groups, the network promoted a full day of New Year's celebrations. A report by Robert Krulwich on the nightly news told audiences that the last millennium had ended as uneventfully as any ordinary day, with most people unaware that a new millennium had even begun. There was deliberation about when the new millennium actually would begin, discussion about the Chinese New Year, and talk about other alternate calendars, all reminders that dates are social constructs and not cosmic truths. Then on New Year's Eve, the ABC network provided continuous coverage of the new millennium, as television crews followed midnight across the globe. Viewers in America on Eastern standard time watched at 8:00 AM as Australians counted down to midnight and celebrated with fireworks (but experienced no millennium crisis). In a comforting effacement of time, television audiences saw the fireworks and pageantry from country to country, sometimes in instant replay, throughout the entire day. As the day progressed, people were reminded to renew themselves with New Year's resolutions. If the resolutions failed, there would be a certain cheer in knowing the new year will come again: world and self are continuously reborn. Finally, in New York, the glittering ball—a symbolic regeneration of the world—descended on Times Square to the exuberant cheering of crowds. Never mind if we happened to look away or were taking a bathroom break, there would be an instant replay later.

Though audiences experience media narratives in archaic time, in contrast, the business aspects of media are defined by linear, one-way time, with emphasis on schedules and deadlines. Commercial television even divides time into discrete segments that can be sold to advertisers. If a thirty-second slot is not sold, it must be filled with public service messages or self-promotion and represents a business opportunity forever missed. Once gone, that thirty seconds can't be reclaimed and sold at a later date.[5] It is the peculiar paradox of moving-image media that one environment contradicts the other. Unlike archaic people, contemporary American audiences experience a mediated mythic time while living in the linear, historic time, which seems to evaporate. The larger environment of contemporary American life is linear and goal-oriented. As audiences annul time through mediated experience, historic time speeds past. George Lucas fans can see *Star Wars* (1973) replayed over and over, even as the moments of their own lives disappear. The paradox is that time can be annulled, but there is never enough of it. Some might observe that print media are as capable as audiovisual media of breaking linear time by allowing the reader to become absorbed in alternate worlds, to review and reread. However, McLuhan's work suggests that print media, with their logical and linear structure, prevent full immersion into archaic time. Print builds messages from letters, to words, to sentences, to paragraphs. This construction, along with grammatical rules, creates a perceptual environment for readers that is quite different from the tribal environment of moving-image media. Clearly, all media create conditions for audiences that can seem different from the physical spaces their bodies inhabit.

Media and Mythic Narrative

Just as media return audiences to archaic time, they also involve them with mythic narrative. Historians sometimes worry about the effect of television docudrama, concerned that dramatization might alter audiences' understanding of an event that has been shaped into a more forceful or entertaining but less accurate account. But such fears only show that historians miss the real intent of these programs. Within the archaic time of the media world, it isn't historical fact but the search for primordial paradigms to which audiences respond. What propels the dramatization of the historical incident on film or television isn't necessarily an attempt to instruct audiences with fact but rather to echo the archetype. For example, Eliade relates how the story of an accidental death in a Romanian village became transformed into a local myth with magical elements, even though the heroine of the story still lived and could dispute the magical elements of the myth (*Myth* 44–46). Similarly, screenwriters will take "poetic license" with true stories because events are important only insofar as they are reproductions of the archetype, bearing orthodox lessons for viewers.

News media frequently allow audiences to share in the process of turning news into myth. As Nimmo and Combs observed of television crisis coverage,

> the viewer-listener accepts the news-tale as only an approximation of truth but suspends belief willingly to share in the real-fiction spun by the narrator. The credibility of the tale, not truth or falsity as such, is the key. Credibility increases to the degree that it conforms to standard mythic plots, especially that of a hero struggling against the odds. (17)

One such contemporary story turned myth is that of Elian Gonzalez, the six-year-old Cuban boy who survived when his boat capsized as it attempted to reach the United States. On Thanksgiving Day, 1999, as Americans celebrated "life, liberty, and the pursuit of happiness" with turkey dinners, fishermen discovered Elian clinging to an inner tube off the coast of Florida. The boy's mother and most of the other Cuban passengers had died in the shipwreck. The story captured media attention because of its mythic, heroic elements and remained center stage because conflicts over custody and ideology kept it resonating in the public imagination. Elian's father, Juan Gonzalez, said he wanted his son returned to Cuba. The boy's Miami relatives, however, began a fight to keep the boy in the United States, claiming that living in a country of political freedom and material wealth should take precedence over parental rights. Months later, television reporter Diane Sawyer interviewed Elian, highlighting the mythic elements of his story: the tragedy of the storm and his mother's death; a magical rescue by dolphins; deliverance into the hands of fishermen on Thanksgiving Day; the appearance of a mother-surrogate. Sawyer told viewers that when a fierce storm overtook the Cuban boat, Elian tried to help the others bail water. As the boat sank, one of the passengers put Elian in an inner tube. For two days, he floated alone, grasping this inner tube. Elian told Sawyer that every time he might have slipped under the water because he was too tired to hold on, a dolphin would push him up. He said that dolphins swam around his inner tube, helping him stay afloat while he repeated a children's prayer: "Guardian angel, sweet companion, don't leave my side day or night. For if you do, I will be lost" (ABC, *Good Morning America*, 28 Mar. 2000). It was as mythic a story as Romulus and Remus being suckled by wolves. As a mythic story, it fired passions in a way that no other refugee story could. Predictably, the news item became television drama in the fall of 2000, when the Fox Family Channel broadcast *The Elian Gonzalez Story*.

By contrast, the mythical elements of the terrorist attacks on the World Trade Center and the Pentagon on September 11, 2001, were so unclear, and the impact was so huge in those earliest releases, that the credibility of the story was hard for most audiences to grasp. This was a story that didn't conform to standard mythic plots, yet did conform to the violent, visual clichés of action films. The mythical elements were problematic because Americans see themselves as heroes, not victims, and the initial repercussions of the attacks were too immense to grasp. Many audiences reacted to the news with numb disbelief. This was too much like a big-budget movie, too much like fiction. Such a story couldn't be real. Over and over again, Americans would compare the tragedy to the special effects sequence in a film.

Thirty-six years before the terrorist attacks on the Pentagon and the World Trade Center, Susan Sontag wrote in an essay about science fiction film a description for the typical film catastrophe that sounded much like the reality on September 11. These imaginary disasters predictably include the discovery of a "monster" among us, the declaration of a national emergency, reports of further destruction, international tensions suspended in view of the global crisis, meetings at the United Nations, and a sense of humanity naked without its artifacts. On September 11, each of these had become the scenarios of news reports rather than the imaginary disasters of action movies.

When the general social environment is stressed, as in the case of potential war, media contents tend to have a yin-yang relationship with social conditions, offering audiences stories that are either highly germane or else escapist entertainment with happier themes.[6] Some of this yin-yang response to media content was evident immediately after the September 11 attacks. Networks canceled violent movies and television programs that dealt with global aggression or nuclear terrorism, replacing these with alternate, less violent programming. This was an effort to be responsive to audiences coping with the repercussions of large-scale social violence. Producers and programmers were concerned that audiences normally immune would be repelled by morbid or violent content in media entertainment following the real terror. By September 13, 2001, the Associated Press reported that Hollywood had postponed the production of movies with terrorist plots. Warner Brothers executives delayed the

October 5 release date of *Collateral Damage* (2001), in which a terrorist bombs a Los Angeles skyscraper. Radio stations circulated lists of songs to be avoided because their lyrics might be offensive in this new environment. Also suspended following the terrorist assaults was the release of an interactive Internet mystery game pertaining to conspiracies and bombings. Sensitivities were too raw.

Forced to report the horror, the only alternative for news media would be to interlace the harsh news with feature stories about individuals involved in heroic rescue, narratives of steadfast family love, and tales of patriotic self-sacrifice. These would be feature stories that were paradigmatic, beloved, and buoying in a time of crisis. The focus of such stories would be sharp enough to grasp emotionally, their archetypal elements clear: brave individuals struggling to save lives buried under mounds of debris; a young woman on an epic journey in a shattered city searching for her fiancé; and the joy of a husband discovering that his burned and battered wife still lived. These features would offer a counterbalance to the detestable necessity for news media to be something of an accomplice in spreading the terrorists' message. As more details became known about United Airlines Flight 93, another heroic story emerged about the bravery and self-sacrifice of passengers determined to bring down the hijackers rather than let their plane crash into another high-profile target. The plane went down in a field in rural Pennsylvania, thwarting terrorists' intentions. As horrifying as the story was, it was also uplifting and inspirational. In it were the mythical elements audiences needed: ordinary Americans being courageous and heroic and doing whatever must be done under extreme circumstances.

As the news media distributed accounts of the September 11 assaults, the public responded with urban legends in a desperate search for some meaning. Intent on finding the larger significance behind such horrendous events, individuals began to see metaphysical messages hidden in the images of smoke and shadow captured by the media. Bizarre stories began to spread days afterward as e-mail gossip. One Associated Press (AP) article took notice of a claim that the face of Satan could be seen in the dark smoke billowing out of the World Trade Center in a picture snapped by freelance photographer Mark D. Phillips, which he had later sold to the AP (Hill). Because the AP maintained that the photo was untouched, consistent with that news cooperative's unyielding policy against modification of photographic content, individuals interpreted the photograph as proof that the terrorists were agents of Satan. The *Boston Globe* reported that newspapers across the country received numerous calls about the photo, demanding to know if it had been doctored (Weiss). *Chicago Sun-Times* columnist Richard Roeper admitted of the image, "there's no disputing the eerie presence of something that resembles an angry human face. But it's quite a leap of faith to say this is the face of Satan. For one thing, how do we know what Satan looks like?" Mainstream media were quick to discredit the urban legends, which included numerology, the examination of occult meanings in numbers—in this case, the date of the attacks—and connections made between the prophecies of fourteenth-century French astrologer Nostradamus and the destruction of the World Trade Center.[7] Conservative Christian leaders Jerry Falwell and Pat Robertson suggested the events of September 11 were God's punishment on an American public too lenient about such things as paganism, feminism, homosexuality, and abortion.[8] This proposition received immediate rebuttal. Websites, Internet discussion boards, and e-mails became rich with debate in the agonized public search for meaning.

Americans celebrated a jittery Halloween in 2001 following the events of September 11. A full moon was set to rise on October 31; the last time a full moon had appeared on a Halloween night had been in 1955, and the next time wouldn't come until 2020. Some people believed that the rare appearance of a full moon on Halloween occurring just after a national tragedy had to be a cosmic sign. Folklore about such a sign made its way into news reports and Internet chat rooms. Adding to the concern was a constellation associated with end-of-the-world beliefs, the Seven Sisters, which was also at the top of the Halloween night sky for Americans. Some people took these two astronomical events as a signal of imminent terrorist attacks or even the end of the world. Fundamentalist Christians warned that this would be a Halloween to stay indoors and shun any entertainment associated with the occult. The Halloween of 2001 was an odd combination of superstitious fears widely disseminated in the media, a deep desire to escape real-life worries in celebration of national unity, and a determination to trick-or-treat no matter what. News reports did note the tendency for trick-or-treaters to forgo the occult costume for the patriotic one.

As weeks passed and the sense of immediate danger receded, many people related that they needed to turn off the news and tune into fantasy, and even some disaster fantasies returned, offering a peculiar relief. As Sontag notes:

> Ours is indeed an age of extremity. For we live under continual threat of two equally fearful, but seemingly opposed, destinies: unremitting banality and inconceivable terror. It is fantasy, served out in large rations by the popular

arts, which allows most people to cope with these twin spectres. For one job that fantasy can do is to lift us out of the unbearable humdrum and to distract us from terrors—real or anticipated—by an escape into exotic, dangerous situations which have last minute happy endings. But another of the things that fantasy can do is normalize what is psychologically unbearable, thereby inuring us to it. In one case fantasy beautifies the world. In the other, it neutralizes it. (464)

But the job of myth is also to energize audiences with archetype, sometimes in propagandistic ways. By January 2002, four short months after Allied planes and missiles began attacks on Taliban and al-Qaida targets in Afghanistan, Americans would respond to the now highly relevant violence of the war movie *Black Hawk Down* (2001) and the fanciful violence of *Lord of the Rings* (2001), making both top box-office attractions. Both movies feature heroic comrades in a struggle against unspeakable evil. However, *Lord of the Rings* presented a struggle embedded in magic and fantasy, showing brave comrades united against an evil force intent on destroying happiness, while *Black Hawk Down* presented a struggle based on real events. On January 21, 2002, on ABC's *Good Morning America*, Captain Jeff Struecker told audiences that the film was a true approximation of his experiences in the 1993 battle of Mogadishu, Somalia, and that the film was germane to America's current war on terrorism. The film depicts a country wasted by famine, torn by civil war, dominated by Sunni Muslims, and bullied by a Somali warlord interfering with humanitarian efforts. The job of American Delta force soldiers was to enter Mogadishu and kidnap the warlord's two top lieutenants so the humanitarian missions might succeed. It was a failed effort, but the film shows the valiant attempt of American soldiers against unspeakable odds. Struecker explained the film's relevance to the Bush administration's war on terror by implying that Americans should not back away from doing "what's necessary." News reports of Washington screenings claimed Vice President Dick Cheney, Secretary of Defense Donald Rumsfeld, and Army Secretary Tom White were enthusiastic about the movie, which renewed patriotic fervor by showing courageous American soldiers fighting dark, bloodthirsty, and drug-crazed foreigners. Movies such as *Behind Enemy Lines* (2001), *Hart's War* (2002), and *Collateral Damage* (2001) that might have seemed too disturbingly violent in September of 2001 would seem highly pertinent by January of the following year and were even welcomed for their depiction of American heroism under fire. By the summer of 2002, Marvel Comics announced a new comic-book series, "The Call of Duty," that would focus on New York City "real-life" heroes: firefighters, police

officers, and paramedics. These new heroes wouldn't be gifted with superhuman traits like Spiderman, Superman, or Hercules but would respond to what the editors at Marvel Comics believed was a "fever to see
these kind of people and heroes immortalized in our type of storytelling"
(Sacks). Reports of the new comic-book series emphasized that these
wouldn't be factual accounts of September 11 or other real events but fictions starring characters who happen to be police, fire, and emergency
medical service workers. The stories would take place in the comic-book
world, where there would be hints of the supernatural.

The Degradation of a Seeker

Media that create myths and return us to archaic time are also important in uniting the national and the global "tribes." Like a tribal society,
contemporary media audiences seem more intimately involved with one
another than they had been before the advent of broadcasting, cable, or
the Internet. The intimacy may be a false one, but the feeling of connect-
edness for audiences is real. After the September 11 attacks, Americans and
sympathetic nations seemed to have become the instantaneous members
of that global community McLuhan had predicted, united against the
worldwide threat of terrorism and eager to participate, to "do" something.
It became clear that America wasn't the only victim. The people who died
at the World Trade Center represented many nationalities. The terrorists had attacked a global society. As spokesperson for the outrage, President Bush spoke of evidence that linked the violence to a fanatic—even
occult—branch of Islam, whose members were hiding out in the caves
of Afghanistan to plot horrors against the global community.

In an examination of political imagery, Nimmo suggests that political leaders will find "a symbol of some person or social group to blame
for social disturbance" and project to the public a symbolic image of this
person or group that will "combine propagandistic appeals with the
threat of force" (267). Though the suicide hijackers had sacrificed their
own lives for their fanatic beliefs, President Bush called them "faceless
cowards" and promised, "Make no mistake, the United States will hunt
down and punish those responsible for these cowardly acts."[9] What would
later become more powerful to the president's imagery than the idea of
faceless cowardice would be the abstract idea of evil personified by Osama
bin Laden. One month after the attacks, the president told the country
in a press conference that "our war on terrorism has nothing to do with
differences in faith. It has everything to do with people of all faiths coming together to condemn hate and evil."[10]

As the war on terrorism commenced, there came the startling discovery that a young American, John Walker Lindh, had been captured as a Taliban fighter. Public moral indignation demanded public denunciation, to reinforce tribal solidarity and bind the nation in what Garfinkel refers to as a "secular form of communion" (316). To offer the public the secular fellowship that seemed so necessary, political leaders and media reports complied in a public "degradation ceremony" to bring shame upon an American citizen who would be in league with such evil. Such a ceremony would show that Lindh and his actions should be clearly understood as eccentric and vicious, and that his betrayal of people and country was no accident. To be successful, the denouncer would need to be a publicly known person acting as a public figure, delivering the denunciation in the name of the "tribe." The denouncer would also need to make the suprapersonal values of the tribe clear and salient. What the denouncer said must be regarded by the general public as "true on the grounds of a socially employed metaphysics whereby witnesses assume that witnesses and denouncer are alike in essence" (318). The coalesced voices of Bush administration officials, reporters, celebrities, educators, and religious leaders speaking through popular media engaged in the denunciation the public seemed to demand. The person of John Walker Lindh would be much less important to the tribe than Lindh as a symbol of wrongdoing that a flag-waving public could denounce with broad consensus.

On December 22, 2002, CNN featured a biographical sketch of Lindh's life, which emphasized his "permissive, privileged, liberal" upbringing: parents who "encouraged their son to find his own path," a mother who "opened up his world to Buddhism and the American Indian religions," in a city "filled with people who believe in free expression and independent thinking." The segment suggested that—like many young Americans—Lindh was a teenager attracted to forms of spirituality associated with the foreign, the exotic, and the fiercely ritualistic. Here was a teen searching for the structure that was not provided by the "progressive" environments of a liberal family, an artistic community, or an alternative public high school. *Newsweek* featured the American Taliban fighter in a cover story that described Lindh as a seeker on a "spiritual journey that had gone awry" (Soloway, Thomas, Breslau, and Moreau).[11] Americans learned that Lindh had trained with al-Qaida, had met with Osama bin Laden several times, had criticized his home country, and had answered the call to jihad before he was finally captured and brought home in shame. By February 5, 2002, a federal grand jury had indicted Lindh on ten counts, including conspiring to kill U.S. nationals and using and carrying firearms during crimes of violence.

Through biographical sketches offered in the media, Lindh's estrangement became evident. He was too rich, too smart, too serious. Here was a privileged young man who condemned comfort and capitalism in favor of deprivation and traitorous violence, who scorned freedom for the rigidity of a regressive fundamentalism. In a statement among the allied voices of official denunciation, Attorney General John Ashcroft outlined Lindh's transgressions, sending the denunciation in the name of the American tribe. On Tuesday, February 5, 2002, at a press conference at the Justice Department in Washington, Ashcroft told reporters:

> It is extraordinary for the United States to have to charge one of its own citizens with aiding and conspiring with international terrorist groups whose agenda is to kill Americans. Today a grand jury examined the government's case and saw fit to charge John Walker Lindh with ten serious crimes based in part on voluntary statements made by Lindh himself. The United States is a country that cherishes religious tolerance, political democracy and equality between men and women. By his own account, John Walker Lindh allied himself with terrorists who reject these values. The United States is a country of laws and not of men. By his own account, John Walker Lindh fought side-by-side with tyrants who recognize no other law than the law of brute force. . . . The reasons for his choices may never be fully known to us, but the fact of these choices is clear. Americans who love their country do not dedicate themselves to killing Americans.[12]

It is difficult to unite a multicultural, multiethnic, multifaith country in global consensus, but the suprapersonal values outlined in Ashcroft's speech are clear. Yet, other voices in media denunciation implied the necessity to also denounce "liberal" thinking. Lindh was not a unique, individual case, these voices suggested, but a symbolic warning. Too much intellectual freedom, too little supervision, divorce, alternative lifestyles, alternative religions, and the lack of structure were the stepping stones to a son's corruption. Finally, authorizing young people to embark upon a serious spiritual quest alone was dangerous business. The sincerity and passion of the fanatic can have an allure for an impressionable young person. Any excessive belief may be dysfunctional for society if it preoccupies individuals and disrupts the performance of a community. The fanatical believer following a vengeful, bloodthirsty god can never be a fit member of the global tribe.

Though Lindh may not have fully accepted the public humiliation of the degradation ceremony, he did "confess his guilt" on July 15, 2002, pleading guilty to charges of aiding the Taliban and possessing explosives. In exchange for his confession, the U.S. government dropped terrorism and conspiracy charges. The courts, which generally control the outcomes of degradation ceremonies in our society, condemned Lindh to two consecutive ten-year sentences, which seemed to satisfy official denouncers. This was more lenient than the life sentence without parole he might have received and too indulgent for some outspoken critics, who wanted to see Lindh's degradation prolonged. The degradation was unsuccessful in the sense that Lindh expressed no public shame or guilt. However, the public denunciation of Lindh was successful in that it ritually separated him "from a place in the legitimate order," defining him as "outside," "oppositional," and clearly "strange" (Garfinkel 318).

Grateful Dead Music and Dead Head Metaphysics

In addition to effacing time, providing audiences with mythic narratives, and connecting the tribe through public rituals, media communication may assist audiences in reaching altered mental states. To achieve this, audience members must be willing collaborators in the mesmerism, allowing the sight and sounds of a media message to synchronize with their minds and bodies like tribal drums.

In the summer of 1989, I produced a documentary on Dead Head subculture, following the summer tour of the musical group the Grateful Dead. The rock band started performing in the early 1960s as the house band for Ken Kesey's Acid Tests, where musicians and audiences experimented with hallucinogenic drugs and musical sounds. Fans of the Grateful Dead developed over the years into a nomadic group, following the band on performance circuits from city to city. The biography of Dead Head subculture reached a peak in 1989. After that year, the band appeared to be in a downward spiral and restrictions were placed on camping near concert venues, and in August of 1995, lead guitarist Jerry Garcia died from complications of drug use. However, in the summer of 1989, the subculture was at a robust stage. By examining the ways Dead Heads used media and music during this period, I will show that the subculture can provide interesting insights about the ways media experiences touch audiences and how these become complicated in audiences' belief systems.

One of the things that impressed me that summer was the spiritual function of music in bringing meaning to the lives of individual Dead Heads and the larger Dead Head community. As I interviewed Grateful

Dead fans both on and off camera, it became apparent that many Dead Heads were more than merely fans of the music; they were devotees. For them, the music surpassed mere entertainment. Though many people used the music for simple diversion, for "partying," it was also what permitted them entry into a subcultural group with its own values, language, customs, myths, and political agenda. Robert Sardiello, a sociology student who also followed the Grateful Dead tour in the summer of 1989, observed that the Dead Head concerts were secular rituals. However, I contend that for some fans, the ritual was hardly secular. For them, the ritual of listening to Grateful Dead music was the sacred agency for mystical experience. For those members of the Dead Head subculture, the band's music was much more than a party accessory or a "joyful noise" celebrating a countercultural lifestyle; instead, the music was the center of spiritual intimacy. Yet, it wasn't the overt messages in the music that were important. The music didn't illustrate or propagate a unified ideology (there was great diversity among Dead Heads about the ways to find meaning in life); rather, the role of the music seemed to be simply to facilitate personal revelation, to act as a lubricant for the apparatus of the spirit. Interestingly, the musical style of the band seemed more conducive to a raucous good time than a spiritual experience. There was little about the Grateful Dead playlist in the summer of 1989 that was overtly mystical either in musical style or lyrics. Some might argue that extemporaneous musical breaks and "drums in space" sequences had New Age or acid-trip qualities, but the Grateful Dead's musical style often was more like Southern blues or country than New Age. It was hardly the stereotype of meditation music. Perhaps—as one Dead Head suggested to me—by juxtaposing familiar Southern rock and blues with fantastical improvisation, the music "freed" the mind to explore new realms, to wander down unexpected and unexplored paths.

The ritual elements surrounding the concert experience and the metaphysical beliefs were conspicuous in the subculture. However, the boundaries of spiritual beliefs and practices were vague, and the main unifying element appeared to be the music. I was surprised by the deep, often unorthodox, spirituality of many Dead Heads. This was evidenced by various religious groups that conducted tail-gate meditations in the parking lots prior to concerts. It was also evidenced by the numerous Dead Heads who asserted their beliefs in the power of crystals, astrology, hypnosis, ritual, or prayer. And it was evidenced inside the concerts by dancers, called "spinners," who, like whirling dervishes, rotated in frenzied circles until the music stopped. Various aspects of the concert experience were like the religious rituals of some premodern culture. Some Dead Heads claimed that the abundant drug and alcohol use in the subculture was a chemical assist in the attempt to find God.

In the summer of 1989, I conducted several interviews with the publicist for the Grateful Dead, Dennis McNally, who compared the wild celebrations of Dead Heads to the mysterious rites in the ancient Greek and Roman culture of Dionysus and Bacchus. These ancient revels extolled altered mental states and the metaphysical joys of drinking, sex, and abandonment of civilization's restraints. In the frantic delirium of a Bacchic orgy, the believer could unite his or her soul with the god. For some members of Dead Head subculture, the music was the principal means for achieving a similar disembodied state, often accompanied and enhanced by drug or alcohol use. The emotional releases I witnessed during concerts were sometimes powerful, frenetic, and—now and again— filled with bliss or agony. In the instance of Grateful Dead concerts, the music served as a vehicle for personal, mystical experience. Perhaps this was but an aspect of the entertainment function. Or perhaps it was something else, something more active and less escapist than I previously supposed any entertainment could be.

Though Dead Heads may have induced psychic events with drug use, there seemed to be a faith in the spiritual reality of these experiences, whether or not they were chemically provoked. Both naturally occurring and chemically induced wondrous events were openly accepted and embraced by Dead Head subculture. Not all Grateful Dead fans are "believers." However, among fans generally there seemed to be an understanding of, and tolerance for, anomalous experiences and the beliefs they produced. Even Dead Head skeptics were indulgent when believers related experiences filled with amazing circumstance and mysterious coincidence that "must be evidence" of a metaphysical world or some "sign of a greater cosmic design." Dead Head customs appeared to deliberately foster this belief. For example, one Dead Head described for me the custom of the "miracle ticket," an expression derived from the lyrics of a Grateful Dead song: "I need a miracle everyday." "A true miracle ticket is when you don't have any money, and you want to see a concert so bad. You need a ticket to get into the concert, and a stranger just gives you one for free. That's a true miracle ticket," she said. Another Dead Head showed me a lucky cardboard sign, which she claimed could produce a miracle every time. Hand-lettered in bright markers on the cardboard, the declaration read, "I need a miracle."[13] Dead Head subculture placed a particular value on giving things to others, so some more affluent Dead

Heads bought extra tickets to give away at concerts, and other Dead Heads showed up at concerts without tickets, hoping for a miracle. There wasn't anything particularly marvelous or supernatural about this system, yet the Dead Head who received her "miracle ticket" when she was most in need of one had her belief in cosmic luck reinforced.

That summer, I began to understand how the images and sensations conjured through popular culture could become the chief instruments for social integration and community orientation, as well as for reinforcing personal beliefs. For many Dead Heads, the music of Grateful Dead concerts had transcendent qualities. Not only did they celebrate counterculture metaphysics, they believed a special karma infused the band, particularly its leader, Jerry Garcia. One bit of Dead Head lore is that in 1971 Garcia, along with some of the other band members and close associates, became involved in tests of "psychic transmission" with a parapsychologist at the Maimodes Dream Laboratory, tests that would leave Garcia with real psychic abilities. In 1989 and again after his death, I heard many stories about the guitarist appearing in dreams of Dead Heads to reveal cosmic truths or relay practical advice. One fan told me that when she was at a concert and Garcia looked out into the audience, she knew he was looking for her and only her. She could feel his eyes lock onto hers and experienced a rush of exultation. Dead Head adoration for Garcia may have been a source of amusement or irritation to the band. In the summer of 1989, McNally complained that "Jerry Garcia is neither the mayor of tent city nor its priest," referring to the nomadic community set up by Dead Head campers.[14]

It was clear that Garcia was a beloved symbol of this community when he passed away in a drug rehabilitation center six years later. Fans gathered across the country to mark his passing with candlelight vigils, prayers, dancing, and music, as well as with promises to "keep the faith." I attended one of these improvised ceremonies, where fans assembled to listen to music, to console one another, and finally to form a candlelight procession to a city park for prayer and meditation. It was evident that this subculture had a profound spiritual constituency. "Keeping the faith" for this group of fans implied that they would continue to congregate, to enjoy Grateful Dead music, and to glorify in the metaphysical joys found through abandoning mainstream social restrictions. For many fans, participation in Dead Head subculture was spiritually healing, a phenomena that Hutson also notes in the rave subculture (53), and that might arguably be an element in any music subculture.

I found it paradoxical that Dead Heads, a group of people who were such avid media users, openly expressed disdain for popular media. Popular bumper stickers on sale in the summer of 1989 urged "Kill your television" and "Reclaim your brain; kick the mass media habit." Yet, many Dead Heads were active readers, dynamic film enthusiasts, and enterprising users of recorded media (audio and videotape). They enjoyed an energetic public-access television network (Dead TV) and were earnestly involved with computer technology (the Well).[15] Many listened to the radio and had favorite (usually alternative music) stations.

Mainstream media often reflected or commented on elements of Dead Head subculture, sometimes in positive ways. For example, the television series *Roseanne* (ABC, 1988–97) made numerous references to Dead Head subculture from the beginning of the series. The show dedicated its 1995 Halloween program to Jerry Garcia. In that episode, a pregnant Roseanne goes into labor while playing with a Ouija board. In the hospital delivery room, all the doctors and nurses are dressed in bizarre costumes, and Roseanne experiences a sense of dislocation. During an intense labor, she has a hazy angelic vision of Jerry Garcia, who tells her to spread the message of peace and love. She returns from this vision to welcome her infant son into the world with the name Jerry Garcia Conner. Several Dead Heads I spoke to would single out specific elements of mainstream media, such as *Roseanne*, as being "okay" but remained firm that most mainstream media contents were to be abhorred.

It didn't take long to realize that much of the disdain Dead Heads expressed for popular media wasn't about the technologies of mass media but about the way mainstream America defined both media use and media contents. One fan explained to me that recorded music shouldn't be used for mindless escape but for "integration with the essence of God." My understanding of this phenomenon of integration was that it was more likely to occur in a concert setting with live music, but that it also happened frequently with recorded music. Though Grateful Dead music rarely received significant radio attention prior to 1986, some Dead Heads claimed to feel "God presence" during Dead Head–oriented radio programs broadcast on college stations. Said one Dead Head, "you can just feel the community [of other Dead Heads] when you hear Dead music on the radio. You know they're listening. Sometimes you can catch the God presence."

Some Dead Heads disdained American mainstream media for their profane uses within a commercial system. They generally felt that capitalism, not the technology, spoiled the mediated experience. Yet, a few Dead Heads were more literal in their belief that mainstream media are evil. I found it disconcerting when interviewing Dead Heads in the summer of

1996 at the Furtherfest concert in Raleigh, North Carolina, to be told by one glaring fan to "shut off my camera" because it was "an instrument of the Devil." This young man with his dreadlocks and torn jeans was not a member of the fundamentalist Christian right, but he seemed to share its sentiments. I tried to engage him in a conversation, but he would have none of it. He believed the medium itself was Satan's instrument and spoke about popular media being the devil's agent. He made it clear that mediated experience, both recording and consuming media material, would damage the soul. He would not let me record an interview. "Kill the TV," he growled before he stalked away.

Drugs, Media, and Occult Knowledge

Historically, a prime goal of the person seeking occult wisdom was to invoke a god or spirit and integrate with the essence of that spirit to the point of complete assimilation or divine union. No longer burdened with personality and mundane human consciousness, the shaman or magician was then filled with perfect knowledge. To achieve this union, the wizard would need to alter everyday perception, which both shapes and blinds the senses. Only with this ordinary "blindness" removed would the seeker be able to fathom absolute wisdom.

One avenue for achieving altered consciousness was through use of hallucinogenic drugs, many of which have been associated with occult practices. The drugs linked with the occult have been of two distinct types: those of the pharmacopoeia, which could cure the physical ailments of a shaman's patients, and those that removed the shaman's human blindness or took him or her out of body to unite with the god. In modern culture, one type of drug became the arsenal of the medical doctor, while the other became the street drugs that threatened society (Shenk). Chemist and religious scholar Daniel Perrine explains that people assigned a sacred power to psychoactive drugs that had profound physical effects.[16] Low doses of some drugs, such as nitrous oxide, distort the usual rhythms of the brain, releasing inhibitions and enhancing perceptions. Psychedelic agents such as LSD produce altered states, resulting in brain-wave patterns similar to those associated with bizarre dreams (Watson 109).

A key motive for modern experimentation with street drugs echoed the archaic shaman's occult aspirations. In the 1960s, Harvard professor Timothy Leary became a leading guru in a transcendental agenda: to expand ordinary consciousness with LSD and break free of repression, whether psychic or political (D. Gates). Leary advocated the use of hallucinogens and gave his students experimental doses of psilocybin, which was legal at the time, as a quick and easy route to divine union. Carlos Castaneda's infamous book *The Teachings of Don Juan: A Yaqui Way of Knowledge* and the other books that followed helped to popularize the association between the use of drugs such as peyote and marijuana and the quest for spiritual wisdom. Those who took part in Ken Kesey's Acid Tests were not simply "kids gone wild," but seekers. As one Dead Head explained his LSD use to me in the summer of 1989, "it's a shortcut to God."

Because film, television, and computer media can also take audiences "out of body," it wasn't long before critics began to compare the media habits of modern audiences to drug addiction.[17] One of the first to suggest that television had addictive properties, McLuhan proposed in 1969 that the technology of television focused audiences' attention inward, promoting a preoccupation with fantasy and inner life (McLuhan and Zingrone 233–69). A decade later, he suggested that television technology might be associated with a generation that sought inner experience through hallucinogens and religious mysticism ("Last Look"). In the late 1970s, Marie Winn associated television viewing with the harmful dangers of drug use, recommending that parents strictly curtail children's use of the medium. Like the dangers of drug use, the risks of television use included obsession, loss of self, physical harm to the body, and misplacement of acceptable goals and real-world skills.

For many Americans, media use became a legal and easily procurable out-of-body experience. Later research found that people who described themselves as television addicts watched television to distract themselves from unpleasant worries and fears, to regulate mood, and to relieve boredom, reasons similar to the motives for using illegal drugs (McIlwraith). Other research reported that subjects experienced "withdrawal" or subjective anxiety when denied television, comparing this behavior to pathological gambling, a behavioral disorder or addiction not manifesting the use of a psychoactive substance (Kubey; American Psychiatric Association; McIlwraith). Critics like Winn stressed the connection between media use and the altered alpha patterns, which also characterize drug use.

In the 1990s, computer addiction also emerged as a disorder suffered by people who were more attracted to the virtual world of the computer than everyday reality.[18] Like preoccupation with television, computer addiction encourages fixations with self and fantasy. Though the availability of television and computer media make them more likely to be associated with addiction, film can also take audiences out of themselves into an altered mental state. The metaphor of addiction as it was applied to media use may be more of an indication of society's ambivalent feelings toward popular media than a clinical phenomenon (McIlwraith). However, if media use alters alpha rhythms, media may fulfill the physiological as well as psychological demands of audiences. A practitioner adept at yoga, meditation, or other means to control functions of the autonomic nervous system doesn't need drugs to alter consciousness. Ordinary people have also learned to enter into a relaxed state with biofeedback or self-meditation techniques. Though some may be skeptical of the near trance brought on by meditation, there are clear benefits. An individual experiencing deep relaxation has less stress, tension, and anxiety. Research shows that subjects who experience the sustained alpha rhythms characteristic of deep meditation are in a relaxed, but at the same time, very alert state, with increased cardiac output and cerebral blood flow (Jevning, Wallace, and Beidebach). This escape from stress also appears to be the state some people hope to achieve more effortlessly through drug or media use. Deep relaxation can dismantle the mind's censors, helping an individual to achieve clarity. This appears to be the goal of those searching for a psychic lubricant.

Some media critics reading this will be quick to point out that the confused masses hooked on the Internet, television, recorded music, or escapist films can hardly have achieved mental clarity, even if their alpha patterns happen to be altered. My point here is not to suggest that media use is any more a quick route to profound awareness than drug use is but to explain that the yearning for the mediated experience, like the yearning for altered consciousness, may be related to an ancient, occult aspiration. It is that yearning for escape from everyday tensions, the desire to lose the ego and yet to feel a surge of control. The same longing for eternal energy and unity with the god the shaman seeks may motivate some audiences to seek out media experience. Through media use, audience members can travel out of their bodies to other worlds and return, though perhaps not always with revelations from the gods. Possibly, the true cause of dismay with popular media is the realization that an experience that holds such promise rarely fulfills the yearning. The occult hope is that unity and knowledge might be triggered through media, like the flash of inspiration triggered by meditation, prayer, or fasting. The disappointment is that such revelation is highly unlikely.

Media: Trickster, Sufi, and Shaman

In his analysis of the media experience, McLuhan tended to devalue content or message in relation to the characteristics of technology. Yet, media

45

provide audiences with both: the lesson through narrative, and the sensation through technology. It is difficult to separate the narratives media supply us from the experiences they provide. Media have dual roles. The Internet is both the sorcerer and the magic. Television is both the teacher and the lesson. Film is both the "trip" and the drug.

Despite multiple roles and functions, media have developed a peculiar personality in the popular imagination. People tend to perceive media as one entity. The evidence of this bias can be found in a tendency for the public to view mass media not as delivery systems for many different messages but as one entity with one voice. Public criticisms are frequently leveled not at a particular newspaper story, radio message, film, or television program, but at "the media." Thus, a frequent grammatical mistake is the use of the plural noun *media* with a singular verb, as in the statement "the media *is* a powerful force in the United States." This grammatical mistake is so persistent and widespread that it's likely to become standard usage. The tendency for media companies to merge into large corporate enterprises that share stories, stars, and information also helps to create a sense of a single, shared media disposition. Finally, the inclination for some audience members to regard media as a companion and shield against loneliness helps to configure popular media as a singular identity.

As one entity, the combined media personality is a schizophrenic one, with contradictory messages. On television, for example, a public service announcement warning teenagers against drug use might follow a comedy program that portrays drug use as harmless high jinks. This integrated media personality is a merger of trickster and shaman; an American version of Mulla Nasrudin, the legendary figure from the Middle East who is stupid and brilliant, greedy and generous, young and old, married and single, a parent and childless, and the proprietor of mystical secrets. Sufis, who believe deep intuition is the only real escort to wisdom, believe this jokester can slip through the clefts in the most rigid ways of thinking to bring an occasional moment of enlightenment (Shah). This blended "media trickster" might also be compared to a character-type created in the early comedy films of Cheech Marin and Tommy Chong.[19] This is the character of a drug user who appears not as a ruthless and dangerous addict but as a harmless, hazy-headed person with good intentions and a sporadic but visionary intuition. In both television and film, this character became a repetitive comic type: a funny, brain-fried individual who had the occasional powerful insight. One of the early television examples of the goofy, drug-using mystic in a sitcom was "Reverend Jim" on the comedy *Taxi* (1978–83). Twenty years later, a similar character, the hippie Larry Finkelstein, provided backhanded wisdom on the series *Dharma and Gregg* (1998–), and Tommy Chong would resurface as another aging hippie, Leo, on *That 70s Show* (1998–). The character often has a shallowly liberal viewpoint, but not always, and his or her friendship comes at a price.

The personality of "the media" that critics so often condemn is seen as both a swindler and a public servant. As a singular, collective personality, the media *is* a comedian to be taken seriously. Though often benign, this personality can be ruthless, greedy, and pernicious. Oftentimes it is self-reflexive and self-critical. As *Taxi's* Reverend Jim observes, "You know the really great thing about television? If something important happens, any-where in the world, night or day . . . you can always change the channel."[20]

Media provide a tribal audience with a schizophrenic shaman whose "magic" involves the sensations fabricated by our technology. Media are our teacher and our lesson, our wizard and the magic, our trip and our drug. Although they are a faceless, corporate media that combine to cre-ate this schizophrenic shaman that audiences perceive, it is individual artists who are involved in the production processes. People make me-dia stories. The next chapter examines the possibility that these individual artists might find "cult value" in modern media production that recalls the archaic artist, who once used art to appeal to a god.

Creating Worlds
The Cult Value of Media Production

Art is a profession, not a shrine.
—Elizabeth Hardwick, *LA View of My Own* (1962)

The Audience as Wizard

*A*ll worlds are created: the social worlds we label "reality" and the fanciful worlds we label "fiction." Both are products of human imagination. Our understanding of the world we know is skewed, seen through a biased intellect and prejudiced emotions. For infants in their cribs, the world is a turmoil of sight, sound, smell, touch, and taste, until they mature and learn to re-create the world for themselves, shaping sensation into a social reality that has some meaning for them (Burke; Ornstein). Surrounding the individual's creative process, social life is like a magic act in a carnival, dependent on the cooperation of many individuals to maintain this illusion we accept as reality.[1] In the act of construing daily life, human beings are very much involved in the process of interpreting and assigning purpose to situations and social interactions that constantly change. Mediated narratives are part of this process as well. As they actively interpret and assign significance to media messages, audience members become producers. Though my interest in this chapter is largely the human skills united in the "cult process" of creating worlds, it is important to observe and honor the audience's craft of re-creating and imaginatively living in those alternate worlds, perhaps discovering something of value to take back into that larger social fiction in which most of us collaborate. Audiences must be active and willing participants in the process, for audiences ultimately produce meaning.

My emphasis here is primarily on narrative storytelling through film and television. However, I should note that emotional transmutation for audiences isn't limited to narratives but can involve any type of mediated expression. For example, I have a colleague who found herself moved to tears by a Gap commercial aired on television during the fall of 2001. The spot featured Carole King and her daughter, Louise Goffen, singing "So Far Away," which has been a signature song for King. The spot doesn't immediately show King, letting Goffen sing on her own until—toward the end of the spot—the camera reveals that King accompanies her daughter on a white piano. Goffen finishes the spot saying, "My first love. My mom." The commercial evoked for my colleague thoughts about parenthood, about the often unseen support of a parent for her child, and about a grown and independent child reconnecting to her parent through the adult pursuits of art and ideas. My colleague was surprised by her own emotional reaction to an advertisement, relating to this spot in ways she had not thought possible. It was—after all—thirty seconds long, quite earnestly "hip," and "for Pete's sake, it was a television commercial."

It's important to notice that as audiences search for and find meaning in media productions, these productions no longer become simply commercials or merely entertainments. On some level, that larger search for meaning guides all the mediated experiences audiences consume. Media messages become either pathways or obstacles for audiences in that search. For each audience member, meaning is unique, personal, solitary, fulfilled by that individual's singular interpretative response. Audience members may find much to hate and much to condemn about a film or television program. In this case, the contemptible media message helps them reassert their own righteous view of the world through their condemnation of the poor effort presented in the film or television narrative. Only when audiences abandon the search for meaning do mediated messages become merely the arbitrary Babel and diversion of a universe in which there is no faith, no point, and no purpose and where "nothing" is all that truly exists.

Producer as Wizard

In the early 1980s, my college friend Travis Hardison was following the advice of some movie industry professionals to get "hands-on" filmmaking experience by taking a job in the production of pornographic films.[2] Because Travis had a little technical experience in college theater and had also worked for a small television station in Alabama, a producer of sadomasochistic pornography hired him to help create special effects for sadomasochist movies. Travis described himself as a "sorcerer's apprentice" to a producer with an international reputation for truly depraved

49

work.[3] This "sorcerer" was an undeniable porn-industry wizard, who liked to think of himself as a "Carlos Castaneda of the flesh," unveiling the true mysteries of bondage and pain that straight people would never grasp. Yet, Castaneda's legacy is considered by some anthropologists to be that of a creator of hoaxes rather than a revealer of truths. The same might be said of this sorcerer of pornography, whose work was more illusion than revelation. The pornographer's ability to create exotic, realistic-looking locales and sordid, vicious fantasies in a low-rent basement impressed my friend. This was material that would be scary, squalid, and secretive, though nothing but the nudity was real (and even that might be distorted or enhanced). The blood was an amalgam of Karo syrup and red food coloring. The cruel spikes on instruments of torture were made of soft rubber that caressed rather than pierced. Theatrical knives had disappearing blades that never cut, and the savage-looking whips that snaked across bare flesh never flayed any skin. Welts, wounds, and bruises were manufactured with makeup. A hair care product such as cream rinse substituted for semen because "it's pearlescent and creamy and always available with a squeeze and a squirt" (F. Burch 70). Careful edits gave the impression of terrible events that never happened, and even the screams of excruciated delight were dubbed in with sound effects or left MOS for the viewer's imagination.[4] Though most pornographers will wash their sets with light in order to reveal every bare detail, this producer understood the merits of chiaroscuro, lighting at angles to create mood. His oeuvre of sculpted light and meticulous detail—rare for the porno of the time—created credible milieus where men and women tortured each other using bizarre and terrifying instruments or flogged themselves into bloody ecstasy.

> Venetian blinds and drapes were hung against blank walls and, because [the audience] expected a window to be there, [the audience would] never know there wasn't one. "No smoking" signs in three languages and foreign editions of a couple of newspapers produced . . . the feeling of being in some unnamed South American dictatorship. (69)

Travis's work in sadomasochistic pornography reflected Sparshott's observation that "a photographic image is not so much a true [vision] . . . as a convincing one" (287).

The finished work, edited 16mm films, would then be smuggled into Switzerland, duplicated into a PAL video format so they would seem to have been locally made,[5] and finally sold to American tourists furtively searching the streets of Amsterdam for the really hard stuff, because such perverse pornography couldn't possibly have been made in the United States. As the pornographer's apprentice, Travis learned that beyond our ordinary world is an extraordinary one, where sweaty eccentricities and pathologies are serviced with the darkest illusions. But as he observed, for "some people, if it *looks* real, it *is* real" and on some level *becomes* real (F. Burch 69).

I believe Travis told me these stories about the seedy world of warped porn hoping his tales of fake breasts being guillotined would provoke from me outraged feminist rhetoric. Sometimes he succeeded, but more often my response was shocked silence. In those days, I was both a tireless defender of First Amendment freedoms and an enthusiastic advocate of feminist ideology, positions that seemed to be at odds with each other in the case of hard-core porn. Telling me about his adventures in the back lot of sadomasochistic sex, Travis was able to enjoy my discomfort and indulge in some macho boasting about all the naked women he saw as a regular feature of his work. Yet, I believe he also told me these stories because he was searching for a perspective from which to understand the events himself. In addition to the teasing and boasting, there was an attribute in his telling of these narratives that sounded something like a perplexed anthropologist, a man who really wanted to be a Hollywood-style filmmaker but who had blundered into this dark subculture to become a participant observer of faked sadistic rituals. I believe that Travis shared with me a philosophy that words, visions, and ideas are sacred things. So, was his pornographer turning the sacred into the profane, or making the profane sacred? Travis admitted that as a filmmaker, his boss was no Orson Welles or Alfred Hitchcock, but he was struck by the man's ability to create veraciously nasty and disturbingly credible films. It impressed me that a producer of porn might consider his work to be a form of fierce art and judge himself to be a visionary auteur. It's equally surprising that a pornographer would develop a respect for craft, attempting to make himself a master of dark technique, the proficient wizard of a sexual *Grand Guignol*, so that his work would be as much a mirage as any major Hollywood film. However, knowing the market and audience, this pornographic producer kept certain elements deliberately unpolished so the work would retain the mangy imperfections of a furtively made, low-budget production, qualities that contributed to making the on-screen action seem genuine.[6]

Once, as Travis was explaining to me in detail how he had achieved a particularly graphic and lurid effect, I mentally flashed on a photograph I had seen of an ancient Mayan painting. The painting depicted a priest

brutally sacrificing a man; a horrid image, but one respected by archae-
ologists because it revealed something about the beliefs and practices of a
once proud and powerful culture. For me, Travis's description of the sadomasochistic film resonated with this painting of an ancient and bloody
ceremony. Perhaps the major difference between the sacred image and the
profane one is that the sacred image is created to honor the pathologies
of a god, while the profane image honors the pathologies of humankind.

Unlike ancient artists, modern media producers tend to be more interested in human pathologies. This was obviously the case with the sadomasochist pornographer. Perhaps central to the public outrage against
media pornography is that it celebrates the lewd by awarding obscene
narratives permanence in the fixed agency of film, video, or print, when
the gut feeling of many people is that only "worthy" stories should be
saved in media that can transcend time and space.

Media and Supernatural Transmutation

The ancient wizard's goal was transmutation, but not the kind that is a
natural occurrence. Water can freeze into ice, or it can boil, releasing
steam. Eggs hatch into chicks, down transforms into feathers, and baby
chicks grow into adult birds. The wizard's concern was with producing
changes that are not naturally occurring and guiding those supernatural transmutations in a desired direction, such as taking a base metal and
turning it into gold. Yet, the legitimate wizards and alchemists of ancient
times were supposedly less concerned with turning lead into gold and
more concerned with turning matter into spirit, because their search was
for the "elixir of the soul" (Coudert 81). The goal of the media producer
is also transmutation, turning imagination into "reality" through the
various elements of production.

Not all medieval alchemists or ancient wizards belonged to a spiritual
league: many were chiefly interested in gold. The same might be said of
contemporary media producers whose goal is the transmutation of moving image and sound into story. Many of them are interested not so much
in the story or the message but in the gold. For example, the pornographer who liked to consider himself the "Castaneda of the flesh" was clearly
in the sadomasochism business for the money. However, on some level,
the goal of any producer is to compose a fictional universe or reveal an
existing one through the manipulation of creative and technological elements. When media makers are successful, audiences can become emotionally or intellectually engaged, even transformed. Because of this transforming power of media, we have seen that one of the continuing and

pervasive fears has been for the directions in which audiences might be transformed as a result. Clearly, not all productions are "elixirs of the soul." In medieval times, the Devil himself was considered to be a master of transmutation (Coudert 76). However, nothing beautiful, good, or meaningful is said to have emerged from his work, though he was believed to be among the greatest of adepts, a wizard above all others.

Sacred or profane, media producers create for audiences alternate realities that they hope will resonate with the realities audiences create for themselves. Though much of any producer's work is illusion, in many ways the wizard's magic or the alchemist's transmutation is a better analogy than the magician's sleight of hand for what producers and directors hope to do. The ancient alchemical tradition was an occult one, used to both discover and control the spiritual and temporal disposition of reality. The alchemist's goal was to transform rather than fool, to discover that which is rare within the mundane, and to reveal or create something precious from commonplace materials. I believe these are also the ambitions behind most film and television producers. Even Travis's perverse pornographer wanted to do more than dupe his audience; he wished "to get them off."

Cult Value and Media Production

In an exploration of how mechanical reproduction separated art from its basis in ancient sacred ritual, Walter Benjamin examined the issues of a formulaic approach to film production and the relationship of film production to the production of art. He observed that the art of prehistoric times is presumed to have been an instrument of magic. Though primitive peoples may have seen the cave paintings a primitive artist created, it was not necessarily a human audience the artist hoped to impress. The primary audience was the god or the spirits the artist meant to influence through the work. The ancient artist through his or her work became an intermediary between the gods of creation and the uncertainty of everyday life. The ancient shaman involved in a ritual of ceremonial magic, dancing, drumming, or singing was not simply putting on a show but was caught up in a mystical drama, inspiring the shaman's own transformation. This gave art its "cult value" in a community of worship and ritual. Over time, human beings supplanted the gods as the intended audience for works of art until—with the development of photography— "exhibition value began to displace cult value . . . but cult value does not give way without resistance" (738). According to Benjamin, the cult value of photography remained for people as late as the early twentieth century, when grieving households would commission photographs of deceased family members. Photographs of the dead were a popular method for keeping alive the memory of the ancestor (Ruby). The cult value in these portraits of the deceased came for the families who commissioned the photographs. Benjamin doesn't discuss the cult value of the process for a photographer who posed the dead body for its portrait. But having had several occasions to videotape dead bodies in the process of covering breaking news stories, I believe the process is a sobering experience, if not a sacred one. Benjamin claims that the making of these portraits of the deceased was a last holdout for the cult value in photography before the age of mechanical reproduction finally separated photography and film from its sacred footing.

Though film theorists were eager to classify film as art and seemed desperate to find ritual elements in it, Benjamin argues that there is very little sacred significance in the production and display of film. He suggests that film (and by extension, television) separated from cult value so much that the narrative film might be compared to "any article made in a factory" (742). For example, he observes, replacing the audience with a camera cancels the cult value of performance and reduces the actor to a mere "stage prop," or glorified model, cast in a role for his or her physical characteristics. Unlike theater, the actor's performance in a film will be constructed from many separate takes, as a product on an assembly line is composed of several distinct parts.

> The film responds to the shriveling of the aura with an artificial buildup of the "personality" outside the studio. The cult of the movie star, fostered by the money of the film industry, preserves not the unique aura of the person but the "spell of the personality," the phony spell of a commodity. (742)

Benjamin compares the camera operator to a contemporary surgeon, and the artist to a traditional shaman. The traditional shaman who healed a sick person by laying on his hands knew the total person he was attempting to heal, but the surgeon may not even know the name of the patient whose flesh her scalpel slices. Likewise, according to Benjamin, the traditional artist creates a whole picture; the camera operator captures only fragments, which will later be assembled by a team. In this view, producers and directors are little more than administrators in a manufacturing process.

Unlike the production of art, which is transcendental, the criticism argues, media production is perfunctory and mechanical, like the fabrication of parts for any consumer product. There is an implicit suggestion that if media productions are truly to be called art, they ought to be spiritually and morally uplifting, instructive, and therapeutic, like religion, and that there must be cult value in the full process. The persons involved in media production should be able to become fully submersed in the activities and temporarily elude the dominance of the ego. There is an implication that all the hopes, fears, and valiant chronicles we compose through moving-image media ought to amount to a form of prayer. From production through distribution, a film or television program must be made for the spirit, not the gold. Producer and audience must be equally moved by the work, so that the alchemical goal of finding the "elixir of the soul" through production emerges at the end of the process with discovery of "self." Or as Jung might have expressed it, having found the "spiritual regeneration" that is a by-product of transmutation (35). Lose ego; find self.

Film and stage actor Anthony Rapp disagrees with the mechanistic assessment of film production, at least so far as screen acting is concerned:[7]

> It's true that the film actor doesn't follow the same trajectory of performance as he might when acting on the stage, but the film actor has the opportunity to tightly focus his performance within the shot and within the frame. Film acting requires a technique that is concentrated in the moment and in the character. It is intense and centered work.

Rapp claims it is possible for the actor to achieve transmutation under these conditions, to become a character and feel that transformation even within a short, exclusive moment of performance that seems disconnected from the larger story. However, it's not always possible to know if this intense moment of transmutation into another person and an alternate life will be a moment that makes the final edit of the film. "When I see the premiere of a completed film, I see it from five different perspectives," he explains.

> I see the film I saw in my head when I first read the script; I see the film from the perspective and kinetic experience of my character as I developed him; I see the film as we were shooting it, with its many possible moments and performances; I see the film in its final edit with those possibilities omitted; and lastly I see the film as audiences react to it. But it is possible in screen acting to feel and understand an intense transformation [of self to character].[8]

In a text on film directing, author Steven Katz suggests that media production isn't simply the manufacture of parts to a specified blueprint.

He believes media artists *rarely* have a specific goal in mind at the beginning of a work, so that the "process of visualization is actually the search for a goal rather than the attainment of one" (4). This sounds something like the reclamation of "cult value" in the production process.

Katz proposes that being able to re-create a film precisely as it has been imagined has little to do with the creative process, nor does it "sound like much fun" (4). This doesn't necessarily negate the preproduction planning and mapping of a project but permits the production to transform and become, allowing both people and project to evolve through the process. The process develops as more of a journey of challenges than a series of routine tasks to be completed and problems to be solved. This suggests that if media productions are to deliver on the inherited promise of art, they should provide avenues of transcendental escape for everyone—not just audiences. Transmutations should occur below the line, for best boys and gaffers, as well as above the line, for writer, producer, director, and cast.

Transmutation and the Processes of Media Production

Through the process of making a film or television program, an ordinary human being can take control of objective time: the running time of a program and the timing of sequences, scenes, and shots. The adept can learn to control subjective time, the emotional pace or perceived speed of an on-screen event and the rhythm and flow among shots, scenes, and sequences. Materials and performers can be manipulated to create the impression of worlds, people, and events that never physically existed. As observed in chapter 2, the fixed characteristics of media allow writers, producers, and performers to continue a discourse with audiences long after death.[9] Even so, the work of media production happens in linear time, with budgets and schedules for cast and crew. Unlike archaic time, production schedules deal with the limited resource of a linear time that cannot be continually reproduced. I can make a similar statement about production budgets. Still, some will argue that media production is more than the assembly-line manufacturing of a product, but a ritual process with transformative possibilities for those involved.

The art of creating truly effective media is something of a puzzle. Even with the numerous how-to books, college classes on media production, and weekend seminars peddling to the general public the idea that "you, too, can become a Hollywood director," the ability to engender the transformation of sound and image into credible and moving productions remains elusive for most. Though amateur media producers and even audiences may think they know what it's like behind the scenes in the making of a movie or television show, like the transmutations of ancient alchemy, the transmutations that occur through modern media production remain something of a mystery. Sometimes the process works, and producers achieve the "elixir of the soul," masterpieces that can mesmerize and transform audiences for generations. But many times the process falls short of this ambition. Even though the techniques and mechanics of production and the behind-the-scenes secrets of the producer's transmutation may be acknowledged or even revealed to audiences (often through "making of" documentaries),[10] these techniques are rarely apparent in the final creative work, particularly if the work attempts a style of realism.[11] In composing a realistic, mediated world, the full processes of production stay hidden. Media production may have become more accessible to the general public, as many households own video cameras and even desktop computers with video editors, yet the creation of believable worlds is still predominantly left to the hands of a masterful few. These are individuals who can access the tremendous resources necessary for production and can persuade investors to bankroll the project.

Along with the ability to raise sufficient capital investment, modern media producers are also individuals who can marshal the diverse skills of technicians and artists to bring the inanimate script to "life." These individuals take vision and performance and turn them into film, video, or digital media, creating a visual language often as elusive to reproduce as the text of spiritual transformation written by a wizard.

On close inspection of the process, it seems wondrous that any type of media composition succeeds in communicating a message or story. At every level of production and distribution, from the internal conception of a script in an author's mind to the broadcast or screening of a completed program, there are multiple opportunities for communication—and the media project—to fail. Even that most basic communication level, the intrapersonal level of communication where individuals think or talk to themselves, is fraught with the traps of miscommunication. The work of many psychiatrists, counselors, and therapists is a direct result of problems at that intrapersonal stage, because individuals can misunderstand their own desires and intents. Advancing upward through the communication levels, from intrapersonal, to interpersonal, group, and organizational, on up to messages intended for large audiences, the opportunities for misunderstanding and "noise" compound, as more people become involved in the production process and as elements like language, experience, and perception become more and more diverse. It is a significant feat when all the players on a media production team share a similar understanding of the project and what needs to be done to accomplish each task. That an audience of strangers can sit together in a darkened theater and respond similarly to an event on the screen, or at least have a mutual understanding of what they've seen, seems nothing short of magical.

A Grammar for Magic

Like adepts hoping to uncover the secrets of the masters, film theorists hope to uncover the secrets of film communication, to reveal the complex relations between cinematography and image, between the human eye and the camera lens, between the actor's mediated performance and an audience's understanding of it. How do interrelations among the various elements of production and the assorted cues prompt audiences' emotional response and appreciation? How does the filmmaker create a world and absorb audiences into it?

Some theorists believe the filmmaker uses form to involve spectators (Arnheim; Eisenstein; N. Burch). With a self-sustaining structure, with pattern and cadence, media substitute their own forms for the chaos and clutter of the natural world. The filmmaker takes the world's turmoil of sensations, abstracts two (sight and sound), and shapes these sensations for audiences. Arnheim saw the frame as a major organizing principle in film, as did theorists Bazin and Mitry. The frame devises a way of looking; the filmmaker places some objects on screen and conceals other objects from view. Thus, the frame becomes a mechanism for sorting, directing, and simplifying experience. The frame can be comforting to audiences searching for meaning, showing us where to look. It can be a wonderfully powerful device for defining an image, producing an unavoidable position from which audiences see, bounding, limiting, and perhaps clarifying the view. It is the director who is most challenged by the frame and the off-screen space beyond it: the space outside the edges of the frame, the space behind the set, the space in back of the camera (N. Burch). Directors can use the selectivity of the frame to deliberately exclude elements, involving audiences in the mystery of what lies beyond. Visually introducing a previously excluded element into the frame can create marvelous effects, as audiences suddenly become enlightened.

For other media artists, "seeing" is the magic of light: the control, the quality, and the directionality of light on objects. Lighting becomes the compound that brings meaning and emotion to an image. Like the power of the frame and the shot, producers suffuse the idea of light with the authority to shape emotion, connecting to themselves and audiences on basic levels. In the introduction to his lighting text, *Matters of Light and Depth*, author Ross Lowell comments that

> light has a profound influence upon living things. It controls appetites, health, and moods. The changing proportion of light and darkness in each day regulates our biological clock and informs some species when to crawl into a cave, others when to fly across an ocean. Without light we would have no seasons, no plants, no life, and—most serious of all—no television or movies. (12)

Lighting designer Dave Viera compares the term he uses to describe the visual quality of light, the *feel* of that light, to the jazz expression *soul* (xv). Both are vague terms, suggesting that intuition and emotion must be part of the process of putting light into the frame.

Some producers stress the importance of movement, expression, and performance in production (Katz), or additional elements of mise-en-scène, such as costumes, sets, and objects. For some, the magic of visual media is in the editing: the graphic, rhythmic, spatial, and temporal relations between shots (Eisenstein; Geuens). For others, sound is crucial (Weis and Belton). Most concede it is the combination of elements that creates the alphabet of film and television grammar through which a producer creates visual poetry (Mamer; Zettl; Douglass and Harnden). By controlling the elements within shots, by combining and arranging the shots themselves, producers can create complete pictures, pure macrocosms. As with the ancient alchemists, who believed the correct ritual that used the correct incantation and proper combination of elements would yield them the riches they so desired, the tradition of formative film theory is rooted in analysis of the proper methods through which to write the "language" of film that generates the magical effect. J. Dudley Andrew observes that formative theory and its emphasis on technique can reduce media production to a mechanics of correct choices:

> Classrooms are teeming with students demanding to know the secrets of the screen, and introductory textbooks by the score, all of them necessarily in the formative tradition, have appeared to answer this student need. Characteristically such books are divided into chapters on composition, camera, lighting, editing, sound, color. . . . Each chapter enumerates the various possibilities for artistic control in its domain, underscoring the "unnatural" (or specifically "cinematic") aspects of the medium. (77)

Not only are specific chapters devoted to explicit aspects of production, but whole books and courses are devoted to one area of the production process, so that students might specialize, becoming editors, lighting designers, or cinematographers. In the professional arena of the big-budget, Hollywood production, the emphasis isn't on one wizard, but the united forces of many, which is often why the search for media "gold" requires such a large investment of it.

There is always the hope that revelation will come through careful attention to formula and prudent regard for detail, but in particular, through that understanding of the special language that leads to mastery of the craft. Film theorists have looked to the rules that make language work for a grammar of film that would help film "speak" clearly to audiences (Metz). But just as following the rules of grammar may not guarantee great writing, careful adherence to "film grammar" may not guarantee a great film. The ancient alchemists warned against the trap of simply following a formula, for knowing the formula doesn't necessarily mean knowing the secret, and even well-meaning textbooks can be misleading. A seventeenth-century guide advised, "Avoide you Bokes written of Receipts, for all such receipts are full of Deceipts" (Ashmole 9). This suggests that the ancient wizards were jealous and ready to mislead each other. There is an additional suspicion that a good bit of guiding and achieving of transmutation is pure luck, perhaps destiny. Some people seem to be born adepts; it is their fate. Others may try but never achieve success, no matter how skillful they are or how carefully they follow the award-winning script or surefire production formula. There isn't even any guarantee that the master producer or director who turned "lead into gold" on one project will be able to repeat this success in the next. "*Sapienter retentatum, succedet aliquando*" (that which is wisely tried again will succeed sometime) reflects the belief that occasionally achievement of the desired transmutation seems arbitrary, even for the master (Coudert 92). The sequel may not be successful.

Cult Value in the Production of an Independent Film

In March of 2002, I had the chance to produce a narrative I had written, *Dead Write*. This was an opportunity to see from an insider's perspective if any cult value remained in the production process for the cast and crew in a contemporary production effort. This was to be a complex production, shot on a soundstage, mimicking Hollywood processes and following union production rules, but would remain at its core an educational endeavor. On the first day of shooting, the first assistant director (AD) would remind everyone not to forget that this was an instructional process, that learning was as important as product. Any question was legitimate. Any student or faculty member could call time-out for a question, as long as the question didn't interrupt actual filming.[12] The educational parameters for this project meant that the process would have some fundamental differences from a professional, commercial production, but there would be enough similarities that if cult value could be observed in this production, it might be present in others as well.

The story of *Dead Write* is hardly metaphysical: a murder mystery that draws from film noir traditions for its aesthetic. During principal photography,[13] the set was filled with students and some professionals, and there was much horsing around and wisecracking as professionals and students from three different colleges began to form friendships. The ability of strangers to make friendships and form emotional ties during the production process, to become in essence a tribe, may be one remnant of the cult value in media production, and it was distinctly reflected here. Within the first weekend of shooting, crew members began to develop their own insider jokes, language, and nicknames related to this specific production. There was much back rubbing, hugging, and making of emotional connections that transcended allegiances to a particular college, craft, or production role. Yet, within the joking and horseplay, cast and crew maintained a respect for the project and the process. As in tribal distinctions, some positions had more authority, but all were honored as contributors. When the first AD called "lock it up," concentration immediately reverted to the set and the "for picture" priority. As many as thirty people on the soundstage would be completely silent and focused. The moments that impressed me the most were when the sound mixer requested the recording of room tone. When the first AD called for silence for the minute or so of recording room tone, no one moved. (See fig. 3.1.) I looked around the room and saw people frozen, barely breathing, some with heads bowed. It was a moment of secular silence, yet the completeness of that silence, the alert attention to it, seemed intensely powerful, almost sacred. Here was a crew committed to craft, unwilling to make mistakes that might compromise the overarching artistry of the project.

Although the preproduction planning on this project had been extensive, there was plenty of evidence that the process was not simply following a preset plan overlaid with a formula. My co-producer, the production techniques instructor and director of photography for *Dead Write*, Michael Corbett, echoed Katz's sentiment that the process of visualization is more a sense of discovery of the shot than the application of formulaic "rules" of composition. While the "rule of thirds" and other visual

Fig. 3.1. Preparing to record room tone creates a moment of secular silence. Photo by E. D. Edwards.

grammar were a part of Corbett's thinking, they were not the principal guide in determining the placement of the camera or the framing of a subject. Camera placement and framing seemed to be primarily discovered during rehearsals, teased from the emotion of a moment, rather than proscribed by a system of rules or a preset plan laid out by the student director, John Lay. (See fig. 3.2.)

In my own role as a producer, concerns for budgets, schedules, and Screen Actors Guild contracts were frequent reminders of the business demands of media production. Yet, as abstract words on paper began to take on physical form—movement, texture, and emotion—those business

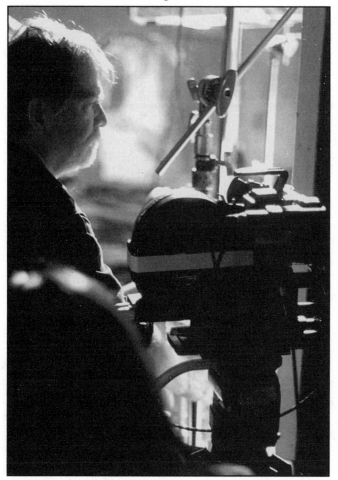

Fig. 3.2. For cinematographer Michael Corbett, emotions in the scene as well as rules of visual grammar determine the composition. Photo by E. D. Edwards.

concerns became less important. Interviewing various members of the cast and crew afterward, I learned that for some of the student crew there was pleasure in knowing in a direct and kinetic way how alternate film worlds came to life, even if they had no firm plans to seek out careers in media production. Like being an apprentice to the master alchemist in a laboratory, they found that even seemingly minute tasks took on special significance in the larger design.

As an independent and educational enterprise, the production of *Dead Write* may not be an accurate representative of a more generalized and professional media production process and its retention of ancient cult values. Though there were financial pressures, they were nothing like those associated with multimillion-dollar projects. Fewer financial pressures may have provided more freedom for exploration. Because the project honored the educational value of process, mistakes didn't have the power to damage a career but were regarded as opportunities for learning. Finally, this little murder mystery was clearly a secular product, not intended for the eyes of a god. If there was a prayer embedded in the celluloid, it was a prayer for the better understanding of the process, leading to opportunities to create bigger and better mediated worlds.

My second experience directing a narrative film under the same conditions illustrated that production dynamics change with each project. In 2004, I wrote, produced, and directed *Root Doctor*, which had at its core a statement about belief and disbelief in the supernatural. Though this film did have a metaphysical message, the crew included an element that was less respectful of the production process and more interested in partying and picking up girls. I've noticed similar attitudes in crews I've worked with or observed in professional and commercial productions, where some crew members were more concerned about the next dinner break than the job at hand. Even so, many members of the cast and crew of *Root Doctor* seemed determined to find the cult value of this experience, though they likely wouldn't have used that term for it. A tribal bonding similar to that of the *Dead Write* crew occurred for some, but not for the entire company. One actor confessed to a feeling of intense loss at picture wrap. When the art department began to dismantle the set, and she realized that the ritual aspects of congregating for the purpose of this production were about to disappear forever, she was profoundly sad, even though picture wrap should come with a sense of accomplishment and anticipation of seeing the final film put together.

Art Versus Business

Some film producers suggest that the mechanics of media production contain nothing remotely resembling the sublime, and they shouldn't. One producer told me bluntly:

> The specialist on a media production team can't expect to be uplifted or find unity through the process of his work. The idea is simply silly. Do you expect your accountant to be inspired while doing your taxes? Each person has a job to do and that [job] has nothing to do with spiritual fulfillment.

Another said, "I don't see the connection between art and religion. Andy Warhol was nobody's priest." However, some members of production crews think differently. "I didn't get into this business for the money," a script supervisor told me. "I love movies. I love television. When I do my job well, I help make programs better. There's a lot of satisfaction in that. And, yes, that satisfaction may even be spiritual." A grip on another film explained that he found some fulfillment in the community created around a production. "The production community is like a family. You eat together, work together, all centered on this one effort of making a film." A craft services worker dishing out lunch in the mess tent echoed this idea, suggesting that she felt happy to be a small part of creating something bigger, just as the acolyte is happy to serve the master with menial tasks. A media student invited to work on the production of a dance film suggested that even the least important member of a production team might find higher satisfaction, or cult value, in her work. This particular student had the job of wrangling a box of twenty butterflies that had been ordered specifically for the production. Her task was to open the box on signal and encourage the butterflies to flutter upward into the shot. The student waited for her signal with anticipation, but the day was cold, and the butterflies were uncooperative. Most elected to roost inside the box instead of flitting cooperatively toward the camera. With her persistent encouragement, one lone butterfly grudgingly made the ascent, escaping up into the light, posing briefly for the lens, creating a moment and ultimately a shot that would be "magical." The student wouldn't know the full impact of the recorded moment until she saw it edited into the final film, but she found satisfaction in having been part of creating that image.

In her spiritual guidebook to higher creativity, Julia Cameron, who has worked as a writer, producer, and director of independent features and documentaries, definitely considers film and television productions to be art forms. In her estimation, like any art, media production is a spiritual pursuit. Cameron warns artists that

> creativity is not a business, although it may generate much business. An artist cannot replicate a prior success indefinitely. Those who attempt to work too long with formula, even with their own formula, eventually leach themselves of creative truth. (183)

However, Cameron also recognizes that business demands and the financial definitions of success—particularly severe for film and television producers—can become impediments for creative achievement. But she suggests that "the many creatives laboring in fiscal settings should remember to commit themselves not only to projects that smack of the sure thing but also to those riskier projects that call to their creative souls" (184). The implication is that the wealth, power, and accumulation of esteem that are the media industry's measures of success are contaminating forces for art. Attempting to ensure healthy finances by only undertaking "safe" artistic projects, artists not only lose their cutting edge but put their creative psyches at risk. Other producers suggest that weaknesses in a completed film can be directly linked to the inability of some members of a company, whether the writer, actor, or grip, to set aside ego, financial concerns, and perhaps even physical comfort to merge with the cult values of the production process.

Just as some scholars and producers are eager to define film and television as art, there is an equally prevalent attitude of contempt for "artists" who don't understand the demands of business partnerships. Some professional producers will even submit that a person looking for spiritual transformation through the media production process is behaving unprofessionally, putting the project at risk. For these individuals, creativity is not a spiritual practice, but a financial one. In a textbook on production management, Richard Gates reminds us of an old Hollywood proverb regarding monetary success and filmmaking: "If you earn money, it's an industry. If you lose money, it's an art form" (7). In a commercial culture, the application that loses money is rarely the one we venerate.

Film and television director Andy Cadiff levels additional doubt about the potential of commercial film and television productions to create environments for inspiration and soul-changing transmutation for cast and crew. He describes directing a television drama as similar to "hosting a dinner party, where someone else decides on the guests, the menu, the date, the time, the attire, the topic of conversation, and the entire purpose behind the occasion."[14] Other directors and producers have echoed the sentiment behind his analogy, suggesting that to get through the media production process requires a form of "stoicism," or an indifference to the pain that will surely come from long hours, bad food, and cranky co-workers. "Film and television production isn't about passion and transmutation," one filmmaker told me, "it's about endurance." He thought a moment and then added, "Transformation. Passion. Inspiration. These are nice myths, but only a true stoic can make a movie."[15]

Stoicism, Passion, and Media Production

When my daughter was still in elementary school, she developed a definition of stoicism that seems in tune with a popular use of the word. "A stoic," she told me, "is someone who doesn't whine, or cry, or dig in her nose." Though the definition is cute and squarely approaches contemporary common usage, the philosophy of the stoic wasn't simply about developing an indifference to irritation or pain. More important than the ability to withstand annoyance was the stoic's doctrine of passion, a distinctive theme of the ancient philosophers. I mention the stoics here because their ideas seem connected to the peculiar dialectics that emerge in discussions of media production: art versus business, transmutation versus construction, communion versus product, and—finally—reason versus passion.

The classical stoic was not a champion of passion; this wasn't because the stoics believed passion was bad for business, but because they were convinced that passion was bad for the psyche. Passion was a "perturbation of the soul . . . which consisted in an excessive or overpowering impulse . . . irrational and insubordinate to reason" (Gardiner, Metcalf, and Beebe-Center 64). To the stoic, the passions—those irrational impulses of desire, appetite, fear, pain, grief, anger, hate, and delight—were like spiritual diseases. Free of passion, the soul was strong and in control. Infected with passion, the soul became weak and confused. For the stoic, the transformative force was logic and reason. The stoic might approve of instructional films with droning narration of fact, products that are unlikely to infect the soul. Produced in the 1950s and 1960s and projected for squirming school children for the next few decades, these sorts of films were not likely to inflame communicable passions in young audiences.[16] For the stoic, it was logic that kept the soul healthy. Intense emotions, such as those that can be ignited through drama, were an invitation to corrupt the intellectual processes and tempt spiritual pollution. For drama, the transformative force is emotion and passion, even hyperbole, the very things the stoics found contaminating. A substantial amount of contemporary mediated communication depends on drama. Movies, television programs, and advertisements all rely on the conflicts and passions of drama. Even news stories are constructed around the principles of drama: the report of conflict and consternation. For producers to embrace stoicism would put them at odds with much of American media content.

In contradiction to the stoics, the eighteenth-century Romantics recognized emotion and passion as important guides and inspirations in life, assigning feeling "a coordinate position with intellect and will" (Gardiner, Metcalf, and Beebe Center 244). According to this viewpoint, passion doesn't contaminate the soul but enriches it. Passion also found champions later among film theorists. Though some looked to uncover a grammatical structure in film with "rules" to guide the production process, others believed visual media operate beyond the control of verbal logic. Moving images may not be a rhetoric we can reason through but visions we can feel. Legitimizing passion this way warns against the crushing force we often concede to reason.

Contemporary producers frequently tell of their "passion" for film and television. Film schools seek students with "a passion for story" or a "passion for film." Workshops in film and video production often promise to "ignite student passion" for filmmaking, suggesting that the process of production is emotional and transformative. Sometimes included with the requirement of passion is the additional suggestion that students should have entrepreneurial or business interests as well, that the two are not mutually exclusive. In *Emotional Intelligence*, a text on business leadership, author Daniel Goleman also suggests that emotion, reason, and intelligence are best combined. Goleman tells us that the human ability to understand the world of ideas is predicated on the ability to understand and control emotion, and that emotion, rather than reason, guides our best decision making. This suggests that even the world of business is not all cold, hard logic but incorporates passion and creativity.

A great deal of my discussion about the cult value of media production has gone into exploring the distinctions between industry and art, craft and magic. Yet, the distinctions remain uncertain. The production processes themselves may not clarify matters. The industry that creates "mere entertainments" operates within familiar territory. That familiarity arises from a combination of standard craft, routine processes, and familiar content. Art seems to be about taking risks, about forays beyond the familiar, and about the recognition that transmutation may not be a comfortable process. One position seems mechanical, the other seems organic, though the reality of production may be a continuum between the two. Sometimes one path fails where another succeeds. It isn't easy to distinguish between them which will guarantee the best route to the "elixir of the soul." However, having been privileged to use a variety of media for a variety of productions and purposes, I must say I believe producers do feel a bit of the wizard's power in controlling a media universe, even if the control is not absolute, if that universe is a synthetic dimension of the larger social fiction, and if the god honored is a commercial one.

I should conclude by noting that not all philosophies of production fit neatly into the discussion of the production process as routines of business versus the transformations of art. The process of production is one fraught with the potential for mistakes. Rather than allow for that possibility, some producers find it more comfortable not to seriously attempt either art or commerce but instead try to create a following from a like-minded audience that can appreciate a lampoon of art with an intentionally "bad" aesthetic. These producers display their mistakes, flaunt them as purposeful, and hope they can demystify for everyone that "occult" process of producing alternate realities. A producer can get over failed attempts of transformation by denying the transformative possibilities up front. Intentional "mistakes" are far less painful than real ones. I recently had the opportunity to interview a production assistant working on a low-budget film with just this attitude. "There's nothing magical about making a movie," he told me.

This movie won't change anybody's life, either while we're making it or afterward. It probably won't even make us much money. The movie we're making is like a farce, a joke on the whole business. It's stupid. The people who will watch this film know that. They'll just laugh . . . No suspension of disbelief, like you say. And the people making this movie are laughing, too. Life is a joke, and so are the movies. No alchemy here. You can't take stuff so seriously.

Part Two

Magic in the Message

Evil, Enchanting, Divine, and Ecstatic
A Century of Witches in Moving Images

Witchcraft was hung, in History,
But History and I
Find all the Witchcraft that we need
Around us, every day.

      —Emily Dickinson, "Witchcraft was hung, in History" (1883)

On an October night in a suburban Greensboro, North Carolina, home in 1998, four teenage girls have a sleepover. Dressed in black, with candles blazing, the girls pop a copy of *The Craft* (1996) into the videotape player and begin to recite an incantation along with the characters in the film. This was a reoccurring event, a ritual that included—among other things—watching segments of the film over and over, chanting, and burning candles.

The mother of one of the girls told me that all the parents were aware of what was happening at these sleepovers. Though not thrilled with the girls' activities, the parents decided not to make an issue of them. The father of one of the girls was an experienced and well-respected educator, certain that his daughter's fascination with witchcraft was only a phase. As it turns out, the father was right. The teens graduated from high school and have since gone on to college. The lure of both film and ritual seems to have been temporary, receding after the girls matured and moved on to other interests.

One mother believed her daughter's witchcraft episodes had more to do with rebelling against the powerlessness of female adolescence than a sincere belief influenced by watching a movie. "Adolescence is a generally troubling time for girls," this mother observed, making reference to Mary Pipher's celebrated book about the difficulties of female adolescence, *Reviving Ophelia*. She continued:

Girls have to cope with their changing bodies in a culture with a definition of beauty so impossibly narrow that most young women feel excluded. They have to cope with a society that doesn't seem to value the self of the girl as important.

This Greensboro mother felt that teenage girls and young women may become attracted to witchcraft as a way of rebelling against authority and social conditions that seem stacked against them. She believed her daughter and the other girls used rituals learned through books and movies to create tight friendship bonds and a sense of community that was important to them during a stressful period of change. "But to this day, I haven't been able to get all the black wax off my daughter's bedroom floor" (Maine).

The Greensboro teens weren't alone in their fascination with witchcraft. A 2001 Gallup poll suggests that 26 percent of the American public believe in witches, a substantial increase over the 11 percent who said they believed in witches in 1978 and the 14 percent in 1990.[1] It isn't clear exactly what kind of "belief in witches" the Gallup poll is measuring. Obviously, Wiccans and other groups claiming to be witches *exist*. The social reality of witches was genuine enough in February 2001 to cause political concern when President George Bush launched his faith-based initiative, a plan that would award religious organizations taxpayer dollars to support charities. Opponents of the initiative worried that since the Constitution requires equal treatment for religious groups, people who practice voodoo or Santeria, as well as Wiccans, satanists, and various other alternative religious groups, might be eligible to apply for government contracts. These concerns, among others, kept Congress from rallying behind an initiative that was to be the cornerstone of Bush's "compassionate conservatism."[2]

Possibly what the Gallup poll measures is not whether the respondents believe witches exist, but whether respondents believe the ritual magic that witches practice has any real effect. If this is the case, poll results indicate a measurable increase in magical thinking at the turn of the twenty-first century. News reports suggest a growing interest in witches particularly among teenagers since the late 1990s, citing the popularity of spell books, movies, and television shows about witches as evidence (Ault; La Ferla; Mulrine). Movies like *The Craft* and television shows like *Charmed* (1998–) and *Sabrina, the Teenage Witch* (1996–2003) emphasize the adventures of witches who have the magical powers to fight evil or get "the best table in the school cafeteria" (Flanigan). While many of the teens attracted to witchcraft are girls, the idea of possessing magic and personal power also attracts boys, particularly those who may feel marginalized. Witchcraft seems to have particular appeal for teens who are self-styled rebels or who feel socially disconnected (C. Edwards).

Not all adults are as tolerant of their teens being exposed to ideas about witches or dabbling in "the craft" as the Greensboro parents who decided it was only a phase their daughters would outgrow. One North Carolina middle school confiscated books on witchcraft from girls accused of casting spells on other students (Smith). Similar stories nationwide indicate a determination among some school officials to root out witches (Ingold; Lam; La Ferla; Kaminer). In another North Carolina case, a high school suspended one of its teachers for practicing Wicca. The school administration worried about the effect of such beliefs on susceptible adolescents ("Wiccan Teacher"). Christian Internet sites continue to warn parents about the dangers of letting their daughters flirt with the occult, accusing popular films and television programs, along with books such as Silver Ravenwolf's *Teen Witch*, of producing a widespread, dangerous interest in Wicca and witchcraft. Whether or not parents, schools, and communities tolerate these interests, observers have noticed an eager following among teenagers infatuated with the stylish new image of witches portrayed on television shows and in the movies.

One of the biggest media events at the turn of the new century was the Harry Potter series, books credited with connecting millions of children and teens, especially boys, to the pleasures of reading. Some educators praised the series of books for a creative use of language, even as some schools banned the books for association with witchcraft.[3] A film based on the first book would become a record-breaking box office success story in the fall of 2001, generating a wide variety of merchandise from toys and games, to clothes, bedding, and lunch boxes, in time for the December 2001 holidays. Throughout the twentieth century and into the twenty-first, moving-image media presented audiences with a constant discourse about witches and a parade of sometimes opposing ideas and images about the nature of witchcraft for audiences to negotiate. It is that aggregate conversation I will examine in this chapter. However, in order to be able to say which films and television programs have contributed to the public discussion, it's important to have a definition of the word *witch* that includes the various possibilities.

Definitions of *Witch*

In a lavishly illustrated reprint of her 1981 title *Witches*, Erica Jong claims that "to understand the word 'witch' is to understand anthropology, history, the history of religion, [and] the history of relations between the sexes" (14). Dictionaries reveal some of the complications and contradictions with a definition of *witch*. The most neutral definitions in *The Oxford English Dictionary*, *Webster's Dictionary of English Usage*, *American Heritage*, *Chamber's Concise Dictionary* and the *American College* dictionaries suggest that a witch is a person, especially "a woman, who professes or is supposed to practice magic; a sorceress" ("Witch," *Webster's* def. 1). However, dictionaries also indicate that the witch's supernatural power may be a result of a compact with evil spirits; the witch practices the "black arts." In contrast, the word *witch* can also refer to someone who practices the neopagan religion of Wicca, which claims to be a positive creed, one without structure and dogma, but whose practitioners have a shared reverence for nature, belief in goddess spirituality, and a world filled with powerful energy that can be harnessed through rituals, talismans, charms, and spells (Berger). Secondary dictionary definitions omit the supernatural element, defining *witch* as "an ugly, ill-tempered old woman" ("Witch," *American Heritage* def. 1). In slang usage, *witch* is sometimes used interchangeably with *bitch* as an insult, indicating a sexually aggressive, vindictive, or malicious woman. Yet, the word that is synonymous with *hag* can also refer to "a bewitching or fascinating woman or girl" ("Witch," *American Heritage* def. 3). The word can also signify independence. Echoing the self-empowerment associated with New Age witchcraft, a Halloween card printed and sold by Recycled Paper Greetings in 2001 displays the drawing of a witch whose typical costume is enhanced by the cartoon character's saucy and knowing expression. Inside, the card explains that *witch* is not just a word, it's an "attitude." Images of witches and witchcraft reflected in the media suggest all the dictionary possibilities, slang uses, and more.

Some films and television programs will use the term *mortal* to distinguish between witches and those people who have no magical powers. However, even though the spells of witches may be said to prolong youth and life, most media depictions of witches suggest they are human and mortal, capable of dying or being killed. For example, the television series *Charmed* and *Bewitched* (1964–72) use the term *mortal* to refer to people who have no gift for magic. Yet, in *Charmed*, it is clear that the sister witches are mortal and could be killed by the many demons who confront the young women with murderous intentions. The mother and grandmother of the sisters are also witches and are both dead, though the sisters can summon their ghosts for advice. The fourth season of the series emphasized the mortality of the witches, when demons murder

76

sister Prue, and the season begins with a Wiccan funeral. Though no witches were murdered on the sitcom *Bewitched*, this television show also portrayed witches who have mortal desires, motives, and frailties. For example, the mortal shortcomings of Aunt Clara (played by Marion Lorne from 1964 to 1968) were obvious as the aging witch became increasingly forgetful, muddling spells and creating havoc as she advanced in years. The Harry Potter film series also makes the mortality and humanity of witches evident, inventing a new word, *muggle*, to characterize human beings who don't have magical abilities, as opposed to those who do (witches). Both witches and muggles are mortal.

Frequently, the witch is considered to be female, with the male counterpart referred to as a warlock, wizard, sorcerer, magician, shaman, or witch doctor. However, some apply *witch* equally to male and female (Wilson 14). For the purposes of constructing the filmography of movies and television programs about witches at the end of this chapter, I define the witch as a person—either male or female—who either uses magic to influence events, believes she (or he) could use magic to influence events, or has been accused by others of using magic to influence events. *Magic* in media depictions is defined as the ability to command or manipulate circumstances through spells, charms, divination, or the mastery of powers beyond the control of ordinary people.

Films and television programs depicting magicians who use sleight of hand for entertainment are excluded from the filmography unless other characters accuse the magician of witchcraft or the magic is depicted as "real" within the narrative. Under this definition, Christian faith healers, who work cures through prayer, might also seem to be witches.[4] However, because orthodox faiths object to the idea of witchcraft, I excluded examples of films that might depict miracles attributed to Christian, Jewish, or Muslim prayer. Beyond an association of witchcraft with the Devil, a prime Christian objection to witchcraft appears to stem from the witch's defiance: the sorcerer's craft is an expression of individual will rather than obedience to God. Witchcraft allocates to an individual the command over supernatural forces that many Christians believe should be left to the authority of God. A Christian faith healer will not take credit for his or her work, because a prayer is a plea and an affirmation of faith rather than an act of magic. For example, in the film *Household Saints* (1993), Lili Taylor plays the character of Teresa Santangelo, a girl who prays incessantly, plays cards with Jesus, and seems surrounded by miraculous events. However, because her actions are those of devotion and submission, other characters in the film consider her a saint or mentally disturbed rather than a witch. Unless a character in a film makes an accusation of witchcraft against another character, or unless witchcraft is in some way central to the film, movies that depict faith in prayer and submission to orthodox religion are not included in the filmography. This means a film like *Leap of Faith* (1992), in which a fraudulent faith healer finally seems to work a miracle cure, is omitted from the filmography. Likewise omitted are movies like *The Apostle* (1997), *The Miracle Man* (1919, remade in 1932), or *The Third Miracle* (2001), where characters believe in the power of prayer to produce marvelous results.[5] Although Christian faith healers and other orthodox characters are not considered to be working magic and are excluded from the definition of witches, Christianity and devout Christian characters, as well as characters of other orthodox religions, are frequently featured in films depicting witches.

I assembled the filmography by searching plot descriptions and reviews for the keywords *witch, warlock, shaman, wizard, spell, potion, sorcerer, hex, magic,* and *charm* and then eliminating any film, video, or television program that didn't depict in some fashion the idea of a human being with the supernatural ability to influence events. I included foreign films and television programs if they received distribution in the United States. Movies and television programs are listed once, at the time of initial release, even though the show may have been rebroadcast on television or re-released for home video distribution in later decades. Television series based on witches, such as *Bewitched, Sabrina, the Teenage Witch,* and *Charmed* are counted only once in the filmography, though they represent multiple episodes featuring characters that use magical powers. Excluded from the witch filmography are movies that focus on supernatural elements that do not include a human being working, attempting to work, or believed to be working in the magical arts. For example, films and television programs about ghosts, genies, mermaids, monsters, fairies, dragons, and vampires are omitted from the list unless they also depict a significant witch character.

Frequently, occult folklore will overlap in film and television presentations. Sometimes a character will be a mixture of folklore elements, such as a witch character who is burned at the stake and returns as a vengeful ghost. Such films as *Witchery* (1988), *Devonsville Terror* (1983), *Superstition* (1982), and the *Blair Witch Project* (1999) are examples of films that blur the distinction between the ghost and the witch. In these films, the witches may be dead but continue to work curses against the living. Some films make a connection between the vampire and the witch, but the vampire character generally becomes a blood-drinking monster after death, rather than a character who resorts to the magic of spell, incantation, curse, or ritual to fulfill personal desires. The Warner Brothers television series *Buffy the Vampire Slayer* (1997–2003) is an example of a show that combines both witches and vampires and occasionally other supernatural creatures, such as monsters, zombies, demons, and werewolves. Ostensibly about a teenager who battles and destroys vampires, the show also features a central returning character, Willow Rosenberg (Alyson Hannigan), who describes herself as a Wiccan and uses powerful magic to assist her vampire-slaying friend in fighting evil. *Twins of Evil* (1972) is another film that blends ideas about witchcraft with vampirism, accentuating the antics of a Satan-worshipping count who sells his soul to become a vampire and a puritanical fanatic who hunts down witches. Similarly, though the featured character on the original soap opera *Dark Shadows* (1966–71) and the remake (1991) is the vampire Barnabas Collins, along with ghosts and other supernatural images, the soap also features a witch, Angelique (played first by Audrey Larkins and later by Lara Parker), who is the vampire's nemesis. Therefore, the filmography includes movies and television programs in which the occult discourse isn't exclusively about witchcraft.

The filmography excludes depictions of witches in television commercials, though images of magical men and women appear frequently in advertisements. This was especially true in the 1990s, when witches advertised items such as clothes washers, vacuum cleaners, candy, lotion, sports equipment, cars, chicken wings, and hair care products. Such imagery tends to evoke a type of fairy-tale witchcraft, suggesting that a product could bestow magical power upon a consumer. For example, a 2001 Thermasilk commercial uses the image of a beautiful woman in black, who flies through the air and discharges magical sparks from her fingertips, to advertise a hair-styling product that promises to let consumers "master the power of heat." Similarly, a commercial for Wizard air freshener features a woman wearing a black shell and Capri pants, vowing to rid a room of demonic smells. Another advertisement features a beautiful voodoo queen on the lacy wrought-iron balcony of her New Orleans French Quarter apartment. She casts her spell and is soon sitting in a car with pro golfer Tiger Woods, who turns to the camera with a grin and tells the audience, "I *love* this town!"

Though I attempted to develop a comprehensive list of witch narratives, I excluded obscure films and programs, shorts, and independent films limited to Internet distribution or local venues, films in which the witch character plays a conspicuously minor role, and various television news features and talk show programs about witches that are often broadcast around Halloween. Likewise, I excluded many single-episode depictions of witches within a television series more frequently focused on other character types and films with very brief references to witches.[6] Though this type of imagery is clearly part of the media discourse on witches, I confined my list to narrative and documentary programs in film and television. Finally, if none of the keywords used to compile the filmography were used to identify a show in any of the sources I consulted, this fault in the methodology may have caused some films and television programs with depictions of witchcraft to be left out of the final list. This makes the filmography a modest account of the opportunity for American audiences to be exposed to the discourse on witchcraft offered through moving-image media.

A search of resources including *Cinemania* (1998), *Videohounds Golden Movie Retriever* (1998), *The Video Source Book* (1996), *The AFI Catalogue of Feature Films* (2001), *Bowker's Complete Video Directory* (2000), and the *Internet Movie Data Base*[7] yielded more than 700 films and television programs featuring characters that either used magical powers to influence events, believed they had these powers, or were accused of doing so by other characters. Film and television depictions of the witch aren't confined to one genre. Witches are featured in cartoons, documentaries, sitcoms, action adventures, dramas, horror, science fiction, children's programming, soap operas, and fantasy. Based on data from the filmography, table 4.1 shows the number of films and television programs with witches in them by decade of release. Evident from the table is the increase in such films and programs over the years, most likely attributable to the general increase in distribution outlets. However, it is interesting to notice the jump in the distribution of witchcraft movies, from 40 films in the 1950s to 125 films during the decade of the 1960s, a time when feminism became a highly visible and vocal movement. There would be a steady increase in witchcraft as a topic explored by film and television over the following decades, but never quite as significant a jump. The table includes a few films released as late as 2002 that had begun production and publicity in the previous century.

Popular Media Portraits of the Witch

Analysis of the filmography revealed eight noticeable portraits of the witch, according to the type of emphasis a film or television program placed on the dominant witch character, or the prevailing statement the show made with regard to witchcraft. The types of witch portrayals include:

Table 4.1. Number of Films and Television Programs Containing Witch Characters

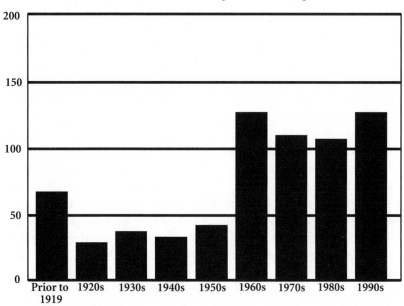

Note: Total number of films included is 732.

the *historical witch* (attempting to describe real historical events and people); the *dubious witch* (stressing skepticism about the witch's magic); the *satanic witch* (emphasizing the witch's devotion and servitude to the Christian Devil); the *fairy-tale witch* (emphasizing the singular witch with legendary magic, usually the benefactor or adversary of a youthful protagonist); the *shamanic witch* (accentuating the exotic "otherness" of foreign beliefs); and the *New Age witch* (stressing the healing power, independence, ecofeminism, and/or goddess worship of the witch). Some media images emphasize the challenges of the maiden or young witch, a type of portrait I categorized as the *ingenue witch*. Portraits of the ingenue witch place emphasis on the young witch's discovery of self and magical power.

A final category emphasizes the sexual appetites or seductive powers of the witch, a type of portrait I call the *enchantress*. Though often portrayed as a beautiful young woman, the enchantress may also be a crone, an ancient creature who maintains a powerful sexual appetite, seducing young men through deception, force, or uncanny charm. What signifies this type is the witch's seductive power, even if the witch character herself may be unaware of that power.

Though these eight categories may not be discrete, and a film might feature more than one type of witch character, each category accentuates a different aspect in the portrayal of witches, and usually one aspect will predominate in a film or television program, even where attributes seem mixed or the show features more than one type of witch character. To categorize a film or television program as depicting one type of witch over another, coders considered the broader intentions of the program or plot and the predominant characteristics of the principal witch character. For example, the ingenue witch might be placed in a fairy-tale setting, but if the film emphasized the inexperience and self-discovery of the witch, the film would be classified as an ingenue witch portrait. However, if a film or television program portrayed an adolescent witch as the self-assured master of satanic secrets, the classification became a satanic witch portrait. Similarly, if a film appeared to stress the exotic beliefs of a young witch from a foreign, or "other," culture more than her youth, inexperience, and self-discovery, coders classified the film as a portrait of the shamanic witch.

Throughout the century, the most predominant images of witchcraft were portraits of the fairy-tale witch. The second most frequently occurring portrait was the satanic witch, followed by the exotic other of the shamanic witch. (See table 4.2.) Of the total number of films and television programs evaluated by coders, 139 could not be classified as definitely emphasizing one category or another. In these cases, the film or television program either could not be screened, there was not enough written information about the film to determine a classification, or no single portrait of the witch dominated the narrative strongly enough for classification.

Certain types of depictions tend to cluster into one genre or another. For example, portrayals of the satanic witch tend to cluster in the horror genre. Portraits of the enchantress appear in horror but may also be found in comedies, adventures, and romances. The fairy-tale and ingenue witches are likely to be discovered in adventures, fantasies, cartoons, and children's programs. Portrayals of the dubious witch tend to group into dramas and mysteries. Sometimes a popular witch character, such as Medea, may have the qualities of the fairy-tale witch in one film, of the enchantress in another, and of the shamanic witch in yet another. A film's assessment of the witch as "good" or "bad" is often mixed within a category, though satanic witches are usually portrayed as bad, while film portrayals of ingenue and New Age witches are often more sympathetic. The magic employed by witch characters is largely neutral but may be evaluated by the witch's intentions. For example, the "good" witch Sarah

Table 4.2. Witch Films Categorized by Type

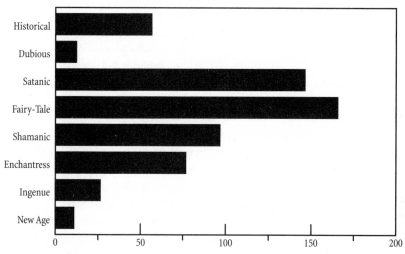

Note: Total number of films categorized is 593.

in *The Craft* may use the same magic or rituals employed by the "bad" witch Nancy, but with more virtuous motives.

The Historical Witch

Films and television programs that portray the historical witch attempt to record and analyze actual events regarding witchcraft, providing historical background, historical description, or both. These shows frequently take the form of documentaries, investigating some historical "truth" about witches and witchcraft or examining specific cases. I include all documentaries about witchcraft in this category, even though viewers may dispute the truth of the account presented by the documentary. The documentary typically makes a claim to accuracy and attempts to add to the historical record, even though it may contain distortions, errors, or false information.

Portraits of the historical witch may also be found in docudramas or dramas that reenact a period of history, offering accounts of real people accused of witchcraft, such as Joan of Arc or the victims of the Salem witch trials. If a film makes reference to an actual historical event but puts emphasis on aspects other than the historical account, I categorized it differently. For example, films like *Burned at the Stake* (1981) and *Love at Stake* (1987) are not considered depictions of the historical witch, even though the films make reference to the Salem witch trials. Films that allege to be "inspired by" real incidents but that contain disclaimers that no real characters or events are represented also were not classified as depictions of the historical witch.

One of the earliest documentaries to present a history of witchcraft is the Swedish film *Häxan*, known in the United States as *Witchcraft Through the Ages* (1922). (See fig. 4.1.) The commentary comes in the form of intertitles,[8] though a 1960s version of the film also features narration by William S. Burroughs. With drawings, woodcuts, and extensive reenactments, the film presents a history of witchcraft with emphasis on the period of the Inquisition. According to Burroughs's narration, a popular belief of medieval times was that witches were people who succumbed to temptation and made unlawful contracts with demons. Though the documentary presents a skeptical viewpoint, it illustrates medieval beliefs with elaborate reenactments. In one scene, a devil summons a beautiful woman from her bed. Another scene shows a convent where a demon has caused an infectious madness among the nuns. The film ends by suggesting that "today" (the film was made in 1922) we know that demon possession is a form of mental illness and that belief in witchcraft is a problem of the intellectually feeble, people susceptible to superstition or emotional confusion.

Fig. 4.1. The historical witch in the documentary *Häxan* (*Witchcraft Through the Ages*, 1922). One of the first documentaries about witchcraft, it used extensive reenactments, as in the pictured ritual. Photo courtesy of Photofest.

Like *Häxan*, the 1955 documentary short *Black Cats and Broom Sticks* tends to be skeptical about the supernatural elements associated with witchcraft. It examines the widespread belief in the supernatural with a sense of astonishment that such beliefs endure. Similarly, the CBS documentary series *You Are There* (1953–57) presented an episode on the Salem witchcraft trials. Skepticism about satanism and the witch's alleged supernatural ability is clear in this segment. During the mid-1950s, the Salem witch hunts would come to allegorically represent the McCarthy crusade against communism.[9]

When the flamboyant founder of the Church of Satan and author of the *Satanic Bible*, Anton Szandor LaVey, appeared on the scene in the 1960s, witchcraft began to become connected with contemporary counterculture movements. LaVey became a self-created celebrity during the decade, which helped him land roles in the feature films *Rosemary's Baby* (1968) and *The Devil's Rain* (1975). Documentaries such as *Satanis* (1968) and *Witchcraft (White Angel . . . Black Angel*, 1970) also publicized LaVey's movement. The last of these, *Speak of the Devil* (1995), featured the life and times of "the Black Pope" before he died in 1997. LaVey's church apparently didn't sacrifice babies, but it did preach living for the moment rather than for an afterlife that might not exist. The movement also used reversed symbols and lots of black as emblematic of rebellion and free-thinking. *Vali* (1967) is another documentary celebrating the freethinking and bohemian lifestyle of a self-proclaimed witch, Vali Myers. The cinema verité film records her occult rituals and ministrations of a love potion, though the film places more emphasis on her artistic nature than satanic influences.

The feminist voice began to emerge in the 1970s, with documentaries such as *Witches: New Fashion—Old Religion* (1972) and *Witches of Salem: The Horror and the Hope* (1972). The feminist voice continued to be an aspect of succeeding documentaries through the 1990s. For example, a 1986 ABC television documentary anthology, *Secrets of the Unknown*, featured a segment on witchcraft that replayed images from the 1922 *Häxan* documentary as visual "witchy wallpaper" for the narration of host Edward Mulhare. Promising to reveal what a witch really is, Mulhare takes viewers back "to an ancient time, when magic was a way of life and the old gods battled for the hearts and minds of humanity." Though the program doesn't credit Egyptologist Margaret Murray, it does present her theory that modern witches are descended from an ancient pagan goddess worship. This is also the idea behind the Wicca movement of Gerald Gardner (Hutton), who is mentioned in this episode.[10] The program includes interviews with modern witches who explain that devils and demons are not part of the Wiccan belief structure. The episode suggests that the purpose of witchcraft is not to control black magic but to draw cosmic forces into the individual witch through rituals and charms, helping the witch to find herself and her power.

Laurie Meeker's documentary *Remember the Witches* (1985) provides audiences with a similar treatment of the subject, though more openly feminist and less candidly sensational. Narrator Julie Akers tells audiences that the practice of witchcraft "has its roots in the old religion—an ancient, pagan religion older than Christianity, Judaism, and Islam—a religion before Buddhism and Hinduism." According to this documentary, it was the misogyny of medieval Christian culture that drove witches into hiding until they were able to emerge in a more tolerant and enlightened twentieth century, "with knowledge of positive magic that awakens the divine spark in each of us."

Several documentaries produced in the 1990s cultivated the link between witchcraft and Wicca, denying any connections between witchcraft and satanism. A Lifetime cable channel presentation, *Intimate Portrait: Witches* (1998), uses a combination of dramatizations and interviews to present a history of witches, with an emphasis on modern-day practitioners of Wicca. Three programs produced by the National Film Board of Canada and directed by Donna Reed place emphasis on goddess worship, linking modern witchcraft to a broader spirituality, women's rights, and environmental concerns. *The Goddess Remembered* (1990) praises the myth of matriarchal prehistory and ancient goddess-worshipping civilizations that were egalitarian. Though some scholars discredit the idea (Eller; Hutton; Davis), the film suggests that the modern Wicca movement is a direct descendant of a persistent pagan religion that survived in secret. *The Burning Times* (1993) examines the persecutions that swept through Europe as a result of the emergence of patriarchal, misogynist societies bent on purging people of ancient pagan beliefs. *Full Circle* (1993) completes the Reed trilogy, examining the tenets of Wicca, reverence for women, creation, and nature. A host of specialty videos produced in the 1990s, such as *Ancient Modern Witch: The Halloween Lecture* (1998), *Witchcraft for Yesterday and Today* (1999), and *Discovering Witchcraft: A Journey Through the Elements* (1998), are clearly made for sympathetic audiences that might aspire to become practitioners of a gentle, New Age witchcraft. A documentary segment in the Travel Channel program *The World's Creepiest Destinations* (2000) presents a commercial side to witchcraft, advertising Salem, Massachusetts, as number four in a list of the top ten creepy places to spend a vacation. *Witch City* (1999) exposes the crass commercialism in Salem, where thousands congregate at Halloween to spend millions of tourist dollars.

Much less sympathetic are films by born-again Christian journalist and evangelical radio host Bob Larson. His documentaries, *First Family of Satanism* (1990), *In the Name of Satan* (1990), and *Bob Larson Live* (1990), connect contemporary factors such as "black metal music" to the growth of satanism and the Church of Satan. These documentaries caution the public to be wary of satanic cults, which are reported to be involved in human sacrifice.

Another documentary, *Paradise Lost: The Child Murders at Robin Hood Hills* (1996), suggests there is a modern willingness to condemn witches, and that a jury in the 1990s might be as susceptible to a witch craze as one in the 1590s. The film uses interviews and trial footage to show how some residents and a jury in the small Arkansas town of West Memphis believed that the 1993 murders of three children had been part of a satanic cult meeting. A few weeks after the murders, a mentally handicapped teenager, Jesse Misskelly, confesses that he had been with two other teenage boys, Damien Echols and Jason Baldwin, who committed the murders as part of a satanic ceremony. There is no physical evidence that links the boys to the crimes, and police transcripts of Jesse's confession suggest the police may have coaxed it from him, supplying him with facts and guiding his story. Yet, some members of the community remain convinced the teens are guilty, imagining the children's murders during a rite complete with homosexual orgies and animal sacrifices.

One of the accused teens, Damien, wears his hair dyed black, admits that he practices the Wicca religion, and has an interest in heavy metal music. Damien's interest in the occult becomes a central element in his trial. Though the teen explains that Wicca is a religion that practices a close involvement with nature and teaches people to harm no one because the "evil you do will come back to you," prosecutors question the benign nature of his beliefs. They exhibit books on satanic witchcraft belonging to the teen and a piece of paper on which he had written the name "Aleister Crowley" as evidence of Damien's satanic orientation.[11] The documentary presents evidence that seems to link the crimes to Mark Byers, the father of one of the young victims. However, West Memphis police had mishandled DNA tests on those bloodstains, making this evidence unusable in the trial. Though the state based its case on questionable testimony and hearsay, the trial ends with guilty verdicts for the boys.[12] Damien says of his hometown, "West Memphis is like a second

Salem." This documentary is a reminder that some communities have yet to embrace the idea of a docile, New Age witch. Because Damien is outspoken, different, and something of a heretic, citizens of West Memphis seem eager to believe him guilty of murder. It should be noted that Satan, the tragic hero in John Milton's famous poem *Paradise Lost*, the same title given this documentary, possesses a similar independent spirit.

The same filmmakers would follow up in 2000 with a sequel, *Paradise Lost 2: Revelations*, documenting the appeal of the three defendants. New evidence included the fact that human bite marks found on one of the children's bodies did not match the bites of any of the three defendants. However, the judge, who also officiated at the original trial, turned down the boys' appeal.

Hosted by Linda Blair, the television documentary series *Scariest Places on Earth* (2001) uses hyperbole, spooky voice-overs with sound effects, and an unsteady camcorder aesthetic to heighten both drama and realism but claims to present accurate stories. One segment from the episode "Rituals of Evil" explores the possibility that the Abbey of Thelema in the town of Celfau founded by the infamous Aleister Crowley in 1920 might still be operating. The segment presents background on the twentieth century's most notorious practitioner of black magic and insinuates that Crowley's admirers may still be following his example, with the use of inverted symbols and the ritual drinking of cat's blood. Much of the historical material about Crowley in the segment is accurate. However, significant portions are more suggestion than evidence, and the overproduced style reduces the program's credibility while it amplifies the drama, making the episode at times seem more like a "mockumentary" than an attempt to clarify or add to the historical account.[13]

Two documentaries produced for television couple accusations of witchcraft with the use of hallucinogenic drugs. An episode from the PBS series *Secrets of the Dead*, "Witches Curse" (2001), focuses on the research of behavioral psychologist Linda Caporael. Caporael suggests that the mysterious illness making people sick in Salem, Massachusetts, in 1692 was actually ergot poisoning. People and cattle may have eaten a crop of fungus-infested rye containing nerve toxins that caused freakish symptoms such as convulsions, bizarre skin sensations, and hallucinations. These are symptoms that in 1692 people believed were the result of witchcraft. Caporael suspects many of the medieval witchcraft cases might be a direct result of ergot poisoning. The documentary episode supports her theory with the case of ergot poisoning in Pont St. Esprit, France, in 1951. After a baker in this small village used contaminated flour, the unfortunates who ate the bread suffered the same symptoms as those reported in Salem: hallucinations, convulsions, and pricking of the skin. Another program, *Real Magic: The Science of Wizardry* (2001), also looks at the effects of ergot while exploring modern fantasies about wizards in ancient Celtic lore. The program proposes that the ancient Druids intentionally used ergot to create alternate mental states that would allow the wizards to experience the fantastic and unite with a god.

The historical witch in narrative accounts. Dramatic films and television programs that illustrate the historical witch reenact famous cases or episodes in history. These include several films about Joan of Arc, such as *Joan the Woman* (1916), *Passion of Joan of Arc* (1928), *The Trial of Joan of Arc* (1965), *Saint Joan* (1957), *Joan the Maid: The Battles* (1994), and *The Messenger: The Story of Joan of Arc* (1999). Also considered historical are dramatic accounts of the Salem witchcraft trials, which include films such as *The Witch of Salem* (1913); *Maid of Salem* (1937); *Les Sorcières de Salem* (*The Crucible*, 1957); and *The Crucible* (1967; 1980; 1996). These dramas generally maintain a skeptical position regarding the accused witch's supernatural abilities.

Four film and television versions of *The Crucible* are derived from Arthur Miller's play about the witchcraft trials of seventeenth-century Salem and the religious hysteria inflamed by repressed sexuality. The message in these films is that greed, revenge, or misguided piety inspired false accusations of witchcraft. The 1996 version maintains skepticism, but it portrays the intention of performing magic as Abigail Williams sneaks into the woods with the servant Tituba and other girls to cast spells. The scene is complete with naked dancing, a frog floating in a cauldron, and the sacrifice of a chicken. In a frenzy, Abigail smears her face with the chicken's blood. After the Reverend Parris finds them in the woods, two of the girls fall into hysterical comas. Abigail warns the others to admit to nothing but the dancing. This drama suggests that the events in Salem weren't caused by the hysteria of ergot poisoning but were the result of bored girls looking for trouble. Other films, such as *The Witch of Salem*, *Maid of Salem*, and *Three Sovereigns for Sarah* (1985), are also inspired by the historical incident.

Witchfinder General (or *The Conqueror Worm*, 1968) describes historical settings and attitudes about witches. (See fig. 4.2.) Set in 1645, during a period of bloody civil war in England, the film depicts the misogynistic persecutor of witches, Matthew Hopkins (Vincent Price), and his sadistic henchman, John Stern (Robert Russel). The two men travel from village to village, exploiting superstitions for personal profit. Matthew

Hopkins was a real historical figure who began his self-appointed career as witchfinder general one year earlier than the setting of the movie. When some villagers accuse a priest, John Lowes (Rupert Davies), of being a witch, his niece Sarah (Hilary Dwyer) offers Hopkins her sexual favors, hoping to spare her uncle. Her sacrifice is useless, however, and Lowes is tortured and dunked. Because the priest survives the dunking, Hopkins finds him guilty of witchcraft and sentences the priest to hang. According to the logic of the witchfinder, if Lowes had been innocent of witchcraft, he would have drowned. The accused person dies either way. John Lowes is an unusual victim for Hopkins, who more often finds women rather than men guilty of using the "black art." Hopkins remarks to his comrade, "Strange, isn't it, how much iniquity the Lord vested in the female." He apparently enjoys torturing the younger women into submission before hanging them. Later, Hopkins brags about "a new method of execution" that will combine torture with capital punishment: slowly lowering the accused witch into a fire, "a fitting end for the foul ungodliness of womankind." At no point in the movie is there even the slightest suggestion that any of the accused witches have the ability to work magic. All are clearly the victims of licentious greed, misogyny, and sadism.[14] The movie departs from historical accounts by focusing on the story of Sarah and having her husband bludgeon Hopkins to death. The two published accounts of Hopkins's death say that he either died of tuberculosis or was himself accused of witchcraft, made to endure the water ordeal, and then hanged (Thomas 301–32; Wilson 113–15).

In both documentary and narrative depictions of the historical witch, accusations of witchcraft are frequently proved false, and the film maintains a skeptical attitude toward magic and the supernatural. With a few exceptions, films portraying the historical witch also tend to be sympathetic toward the accused witch. These films generally appeal to the viewer's logic and reason. Instead of a malevolent character working real magic or a delusional heretic committing horrific acts, the historical witch typically described in films and television programs is a victim of corrupt officials, dishonest neighbors, or religious men who are blindly zealous. The historical witch is a casualty of people driven by avarice, spite, fear, or the desire for power to persecute innocent or misunderstood individuals.

The Dubious Witch

The dubious witch is a character accused of witchcraft, but one whom the film will clearly show as innocent, deluded, or part of an obvious hoax. Films that depict the dubious witch may be given a realistic setting,

Fig. 4.2. The historical witch in the drama *Witchfinder General* (or *The Conqueror Worm*, 1968). This is a loosely rendered dramatic interpretation of a real historical character, a misogynist persecutor of witches in seventeenth-century England who was responsible for the death of many innocent women. American International Pictures. Photo courtesy of Photofest.

however the characters or situations are not drawn from a contemporary case or a genuine historical account. These films are presented as pure fiction.

The characters accused of witchcraft in *The Scarlet Letter* (1995) are clearly innocent. Very loosely adapted from Nathaniel Hawthorne's solemn 1850 novel about the awful consequences of forbidden love and repressed guilt in Puritan New England, the film tells a story about fear and conspiracy similar to that of *The Crucible*. The character Harriet Hibbons (Joan Plowright) is suspected of witchcraft because she is an independent woman, works as a midwife, and is knowledgeable about herbs. Harriet jokes with Hester Prynne (Demi Moore), "the wilds at night are my natural territory, particularly when there is a full moon." Casual jokes and irreverent references are the extent of the sewing circle's relationship to witchcraft. It becomes clear that accusations against the women are part of a vengeful conspiracy. The women have no magical power or contract with the Devil.

In *Swept from the Sea* (1997), villagers living off the Cornish coast during the late 1880s believe Amy Foster is a witch because of her odd behavior. Her own mother tells her, "Bad you were conceived and bad you will remain." Amy collects things found on the beach and creates a "home" for herself in a cave by the sea, behavior that villagers find suspicious. The film makes no suggestion that Amy is casting spells or working magic, rather she is condemned by the illegitimacy of her birth and her own eccentricity to be feared and despised by her family and neighbors.

Even though death is personified as a supernatural character in *The Seventh Seal* (1957), the magical abilities of its witch (Maud Hansson) are clearly doubtful. (See fig. 4.3.) A knight, Antonius Block (Max von Sydow), and his squire, Jöns (Gunnar Björnstrand), return from the Crusades to a homeland wasted by the plague. At a village, the travelers encounter a woman in the stocks. Soldiers tell them she is a witch who has had carnal knowledge of the "evil one" and is to be burned. Because people of the village are so afraid of the witch and her power to infect her enemies with the plague, only a few brave soldiers agree to be paid to execute her, a job that is usually voluntary. The questing knight talks with this woman, who has already been tortured past saving. The knight wishes to know if the reality of the Devil can be confirmed, for if the Devil is real, then God must exist. "Faith is a torment," he says. "It is like loving someone in the darkness who never appears, no matter how loudly you call." The knight gives the witch a drug to deaden her pain, for it is clear she has no special power to save herself. As the soldiers raise her up and light the fire, Jöns questions, "Who watches over that child? Angels? God? Satan? Or emptiness? Look at her eyes. Her poor brain has just made a discovery. Emptiness under the moon." The film makes it obvious that the accused witch has neither magic nor the Devil to protect her.

Set during the 1930s Depression, *Apprentice to Murder* (1988) shows how a fundamentalist preacher, Dr. John Reese (Donald Sutherland), practices faith healing and "battles witches" in rural Pennsylvania. Sometimes Dr. John's healing rituals appear to have a good outcome. Billy (Chad Lowe) comes to him for help, and the preacher's herbal mixture has the desired effect on Billy's alcoholic father. Dr. John's repeated incantation "with his switch and Christ's dear blood, I banish thy pain and do thee good" appears to have a healing effect on Billy's wounds. But when a child dies in his care, Dr. John is arrested for practicing medicine without qualifications, and we learn that he has spent several years in a mental institution. Billy accepts Dr. John's interpretation of these arrests and incarcerations as Satan's attempt to stop his holy work. Dr. John

Fig. 4.3. The dubious witch (Maud Hansson) in *The Seventh Seal* (1957) clearly has no power to save herself, casting doubt on the magical abilities of witchcraft. Janus Films. Photo courtesy of Photofest.

trains his susceptible young assistant to see evil magic in every coincidence. The result is hallucinations and spiraling madness for both. When farm animals sicken and die, Dr. John accuses a neighbor of practicing satanism and placing a hex on various people for his own profit. Dr. John attempts to remove the hex and becomes ill. As his sense of evil oppresses him, he seeks the "strong medicine" of an African American faith healer, Mama Isobell, who practices what looks like a melding of the sympathetic magic of Obeah, or perhaps voodoo, with fundamentalist Christianity.[15] After Mama Isobell cures Dr. John, she advises him how to stop the man who made the hex. The preacher and his assistant return to rid their community of its witch but end up committing murder in the name of Jesus. The film does not suggest that any hexes or magic ever took place but that evil can result from beliefs that are excessively zealous and consuming. Though the film is "inspired by a true story," it doesn't pretend to be the actual account of real events and carries a disclaimer to that effect.

Like films depicting the historical witch, films depicting the dubious witch maintain a skeptical attitude toward the supernatural. Reasonable characters don't believe in the witch's magic. For example, in *The Lady's Not for Burning* (1987), the sensible Jennet Jourdemayne (Cherie Lunghi) is incredulous that the townspeople believe she is a witch: "They accuse me of such a brainstorm of absurdities that all my fear dissolves in the humor of it."

The Satanic Witch

Unlike depictions of the historical witch or the dubious witch, media depictions of the satanic witch are rarely sympathetic, and the film often takes a position where the "magic" the witch possesses is considered "real" within the narrative. This witch character is noticeably involved in Devil worship and doesn't merely harness supernatural forces to her use, she actively venerates the Antichrist. She is vile, selfish, aggressive, carnal, bloodthirsty, and second only to the fairy-tale witch as the most popular witch type in film and television.

The satanic witch depicted in modern media is a character apparently inspired by the *Malleus Maleficarum*, a document written in 1486 and circulated to judges and magistrates throughout Europe to help in the discovery and destruction of witches.[16] Pope Innocent VIII's papal bull ushered the work into the medieval courts, giving this book the highest Church authority. Written by two German friars, Jacob Sprenger and Heinrich Kramer, the handbook for witch hunters defined the witch as a creature who satisfies her lust for power by making a covenant with the Devil. Her pact may involve sexual intercourse, the sacrifice and consumption of newborn babies, and the production of magical ointments from appalling ingredients. Once in league with the Devil, the witch uses forms of representative magic, such as sprinkling water to produce rain or wounding the image of a person in a wax or straw doll, to inflict real pain or sickness on the signified victim. These symbolic actions are a sign to demons, who then make the intended event happen. This definition of the witch sketched by the *Malleus Maleficarum* would remain popular for the next three hundred years, creating the blueprint for the character of the satanic witch in folklore and later in film and television.

Depictions of the satanic witch are largely confined to the horror genre, thrillers, or suspense films. Despite the violence and willingness to shock, horror is generally a paranoid and morally conservative genre, showing audiences what appalling things can happen when people risk defying social customs, question established religious doctrines, or entertain activities that are taboo. This is a genre that suggests the *Malleus Maleficarum* could be right and that the evil of the satanic witch must be uprooted and exterminated at any cost. Film and television depictions of the satanic witch show men and women with intentions that are egotistical, cruel, and contrary to anything wholesome or righteous. The satanic witch is impossible without the idea of the Christian Devil, or Satan.

Media often depict the satanic witch as belonging to a contemporary cult involved in present-day satanic activity. One of the best-known examples of this contemporary and seriously rendered satanic witch was Minnie Castevet (Ruth Gordon) in Roman Polanski's faithful adaptation of the novel by Ira Levin, *Rosemary's Baby* (1967). Considered by many to be a classic, this was the only witch film to rank in the top ten of the American Film Institute's list of the one hundred most thrilling movies.[17] In this film, Rosemary (Mia Farrow) and Guy Woodhouse (John Cassavetes) move into an apartment in New York, becoming friends with elderly neighbors, the Castevets. When Rosemary learns that she is expecting, Minnie Castevet becomes very attentive, bringing herbal drinks and taking a detailed interest in Rosemary's pregnancy. (See fig. 4.4.) What makes Minnie so convincing is her ordinariness. There is nothing overtly dark or sinister about her. Various coincidental clues arouse Rosemary's suspicion. She begins to believe that the Castevets belong to a coven of witches who want to sacrifice her newborn baby. The film does hold out moments of doubt, allowing audiences to question whether Rosemary's beliefs are valid or just the paranoid fantasies of a hysterical, pregnant woman plagued by hormone surges. Ultimately, we learn that Rosemary's fears are all too real; the Castevets and their friends are a coven devoted to the worst possible evil.

More than thirty years later, Polanski would produce another image of modern satanic witches in the film *The Ninth Gate* (1999). This film features a rare-book collector, Boris Balkan (Frank Langella), who is introduced to audiences as he gives a lecture on witchcraft. "A witch," says Balkan "is a person who—though cognizant of the laws of God—endeavors to act through the medium of a pact with the Devil." The millionaire Balkan owns a collection of rare books that feature the same protagonist, the Devil. The most important book in his collection is *The Nine*

Fig. 4.4. Ruth Gordon (*left*) plays a satanic witch manipulating an unsuspecting Mia Farrow in *Rosemary's Baby* (1968). Paramount Pictures. Photo courtesy of Photofest.

Gates of the Kingdom of the Shadows, published in Venice in 1666 by Aristide Torchia, a man who would later be executed by the Spanish Inquisition because he collaborated with Satan. Balkan hires an expert on rare books, Dean Corso (Johnny Depp), to compare the engravings in his copy with the other two extant copies. One of the owners of a Torchia text is the Baroness Kessler (Barbara Jefford), who is herself writing a biography of Satan. She describes modern satanism as "a social club for bored millionaires and celebrities who use the meetings as an excuse to indulge jaded sexual appetites." The baroness further reveals to Corso that she had met Satan as a teenager. "I saw him as plain as I see you now. It was love at first sight." Corso replies, "Three hundred years ago you would have been burned at the stake for saying something like that." The baroness answers, "Three hundred years ago I wouldn't have said it, nor would I have made a million writing about it."

Some horror films make dark connections between satanism and contemporary movements, such as the New Age veneration of nature and self-empowerment. According to these films, self-empowerment is not a virtue but the egotistical door that invites the Devil in, and nature not carefully shepherded can become evil. For example, the film *Little Witches*

(1996) establishes an obvious link between satanism and ancient fertility cults, which the film depicts not as a veneration of nature but as an adoration of evil. The opening scene of the film shows the climax of a fertility ceremony, portrayed as perverted and dangerous. As naked women cavort around a cauldron, a clawed hand emerges from the murky, bubbling depths. This is obviously not the hand of a quintessential god of nature, but the claw of a hideous monster. Only the robed figure of the "Guardian" prevents the "Horned One" from materializing, when she brutally murders his priestesses. The film then moves from this earlier time to present day and a Catholic girls' school. Initially, the character Jamie (Sheeri Rappaport), one of the students in the school, appears to be an ingenue witch, a teenager intrigued with the occult. However, the plot places less emphasis on the self-discovery or developing power of a young girl and strongly emphasizes her malevolent intentions.

Bless the Child (2000) is one of several films in which the satanic witch survives into the new millennium as a horror movie staple. In this film, Rufus Sewell plays Eric Stark, the leader of a self-empowerment group called the "New Dawn," actually the euphemism for a satanic movement. In public, Stark is a socially conscientious man, helping to reform drug addicts and juvenile delinquents with a program that sounds like a popular twelve-step recovery method. But the film quickly reveals that Stark's philanthropy is actually a front for a growing coven of satanic witches who are killing children in their search for a child prophesied to have been born with special powers. Kim Basinger plays Maggie O'Connor, the aunt and guardian of the little girl the coven seeks. This child exhibits supernatural abilities when she resurrects a dead bird. Meanwhile, Stark's group is desperate to find this child and turn her to "the left-hand path" before Easter. They have embarked on a "slaughter of the innocents," a biblical reference to King Herod's soldiers being sent to kill all babies born on a certain date in hopes of destroying Christ. Called in to help solve the puzzling child murders, FBI Special Agent John Travis (Jimmy Smits) connects the various cult symbols left at crime scenes to witchcraft. Though Travis has helped solve occult crimes in the past, he emphasizes that important cases usually end in acquittal of the accused. "The problem of prosecuting occult crime is the judicial concept of reasonable doubt," Travis tells the other detectives. "Motives can be so bizarre, so far beyond reason, that they're hard for a jury to accept." One interpretation of the film could be that self-help organizations like the New Dawn, with its outreach centers that offer a message of self-empowerment, are not to be trusted.

Male characters like Eric Stark, seeking to harness Satan's power for their own pleasure, are not as predominant as female witches but do occur. One common story featuring the male witch (or wizard) is a retelling of the Faust legend. Beginning with the early black-and-white silent films *Faust and Mephistopheles* (1898) and *Faust* (1909; 1923; 1926), this story warns audiences of what can happen when a man seeks wisdom and mastery over the supernatural, even when his intentions are initially good ones.

In the 1926 version directed by F. W. Murnau, the Archangel and Satan wager for the soul of Dr. Faust. In an intertitle, the Archangel (Werner Fuetterer) declares, "If thou canst destroy the divine in Faust, the Earth be thine." Satan proceeds to send a wind of plague that infects the village where Faust (Gösta Ekman) lives. Faust attempts to help his neighbors, but all his medicine and learning appear useless. In anger, he begins to burn his books until he discovers that one ancient text contains a spell to invoke the Devil. It is Faust's eagerness to help humankind that tempts him to perform the ritual. After the circle he makes on the ground bursts into flame, his invocation appears in the intertitle: "I call to thee for help, Spirit of the Darkness: Appear! As thou art called with thy fiendish name: Mephisto, appear!" Once the Devil, incarnated as Mephisto (Emil Jannings), appears, he tempts Faust with youth, vanity, lust, and power. "I'll grant thy request!" says Mephisto. "Thou art my master, I am thy servant." But while Mephisto does grant requests, the outcome is never a desirable one but a cruel perversion of human hopes. At one point, Mephisto visits Marthe Schwerdtlein (Yvette Guilbert), a woman who sells love potions. She is clearly a witch who accepts Mephisto's gifts and improper fondling. Faust falls for Marthe's niece, Marguerite (Camilla Horn), and Mephisto makes it possible for Faust to have the young woman. Things go from bad to worse for Marguerite. Faust kills her brother. Villagers shun her after the birth of her illegitimate child. When her child dies, the villagers decide Marguerite must burn at the stake for murder. Faust throws himself on the fire with Marguerite, and his self-sacrifice cancels the wager the Archangel made with Satan.

Later variations of the Faust story suggest that ego, curiosity, the pursuit of knowledge, and the desire for power are the motivating forces behind Faust and other wizards. However, as in the films *Doctor Faustus* (1967) and *Bedazzled* (2000), it may also be the desire for a woman's love that causes a man to make bargains with demons.

A 1990 film, *The Haunting of Morella*, provides a typical example of a female character drawn to the occult. Set in colonial America, the film shows the sorrows of a young man, Giddeon (David McCallum), who marries a wealthy but ailing young woman, Morella (Nicolle Eggert). Morella becomes intrigued by the promises of occult power to bestow health, eternal youth, and life. Because of her desire for immortality, she becomes deeply involved with satanic practice. She sacrifices a virgin and bathes in her blood. Later, the distraught husband discovers Morella in the midst of a ritual, holding their baby daughter over a cauldron. He is just in time to stop what he believes is a sacrifice. Justice is swift, and Morella is crucified as a witch. Seventeen years later, Morella's disciple, now the governess to Morella's daughter Lenora, resurrects the dead witch. The object is to help Morella return to life by taking possession of Lenora's body on the girl's eighteenth birthday. The movie depicts the witches as cruel, evil, self-centered, and noticeably involved in lesbian sexual escapades.[18]

Other films, such as *Satan's Princess* (1990), also emphasize the lesbian tendencies of the satanic witch. In this film, a renegade cop, Lou Cherney (Robert Forester), must leave the force early because of an injury received in the line of duty. A distraught father wants him to continue looking for his missing daughter, who has been gone without a trace for ten months. Clues take Detective Cherney to the modeling agency of Nicole St. James (Lydie Denier), an agency connected to a young woman found murdered and sexually mutilated. Lesbianism becomes a significant clue to the truly perverse nature of the witch Nicole, who has so seduced the missing girl that she is beyond saving. Like many satanic witches, Nicole is enormously wealthy and powerful, surrounded by devoted minions ready to lay down their lives for her. At one point in the investigation, Lou expresses a sentiment not unique to this film: human law is ineffective when dealing with satanic evil. Though the Inquisition of earlier times had been successful in eliminating thousands of accused witches, Lou makes it clear that contemporary courts are useless. The investigation is personal for Lou because it involves his developmentally disabled son, Joey. Nicole is able to control Joey psychically, even getting him to attack his father. This is another element that gets repeated in films featuring the satanic witch: just as women have a special connection to the supernatural, so do young children, the developmentally disabled, the outcast, and the mentally ill.

Suspiria (1977) is a stylistic version of the satanic witch tale, a story told with stylized lighting, lavish sets, and an obsessive soundtrack of repetitive bells. Suzy Bannion (Jessica Harper) is a young American dancer who travels to Europe to study in a famous ballet school, the Tam Academy. Terrible things happen to her after she arrives at the school. She suffers from weakness, a fellow dancer is brutally attacked and killed, the dormitories become infested with worms, and Suzy is assaulted by a bat. She seeks the help of a psychiatrist, Dr. Frank Mandel (Udo Kier), who tells her that belief in the occult is a form of mental illness. "Bad luck isn't brought by broken mirrors, but by broken minds." Mandel tells her the history of the school: The academy had been founded in 1895 by a Greek immigrant, Helena Marcos, for the combined study of dance and the occult. At the climax of the film, Suzy discovers that the founding coven of the school has survived through the centuries. The coven is malefic, negative, and destructive. The witches' only goal seems to be achieving tremendous personal wealth, though they seem horribly inefficient. Knowledge gives the witches tremendous power, but only to do harm. And the harm they inflict seems to have no real benefit to them beyond a sadistic enjoyment in the suffering of others.

Media images of the satanic witch are frequent throughout the twentieth century, appearing in early black-and-white films, such as *Le Sorcier* (*The Witch's Revenge*, 1903) and *Faust* (1909), and continuing throughout the century. In horror films like *Omen* (1976) and the sequels (1978; 1981; 1991) and *Lost Souls* (2000), witch characters are a present and important pressure but tend to be more of an ensemble force helping to bring the Devil to power. For example, the satanic magic in the made-for-television movie *Omen IV: The Awakening* (1991) largely arises from the young demon, Delia (Asia Vieira), and the satanic forces supporting her. However, the film also features the character of a nanny involved in New Age witchcraft, who attempts to take young Delia to a psychic fair, with horrific results. The New Age witch with her crystals, herbs, and good intentions is powerless against the more potent forces of evil.

Because contemporary audiences may not fully give in to paranoia and traditional, tightfisted morality, horror films often become horror-comedy or bad aesthetic cult films, which allow audiences to laugh at their own superstitions. For example, *The Blair Witch Project* inspired more than a dozen spoofs poking fun at the film's low-budget mockumentary style of production and idea of student filmmakers victimized by the subject of their documentary. Because the film's script or elements of production are weak, bad aesthetics demystify both media production and the supernatural, with the result that both become laughable. Interestingly, both horror and horror-comedy tend to be the genres attractive to adolescent males, who may be lured both by the violence and the patriarchal ideology offered by these films. Many horror movies suggest that the witch who seeks power through supernatural strength must be defeated by a heroic male protagonist, or by a strong female protagonist who accepts that the patriarchal order is the natural condition and that she must fight supernatural forces to defend the status quo.

The Fairy-Tale Witch

The fairy-tale witch is an independent creature without alliance to the Christian Devil. She is, however, antisocial and anticlerical. She frequently lives in a fantasy world where magic bubbles close to the surface, as in the literal fairy tale. Not the antithesis of the orthodox Christian, like the satanic witch, the fairy-tale witch is a character apart. Though she may consort with demonic creatures, the films will render these as fantasy characters, not satanic ones: imps, archaic gods, satyrs, and magical beings. The fairy-tale witch does share with the satanic witch an assortment of potions, cauldrons, herbs, spells, and incantations. And, as in film depictions of the satanic witch, her magic is usually depicted as genuine within the universe created by the film. Adventure films, fantasies, and children's films are the genres most likely to depict the fairy-tale witch.

Famous fairy-tale witches include Merlin, found in films such as *A Connecticut Yankee in King Arthur's Court* (1949), *The Sword in the Stone* (1963), *Excalibur* (1981), *Merlin* (1998), *The Last Enchantment* (1995), *Quest for Camelot* (1998), and *The Sorcerer's Apprentice* (2000); the wicked queen in *Rapunzel* (1951; 1981); Baba Yaga in *Baba Yaga* (1973); the wicked queen in *Snow White* (1937; 2001); Maleficent in *Sleeping Beauty* (1959); and the witch character from the many versions of *Hansel and Gretel* (1909; 1923; 1933; 1951; 1953; 1965; 1982). Of course, not all films and television programs will portray a famous witch character in the same way. For example, Merlin may be sweet and bumbling in one portrait but dark and powerful in another. The 2004 version of *King Arthur* depicts Merlin as a Woad leader and warrior without any on-screen sorcery, though one character does refer to him as a "dark magician." The Merlin character is more frequently depicted in film and television as a fairy-tale witch.

In film and television narratives, the fairy-tale witch may be the guardian of a youthful protagonist, but more often appears as the hero's nemesis. For example, in *The Wizard of Oz* (1939), young Dorothy may have been befriended by a good witch but is more frequently threatened by the wicked one. (See fig. 4.5.) In *Hocus Pocus* (1993), a teenage boy vanquishes the bumbling but malevolent witches that are his enemy. In *The Witches* (1990), another young boy outwits the evil women who are the adversaries of all children, restoring order to the world. Movies and television shows often portray the fairy-tale witch as wickedly selfish, though occasionally one is nice, even virtuous, such as the gentle but bumbling wizards from *Dragonslayer* (1981) and *Willow* (1988) and Merlin in the Disney animation *Sword in the Stone* (1963).

A film will sometimes place the fairy-tale witch in the context of a group, as in the Jim Henson production of *The Witches* (1990), where an assembly of witches convene at a hotel and plot to rid the world of all children. More frequently, however, movies show the fairy-tale witch as a loner, unconnected to a coven. Solitary and often impoverished, she is likely to live in remote forests, hidden caves, or dismal tenement houses. Occasionally, she is wealthy, though isolated in her wealth. For example, the wicked stepmother of *Snow White and the Seven Dwarfs* (1937) seems a detached creature, vainly attempting to maintain her reputation as a beauty. She cannot compete with the youthful perfection of her stepdaughter. It's all or nothing for this witch, who ultimately sacrifices the beauty she prizes for a disguise: that of the ragged, impoverished outcast that is the stereotype of the fairy-tale witch. The queen swallows a potion and transforms into the stereotypical image of the witch, seeking vengeance against the lovely girl who usurped her role as the fairest of them all. In the 2001 version, the wicked queen reverts to the ugly outcast she was at the beginning of the film, the sister of a sorcerer who is disappointed at his sibling's greed. Sometimes the magic of the fairy-tale witch is so powerful that her humanity comes into question. For example, Maleficent in *Sleeping Beauty* (1959), though she appears to have the characteristics of a witch, is described as an evil fairy. Similarly, Miranda Richardson as Queen Elspeth in the 2001 television movie *Snow White: The Fairest of Them All* commands equally powerful magic.

Fairy-tale witches are not confined to long ago and far away settings. In an episode from the children's television anthology series *Goosebumps* (1995), the fairy-tale witch takes the form of a weird relative. In "An Old Story," two brothers learn that their eccentric Aunt Dalia is coming to babysit while their parents are out of town. Aunt Dalia serves prunes in everything she makes, even cookies, which the boys eat and enjoy. But the prunes cause the children to age rapidly (an example of symbolic magic, since eating prunes is a dietary practice frequently associated with seniors, and the wrinkles on prunes evoke the wrinkled skin of the elderly). The boys learn that Aunt Dalia's friends are paying her to change boys into old men so they can become husbands for the elderly women. By accident, the boys eat baby food, which returns them to their normal age (another example of symbolic magic). Then one of the brothers throws a pitcher of prune juice on Aunt Dalia, aging her so rapidly that she is destroyed.

Fig. 4.5. Margaret Hamilton as the classic fairy-tale witch in *The Wizard of Oz* (1939). Metro-Goldwyn-Mayer. Photo courtesy of Photofest.

In *Sinbad and the Eye of the Tiger* (1977), the protagonist is not a child but the heroic young man a child might hope to emulate. In this film, the evil witch Zenobia (Margaret Whiting) magically transforms Prince Kassim (Damien Thomas) into a baboon so that her own son can inherit the throne. None of the court wizards can counter Zenobia's powerful magic. Young Sinbad (Patrick Wayne) takes Princess Farah and Kassim in his baboon form to see the wizard Melanthius, hoping to find a reversal of the spell. Though the wizard provides them with important information, he is unable to reverse Zenobia's powerful magic. Sinbad becomes determined to save Kassim, and subsequently the entire kingdom, from the rule of Zenobia's malicious son. Determined that her son will become caliph, Zenobia does everything in her considerable power to stop Sinbad. However, as is frequently the case in fairy tales, the youthful hero is triumphant.

Because it is a foreign film, the initial temptation would be to classify the Cameroon import *Quartier Mozart* (1992) as an example of the shamanic witch. However, the film, written and directed by Jean-Pierre Bekolo, doesn't accentuate the exotic "otherness" of Mama Thekla or the dangers of foreign beliefs. From the perspective of the film, this sorceress is a familiar part of the folk culture of Cameroon.

The Washington Irving story on which the film *Sleepy Hollow* (1999) is very loosely based portrays a variety of witch types, though the fairy-tale aspects predominate. Rather than a school teacher, the Ichabod Crane (Johnny Depp) of the Tim Burton film is a New York City detective sent to solve a serial murder case in the isolated town of Sleepy Hollow at the turn of the twentieth century. Village residents find murder victims decapitated but never locate the victims' heads. Locals attribute the crimes to a dead Hessian mercenary, the Headless Horseman. Initially, Ichabod is a detective in the manner of Sherlock Holmes, trusting in logic and science over superstition. "We have murders in New York without benefit of ghouls and goblins," Ichabod tells Baltus Van Tassel (Michael Gambon). In the manner of Dorothy observing that Oz is not Kansas, Van Tassel replies, "You are a long way from New York, constable." Unlike Holmes, the skeptical Ichabod quickly learns that he must discard his doubt in the supernatural.[19] The headless German mercenary that has been murdering citizens of Sleepy Hollow is very real in the world this film creates. Christina Ricci plays the enchantress Katrina Anne Van Tassel, who offers Ichabod a book of spells and charms that had belonged to her deceased mother "for protection." Ichabod observes, "there's a bit of witch in you, Katrina . . . because you've bewitched me."

We learn that Ichabod's own mother had been accused of witchcraft. "My mother was an innocent," Ichabod tells Katrina, "a child of nature condemned, murdered by my father. Murdered to save her soul by a Bible black tyrant behind a mask of righteousness." Later, Ichabod consults the Western Woods crone (Miranda Richardson), a type of fairy-tale witch who lives alone in a cave lit by hundreds of tiny candles and who comes to the assistance of the hero. This witch first shackles herself, then beheads a bat, and sprinkles a mysterious powder that creates deep purple smoke, before she becomes possessed by a demon and reveals the resting place of the Headless Horseman. Finally, Ichabod learns it is the Archer Witch (also played by Miranda Richardson) who has brought the headless misfortune to Sleepy Hollow. She is a woman who offered her "soul to Satan if he would raise the Hessian from the grave to avenge me." It is this satanic witch who controls the headless demon, procuring a fortune for herself and getting revenge on those she believes wronged her. Though the film presents a range of portraits of the witch, it is the likeness of the fairy-tale witch that emerges most strongly in this moody, mythical version of *Sleepy Hollow*. Even the self-avowed satanic witch appears to work her dark magic alone, without the support of a coven or on-screen supplications to the Devil.

The Shamanic Witch

The shamanic witch is that category of portrayals that draws from foreign cultures and exotic religious beliefs. Film and television borrow and distort rituals from Caribbean (especially Haitian), African, Native American, South American, Asian, Australian, and New Zealand religious customs to create media versions of the shamanic witch. What unites this category is a film perspective that makes the foreign shaman's beliefs and practices seem bizarre. The shamanic witch tends to be a practitioner of pagan religions often in conflict with the beliefs of the film's hero. The shaman's arcane rituals are either imported from a foreign land or the hero stumbles upon them while sojourning in the shaman's country. The film may depict the shaman's magic as "real" within the world the film creates, but just as often, the powers are questionable or they are defeated by the truth of science or the "more civilized" religious belief of the protagonist.

Medea (1969) tells the story of how a woman who might be considered a holy priestess in her own country becomes a horrid witch when exiled to a foreign land. Opera star Maria Callas, who sang the role of Medea on stage, also starred in this nonmusical film version. (See fig. 4.6.) The film introduces the title character as a respected priestess in her home country who oversees the sacrifice of a young man. "Give life with the seed and be reborn with the seed," she proclaims. Afterward, villagers share the victim's blood, smearing it on plants and dribbling it on the ground to ensure the growth of crops. When Jason (Giuseppe Gentile) arrives, Medea is tormented by a magic more powerful than her own: desire for this handsome adventurer. For his sake, she betrays her family and becomes an exile. When Jason abandons her to marry the princess of Corinth, Medea's nurse reminds her of her own powers. "You are an expert in evil spells. You are different from us. They say that in your land you worked wonders." Corinth, it seems, is still a pagan culture, though with practices different from Medea's home country. Medea's revenge, when it comes, relies less on manipulation of magic and more on a horror conjured by the despairing human heart.

Black Robe (1991) provides an interesting example of the shamanic witch because the film shows the exotic otherness of both the Indian shaman and the Jesuit missionary who comes to Quebec in 1634 to convert the Indians to Catholicism. The film provides another expression of the idea that one culture's priest or shaman is another culture's demon-possessed witch. Lothaire Bluteau plays Father Laforgue, the young French priest sent to the wilds of North America to convert the Huron Indians. He is nicknamed "Black Robe" by the Algonquin Indians, who guide him

Fig. 4.6. Maria Callas plays a shamanic witch expelled from her home country in *Medea* (1969). New Line Cinema. Photo courtesy of Photofest.

and his companion, Daniel (Arden Young), to the Huron settlement. The "magic" of the written word, which Father Laforgue demonstrates, impresses his Indian guides, but they are less impressed with his Christian concept of an afterlife without tobacco, wives, and tangible human happiness. Father Laforgue's beliefs are too abstract for them. His abstinence and other unnatural ways worry the Algonquins, who decide they must find a sorcerer to tell them what to do about the Black Robe. Among the Montagnais, they find Mestigoit (Yvan Labelle), a dwarf shaman with a fiercely painted face, who confronts Laforgue by shaking his gourd and howling, "You are not a man but a demon. Demons fear noise. I curse you, demon." Through sheer annoyance, Mestigoit is successful in getting Father Laforgue to walk away, but only for a short distance and only temporarily. Mestigoit later decides that Father Laforgue isn't himself a demon but is possessed by one and advises the Algonquins not to travel with him.

At one point, Father Laforgue confesses to Daniel, "I'm afraid of this country. The Devil rules here. He controls the hearts and minds of these poor people." Daniel answers, "But they are true Christians. . . . They forgive things we would never forgive." Laforgue argues, "The Devil makes them resist the truth of our teachings." Daniel attempts to explain the Indians' beliefs to Laforgue, but the priest finds these beliefs childish, certain that only Christianity has the answers. Both shaman and priest appear to be ineffectual in changing the bleak fortunes of the Indians. Moreover, Christianity does more harm than good for the Huron converts, who are destroyed by their enemies, the Iroquois. Though the film seems dubious about any shaman's "magic," the dreams that are an important part of the Indians' faith do appear to be prophetic. As Father Laforgue's Indian guide is dying on the same island he had foreseen in his dream, the audience is allowed a glimpse of the wintry spirit that comes to escort him into the afterlife.

A more contemporary portrait of the Native American shaman comes in the Western *Shadowhunter* (1993). The shaman is Two Bear (Benjamin Bratt), an Indian who uses his magical power to commit the crimes of robbery and murder. John Cain (Scott Glenn) is the burned-out homicide detective, a white man who must travel to the Navajo reservation in Arizona to transport this mystic "coyote man" back to Los Angeles. Two Bear escapes from Cain's custody by using his mythical power to "skinwalk," or spiritually overtake another human being. Two Bear is able to confuse the white man with visions, invading his dreams and causing him to become sick. Cain employs the aid of an expert Indian guide, Ray Whitesinger (Angela Alvarado), to track the coyote man across the desert and into the abandoned cliff dwellings of the ancient Anasazi. When Cain expresses doubt about Two Bear's power, Ray tells him,

> What makes you people think your magic is real and ours is hocus-pocus . . . [that] your prophets can raise the dead and part the seas and ours are just bull? Let me tell you something, my friend. Our ancestors have practiced their medicine for ten thousand years. It's real and it's powerful.

Soon there is no room to doubt Two Bear's power, though Ray and Cain manage to best it in the end.

Another portrait of the Native American "skinwalker" comes in the film *The Dark Wind* (1991). State Trooper Jim Chee (Lou Diamond Phillips) is a Navajo who wants to be a traditional medicine man as well as an officer of the law. He teams up with a Hopi detective, Cowboy Albert Dashee (Gary Farmer), to find the truth about a corpse in the desert and a drug smuggling ring. Cultural appropriation goes both ways in this film, with whites commercializing Indian customs and Indians adopting white mannerisms. At one point, Chee must explain native folklore to an Indian boy wearing a Bart Simpson T-shirt, and the boy rejects his native folklore as "gross." Though the film initially places suspicion of the evil witchcraft on a Navajo named Joseph Musket, it shifts to a white man, a "carney hump," an outsider to both Indian and mainstream American cultures who has commandeered what he needs from each. This witch seeks vengeance, something an Indian wouldn't do. As Chee explains, "Navajos believe that when a man does something wrong or destructive or just plain crazy, it's because a dark wind is blowing through him. . . . It makes no sense to seek revenge. . . . Just stay out of his way until it all blows over."

Fait Accompli (or *Voodoo Dawn*, 1998) provides a good example of the shamanic witch that draws on the fascination for religious practices imported to America from Africa, Cuba, and Haiti. In this film, a vicious criminal named Rick (Michael Madsen) learns the secret of a voodoo shaman's power while in prison. Once released, Rick uses his power to get revenge on the officer who arrested him by killing most of the man's family. The officer's son, A. J. Merchant (Balthazar Getty), goes to Queenie, a conjure woman (Pat Perkins), for advice. Set in a foreboding Louisiana bayou, Queenie's house is surrounded with wind chimes made of bones and other mysterious objects. Here A. J. learns that he has been the target of Rick's supernatural power. Queenie tells A. J., "There is no such thing as coincidence." A. J.'s misfortunes come from a man who has "done gris-gris your whole family." Queenie intervenes to repel the "bad luck" Rick has brought to A. J. and his family with her potent magic.

Numerous films feature the shamanic witch in the context of voodoo, including *French Quarter* (1977), *Angel Heart* (1987), and *The Serpent and the Rainbow* (1988), though other foreign beliefs may be brought into the context of these films as well. For example, in *The Serpent and the Rainbow*, early scenes take place in the Amazon basin, where Dr. Dennis Alan (Bill Pullman) drinks a potion given to him by an Indian shaman. This potion causes him to have a vision of his protective animal spirit, but it also gives him the vision of the Haitian witch doctor who will become his spiritual enemy and the focus of the film. Though the magic in the movie is overt, the film does have many scenes that attempt to deal with voodoo earnestly as a religion and a way of life.

Less prevalent, but also part of the discourse on the shamanic witch, are films featuring the Celtic shaman. The pagan rite portrayed in the film *The Wicker Man* (1973) would get a historical explanation in the three-part BBC documentary *The Celts: Rich Traditions and Ancient Myths* (1986) as one of the sacrificial practices of the early Celtic people. "If you want to appease supernatural forces, then you must give them something of value," the documentary explains. "The Druid was the shaman. . . . the more mysterious and arcane his practices, the more powerful he became." According to the documentary, the wickerman ceremony involved human offerings and included people who tossed themselves into the flames in ecstatic self-sacrifice. The documentary suggests that Christianity didn't vanquish Celtic paganism; the beliefs either "petered out" or were absorbed by Christianity, so that, for example, the old religious festival of Samhain would in later centuries be celebrated as the secular Halloween. However, the narrative film *The Wicker Man* suggests that the darkest aspects of Celtic human sacrifice remain extant in modern times among secretive peoples. The story concerns a Christian police officer from the Scottish mainland who goes to the offshore community of Summerisle to investigate the disappearance of a young girl. What Sergeant Howie (Edward Woodward) discovers is a secret neopagan society that survives in the twentieth century and a shaman devoted to the "old gods." The narrative portrays such remnants of ancient Celtic belief as horrific. As an examination of the Celtic historical witch, however, the documentary is less judgmental than the narrative.[20]

African and South American witch doctors, voodoo priestesses, Native American shamans, and mysterious Asian monks with magical forces under their control make up the majority of film and television portraits of the shamanic witch. Many of these tend to position foreign beliefs as sinister or ridiculous, as does *Jungle Goddess* (1948), which shows the superiority of a civilization that created hamburgers and fries over the pagan culture that resorts to magic. Similarly, in the 1957 film *From Hell it Came*, a witch doctor from a Pacific island is the villain, and he is concerned that the American scientists will prove his "magic" to be false. However, the magic in this film is not all explained away by science. An unjustly murdered prince, who had been buried in a hollow tree, does magically return for vengeance. Later films, such as *Indiana Jones and the Temple of Doom* (1984), also position the foreign as malignant. In this fantasy adventure, the hero, Indiana Jones, must save an Indian village from the sinister cult of the goddess Kali, a regressive mother goddess savagely lusting after human flesh. The ideological construct of the savage against the civilized is a frequent theme in films that feature the shamanic witch. Sometimes the film is sympathetic to the shaman. However, just as often the foreign occult influences of the shamanic witch are portrayed as cruel, corrupt, and feminine, whereas Western paternalism is portrayed as a civilizing and purifying male force.

Sometimes a narrative affectionately dominates and appropriates the shamanic position, as does the television movie *The Tempest* (1998), in which a white slave-owner adopts the voodoo beliefs of his slave. Very loosely based on the Shakespearean play of the same name, this version is set in the American Civil War era. Guideon Prosper (Peter Fonda) becomes enthralled with the voodoo teachings of his black slave, Azaleigh (Donzaleigh Abernathy), a Mombo priestess. Guideon ignores his responsibilities, leaving control of his plantation to his corrupt brother, Anthony (John Glover), who abuses the slaves and steals the plantation. Anthony attempts to murder Guideon, who is saved by Azaleigh's magic. However, her magic is not powerful enough to let her save herself from Anthony's bullet. Guideon escapes to the bayou with his daughter, Miranda (Katherine Heigl), and Azaleigh's son, Ariel (Harold Perrineau Jr.). The character of Guideon Prosper combines his mastery over black culture with his affection for it. He studies "philosophy, alchemy, and heathen black magic" to become a master magician. The voodoo power he acquires is not limited to Azaleigh's oral wisdom but is integrated with the white man's superior literacy. The film portrays Guideon sitting in his candlelit shack in the bayou, studying an ancient, apparently Western, text, obviously not something bequeathed to him from Azaleigh. But Guideon's self-doubt begins to weaken his magical power. As a fiery vision that entreats the men to believe in themselves, Azaleigh reappears to Guideon, her pupil, and Ariel, the son who rejected his mother's "mumbo jumbo." Azaleigh tells Guideon, "You have lost your faith. Until you find it in yourself, the magic is lost to you." Guideon rediscovers his powers again in time to help the Union Army win an important battle.

The Ingenue Witch

The ingenue witch is a child or teenager who learns she possesses magical power and must discover how to use that power as she copes with the trepidations of growing up and discovering who she is. In many film and television depictions, she must contend with the wickedness of middle school or high school and the perverse social world of teenagers, where confidence is blighted and young people attempt to become what they believe will best help them to fit in with the social crowd. The ingenue witch is oftentimes an outsider, unpopular and picked on, even by other witches. Children's comedy and fantasy programs contain some of the strongest portraits of the ingenue witch. For example, in the family television movie *The Worst Witch* (1986), the character Mildred attends a prestigious witch academy, where she is bullied by both classmates and teachers. The character of Louise in *Teen Witch* (1989) is also unpopular at her high school. When she discovers that she's descended from the witches of Salem and has inherited their powers, she tries to get revenge on the girls who torment her and teachers who tease her. However, she later decides that it isn't right to "cheat" her way to popularity by using the advantage of magic.

The title character in *Harry Potter and the Sorcerer's Stone* (2001) is also an outcast, raised by "muggle" relatives who hate him and take great care to make his life miserable.[21] Even when Harry Potter arrives at the Hogwarts School, a kind of elite conservatory for witchcraft, several young wizards who are jealous of his talent and notoriety continue to hurt his feelings and fill him with self-doubt.[22]

Not all ingenue witches inherit their magical abilities. In an interesting modern twist to typical hocus-pocus, the title character in the television series *The Secret World of Alex Mack* (1994–97) is accidentally exposed to a toxic chemical spill. What makes Alex Mack interesting is that her magical powers don't come from the occult world of spirits and the supernatural, but from the sometimes equally mysterious world of science. Alex's exposure to this concoction of chemicals proves to be a modern magic potion, the accidental alchemy that gives Alex the ability to transform herself into a translucent glob with the additional power to move objects and "zap" people with small electrical charges. Like the accused witches of the Middle Ages who lived in fear of Church officials, Alex lives in fear of the authorities of the chemical plant, who wish to control or eliminate her illegitimate power. The minions of the chemical plant become a comical Inquisition, continuously searching for the young teen who received this magical contamination. Alex alludes them by learning to use her newly acquired power. However, even with her magical ability, she still lacks the charms necessary to become a favorite at school.

Matilda (1996) presents a young character bullied and neglected by her family. However, this character neither inherits her abilities nor does she receive them as a magical gift. Through her own efforts and sheer mental concentration, Matilda develops her magical abilities and uses them to successfully overcome the cruel domination of her parents and school principal.

Several ingenue witch characters evolved to moving-image media from comic books. Three of the most popular are Wendy, associated with *Casper the Friendly Ghost*; Sabrina, associated with the *Archie* comics; and Sara Pezzini, associated with Top Cow Comics' *Witchblade* series.

Sabrina, the Teenage Witch developed from a comic-book character to an animated series in 1971, to a highly popular live-action sitcom series in 1996, followed by two television movies: *Sabrina Goes to Rome* (1998) and *Sabrina, Down Under* (1999). Another show, *Sabrina, the Animated Series*, would appear on ABC from 1999 to 2001, when the live-action sitcom made a move to Warner Brothers television, where the show had a strong following until it ended in 2003. The series seemed to respond to a teenage fantasy. An ordinary girl (Melissa Joan Hart) learns she is special, having inherited magical abilities. She has one bizarre adventure after another while learning how to control her magic. She zaps herself a wonderful wardrobe, befuddles her friends, visits witchy worlds through the portal of a linen closet, and is able to get occasional harmless revenge on her stuck-up nemesis, Libby (Jenna Leigh Green). She then successfully graduates from high school and moves on to college and another network, where her adventures continue. Sabrina is perhaps one of the best-adjusted of ingenue witches, genuinely liked and admired by most of her classmates. In college, her magic helps her uncover the injustices of an academic system that rewards the school's athletic heroes with undeserved grades. Sabrina herself resists the temptation to "zap" homework papers, because that would be cheating. Though the later episodes of the series have Sabrina living on her own in a house with other college students, she remains an ingenue witch, still learning about her magic and still returning to her aunts for advice and guidance.

Interestingly, one episode of the Warner Brothers television series *Sabrina, the Teenage Witch*, "Welcome Traveler" (WB, 3 Nov. 2000), featured the depiction of a dubious New Age witch, a character called Jim Tom (Richard Kline). In this episode, Sabrina must debunk the self-proclaimed witch and leader of a bogus cult dedicated to the "exploration of alternate realities" and vegetarian nutrition. Sabrina grows suspicious when one of her college roommates, Miles (Trevor Lissauer), becomes enthralled by Jim Tom's philosophy. "Human cells contain the very same primordial elements that compose all heavenly bodies throughout the universe. . . . We are children of the stars . . . discover your cosmic soul," intones a video, while cult members sit on cushions and promise to give Jim Tom all their worldly goods in return for his enlightenment. Over his prescribed dinner of mung beans and rice, Miles tells

Sabrina, "I feel connected to myself, other people, and the universe. I feel whole." To which Sabrina responds, "Get over it," and then sets her resolve to expose the fraudulent Jim Tom. This episode reiterates the idea that a "real witch" does not proselytize, while warning young people about the dangers of cults.

Wendy was an occasional character on Izzy Sparber's *Casper the Friendly Ghost* animated cartoons of the 1940s and 1950s. After Casper starred in a successful mixed live-action and animation movie followed by an animated television series, Wendy appeared in a less successful, straight-to-video release, *Casper Meets Wendy* (1998). As both a cartoon and a live-action character, Wendy has some of the best qualities of the ingenue witch. She is a thoughtful, forgiving, open-minded young girl with high moral standards. She won't allow the prejudices or the wickedness of adults—whether they be ghosts or witches—to cloud her thinking.

The television movie *Witchblade* (2000) evolved from the adventure comic and would become the pilot to the Warner Brothers television series *Witchblade* (2001). In the pilot film, Detective Sara Pezzini (Yancy Butler) is a young, renegade New York City cop. Like many renegade cops from film and television, Sara is a moody, edgy outsider; character traits that renegade cops and ingenue witches have in common. Sara plays by her own rules. In the pilot, she seeks vengeance against mobster Tommy Gallo (George Jenesky), the man who murdered both her adopted father and her childhood friend. During a shoot-out in a museum, Sara makes contact with the Witchblade, a mysterious gauntlet, or armored glove, that has special powers and chooses its wearer. Sara learns that the Witchblade had been used by Joan of Ark and other witchy "warrior" women going back deep into history. The armor demands a blood sacrifice from Sara before she will be truly bonded to its power. Though she is older than most ingenue witches, Sara has still not discovered who she is or how to use her newly acquired magical abilities. Her magic seems largely restricted to dodging bullets and calling forth some extraordinary kung fu. However, the Witchblade also allows Sara the clairvoyant's gift to look beyond the ordinary world, to glimpse and battle against inhuman evil. The pilot makes two interesting statements. The first: only women can wear the Witchblade because "women are more elemental." This is an idea frequently repeated in popular movies across categories: women become witches because of their inherent intuition or superior biological links to life and nature. Sara herself makes the second statement, another idea fundamental to the idea of witchcraft: "Things are more connected than they appear." All things and all events are linked in a scheme that the witch can learn to manipulate. When misfortune occurs, it is dark magic that has influenced a person to be in the wrong place at the wrong time.

Carrie (1976) provides an example of an ingenue witch who finally learns the full nature of her powers and commands them, with the worst possible result. Like many ingenue witches, Carrie White (Sissy Spacek) is an outcast, the daughter of a rigidly religious woman (Piper Laurie), who herself has the look of a witch: long black cape and severe presence. Mrs. White's view of the world is so repressed that she interprets Carrie's first period as not only a reminder of original sin but evidence of Carrie's personal corruption. In her 1991 analysis of the film, Shelley Lindsey suggests that the film offers a masculine fantasy that interprets the feminine as something horrific. Lindsey observes that many cultures have fears about menses, a time when a woman might be polluted or possessed by dangerous spirits. Poised at the threshold of the supernatural, menstruating women might be considered especially treacherous. "Equating Carrie's burgeoning sexuality with her newfound telekinetic power, the film hyperbolizes this connection" (36). Though the film seems sympathetic to Carrie, it ultimately advocates Mrs. White's repressive position by proving her prognostications to be true. Carrie *is* corrupt, a witch with unnatural power and the willfulness to use it for her own horrible revenge. Moreover, the young men in the film are characterized as lacking any strength of character. They are completely dominated by girlfriends, who manipulate the boys into setting the stage for the horror that unfolds. The film could be interpreted as a warning to young men about the dangers of giving in to the whims of girls and a caution against "unnatural" female power.

The sequel, *The Rage: Carrie 2* (1999), is about another ingenue witch with telekinetic power, Rachel Lang (Emily Bergl). This film doesn't link Rachel's power to the onset of puberty. Instead, she appears to have had telekinetic ability from childhood and has even developed a knack for controlling it. This film, like many ingenue films, becomes an intent exploration of school as a rigid and cruel caste system. Living with lower-middle-class, unsupportive foster parents, Rachel is described by her peers as a "bottom feeder" among the high-school social crowd. She's sulky, dark, and tattooed but confesses that "sometimes I wish I could be one of the shiny, happy people." Though she's an outcast, Rachel attracts the attentions of Jessie (Jason London), one of the more popular boys on the football team. Jessie's former girlfriend remarks, "If he's going to be seen in public talking to someone else, he should show some respect. He should show me the respect at least to be seen with someone pretty, someone cool, someone who counts." At this school, the popular boys on the football team are involved in a game where boys tally points for sleeping with certain girls.[23] When Rachel's only friend commits suicide after being used in this game, the boys threaten Rachel, warning her not to talk to authorities about their sexual sports. Misogyny is an obvious element of this film. Young women are both objects in a game and objects of derision. For example, in one scene, the head football coach makes a player drop his pants, remarking that "after that half-assed block, I just wanted to check to see if maybe you had a tampon string hanging between your legs." Rachel ultimately gets her revenge, but at a terrible cost.[24]

One of the most influential depictions of the ingenue witch came with the film *The Craft*. (See fig. 4.7.) Like *Little Witches*, *The Craft* features girls in a Catholic high school, but this school is co-ed, and this film doesn't have the satanic element. Sarah (Robin Tunney) is the new girl in school, and because she is new, she is an outsider. Sarah soon allies herself with three other social outcasts: Nancy (Fairuza Balk), Bonnie (Neve Campbell), and Rochelle (Rachel True). Other students at St. Benedict's Academy have nicknamed these girls "the Bitches of Eastwick" because of their dark outlook, dark clothes, and sullen attitudes.[25] Much of the film focuses on the four girls as they deal with the horrors of high school and begin to experiment with magic in an attempt to gain power and control over their lives. For the ingenue witches in this film, the experiments work. Wiccan Pat Devin, who became a technical supervisor for *The Craft*, said she considered a script in which the Wiccan "Law of Threefold Return" was a major part of the plot and that also emphasized the idea of magic being neutral to be an encouraging new development in Hollywood depictions of witchcraft.[26]

The Craft depicts a deity, Manon, described as bigger and older than God or the Devil. The girls swear no allegiance to Satan, who is mentioned only once in the film when the character Nancy explains, "if God and the Devil were playing football, Manon would be the stadium." Though the film puts forward New Age concepts and had a Wiccan adviser, the portrait offered by the film is clearly that of the ingenue witch, a young person trying to develop a sense of potential, competence, and fundamental worth as an individual in a world that rejects her. It is interesting that in this film about the bonding of social outcasts, the magic that ties the girls together quickly degenerates along with their friendship. Soon the girls are using magic as weapons against each other. The film may be a stronger statement about the evils of high school and the shallowness of teenage friendship than an assertion about the value and vitality of magic in a young woman's life.

Fig. 4.7. Fairuza Balk, Robin Tunney, Neve Campbell, and Rachel True play ingenue witches in *The Craft* (1996). Columbia Pictures. Photo courtesy of Photofest.

The Enchantress

Male characters in movies are often the victims of a seductive enchantress, the witch who commands a potent power to entice helpless men. Though the enchantress may work spells and mix potions like the witches of any category, the emphasis of this portrait is on the witch's beauty, allure, and ability to seduce even the strongest and most reasonable of men. Action-adventure and fantasy films sometimes offer an image of the enchantress when the hero encounters her on his journey. Such a creature seduces the title character in *Conan the Barbarian* (1982), revealing her true nature in the heat of ecstasy. A similar creature in *Kull the Conqueror* (1997) seduces the champion into a corrupt marriage. Another enchantress, Circe, bewitches Odysseus and his men on their voyage (*Circe, the Enchantress*, 1924; *Circe the Sorceress*, 1989; *The Odyssey*, 1997). Often the enchantress isn't interested in a man's love, but in using her seductive power to exploit her victim for other purposes. However, the enchantress may be unaware of her magnetism. Enchantresses can include a range of characters, from Marina, who blunders into love with intuitive magic (*The Butcher's Wife*, 1991), to the faithful, devoted Samantha (*Bewitched*), to the demonic Lilith (*The Serpent's Lair*, 1995). The genres for the enchantress range from romantic comedies such as *I Married a Witch*

(1942), to action films like *The Warrior and the Sorceress* (1984), to dark comedies like *Black Magic* (1992), and soft-core pornography in horror films like *Sorceress* (1994).

An early example of the enchantress comes in the fantasy adventure *She* (1934). (See fig. 4.8.) A skeptical adventurer, Leo Vincey (Randolph Scott), sets out with family friend, Horace Holly (Nigel Bruce), to find the "flame of life" that his ancestor, John Vincey, was supposed to have discovered hundreds of years earlier. In the frozen arctic, they encounter a guide and his daughter, Tanya (Helen Mack), and then make their way to a hidden civilization ruled by a beautiful and mysterious queen (Helen Gahagan), who tells him, "I am she, she who must be obeyed." Like the sorceress in *Death Becomes Her* (1992), this woman has found the secret of eternal youth. Leo discovers that she has lived for more than five hundred years and was his ancestor's lover. The sorceress queen murdered John Vincey out of jealousy, but she now believes Leo is her long-lost lover returned to her. She attempts to sacrifice her rival, Tanya, but Leo rescues the girl. Tanya tells the queen, "Your magic makes you seem young, but in your heart you're old, old." The queen mocks Tanya's mortality, but when she steps into the eternal flame, her magic betrays her, causing her to wrinkle, wither, and die. It's not uncommon in film for an enchantress to lure a hero with false youth and beauty. For example, Morgana (Helen Mirren), the witch who seduces her half brother in *Excalibur* (1981), also loses her beauty when her magic fails.

Though there are early examples of the enchantress, the portraits seem more prevalent in the latter half of the twentieth century. One of the earlier, better known, and certainly more favorable portraits of the enchantress is Samantha, a character Elizabeth Montgomery brought to life in the popular television series *Bewitched*. Montgomery had her first role as an enchantress in the comedy *How to Stuff a Wild Bikini* (1965), but in *Bewitched*, Samantha not only charms Darren into marriage but keeps him enthralled with her week after week during the eight-year run of the show. Initially, Samantha promises Darren she will give up her craft to become an ordinary housewife. It is a promise she will not keep. Darren may think he wants a commonplace life, but Samantha knows better. She surrounds him with magic and conjuring in-laws, but through every bizarre adventure and embarrassing situation her magic creates for him, Darren's love for Samantha remains steadfast. Their marriage appears unshakable, even under the most freakish of circumstances. However, Samantha never uses her magic with corrupt motives. She is usually impelled by love and concern to cast a spell. It is clear that their love is

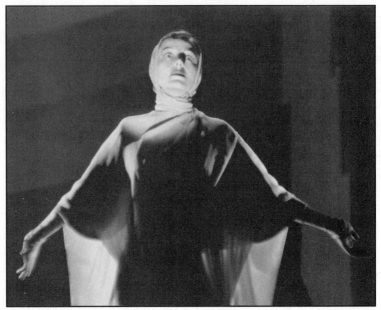

Fig. 4.8. Helen Gahagan as the powerful enchantress in *She* (1934). RKO Radio Pictures. Photo courtesy of Photofest.

reciprocal and that even though her husband is an ordinary man, Samantha honors and respects him, regardless of how much her mother Endora (Agnes Moorehead) ridicules him. This series was, as Susan Douglas suggests, a woman's fantasy.

> In *Bewitched* we have a woman's dream and a man's nightmare. Darren was surrounded by an endearing yet constantly troublesome matriarchy, a domestic situation in which his wife, mother-in-law, and other relatives were witches, endowed with magical powers, which constantly threatened his professional status and his authority as head of the household. (127)

Samantha has everything a woman can desire: a devoted lover, domestic bliss, and the power to have what she likes with the twitch of her nose.

> Young, slim, blonde and beautiful, with practical ideas about what needed to be done in her community, yet a witch, Samantha stood at the intersection between middle-class definitions of the ideal young wife and rebelliousness against those definitions. (128)

The film predecessor to the character of Samantha Stevens in *Bewitched* is the witch Jennifer (Veronica Lake) from the 1942 film *I Married a Witch*. After the enchantress Jennifer and her warlock father (Cecil Kellaway) are burned at the stake and their ashes imprisoned beneath a tree, the seventeenth-century witch curses the sons of the Wooley family to marry unhappily. But lightning from a twentieth-century storm strikes their tree, releasing the spirits of the witches as ghostly smoke. Jennifer reveals her enchantress nature when she says to her father, "T'would be nice to have lips . . . lips to whisper lies . . . lips to kiss a man and make him suffer." Jennifer does take on mortal form as a beautiful blonde, determined to torture the descendant of her old enemy, Wallace Wooley (Fredric March), with a love potion. However, Jennifer drinks the potion by mistake and yields to love herself. Even though she says several times that "love is stronger than witchcraft," it was a potion that initially caused her to become a victim of love.

Similarly, Gillian (Kim Novak) in *Bell, Book and Candle* (1958) uses witchcraft to entrap Shep (Jimmy Stewart) but falls genuinely in love with her victim, which is dangerous for a witch because it means she will lose her powers, her familiar (the cat Pyewacket), and her standing in the magical community. However, the film suggests that this witch is unfulfilled by magic and longs for a more conventional life. She says of witches, "We forfeit everything and end up in a little world of separateness from everyone."

A less humorous portrait of the enchantress using magic to manipulate domestic bliss comes in *The Juniper Tree* (1987). Desperate for a home, Katla (Bryndis Petra Bragadóttir) casts a spell that will win her a husband and later makes a fertility charm so she can conceive a son to make that husband happy. While both spells work, Katla's magic isn't strong enough to fully protect her from a possessive stepson, suspicious of Katla's rituals. When the boy threatens her home and happiness, Katla plots to kill him.

It isn't clear whether the enchantress Lillian Blatman (Rachel Ward) in the television movie *Black Magic* is vulnerable to love herself. However, it is clear that the men who meet Lillian are unable to resist her. Alex Gage (Judge Reinhold) suffers from insomnia and nightmares involving the ghost of his cousin, Ross, who was murdered by a witch. Alex ventures to the town of Istanbul in Frogmore County, North Carolina, hoping to rid himself of these dreams. Here Alex learns that the county got its name when a coven of witches cursed the area with a plague of frogs. At a bowling alley, he meets Lillian and learns she was his dead cousin's girlfriend. Alex is immediately smitten by her beauty and bold demeanor. His cousin's ghost continues to haunt him, asking him to kill the witch, but the smitten Alex hesitates. At one point, Alex replies, "We men have been liberated. We no longer have to believe that every woman is an evil witch bent on our destruction. Paranoid misogyny is out of fashion." The movie reveals that paranoid misogyny might have served Alex better, for he ends up cursed and killed, a ghost in the company of other ghosts murdered by Lillian. While Alex listens to his cousin's ghost call him a "romantic, worthless putz" in an uncomfortable purgatory, Lillian revels in luxury as the wealthy beneficiary of her boyfriend's life insurance.

Though she often seduces men for dark purposes, the enchantress may also seek love for herself. For example, the unfulfilled longing of three magical women in *The Witches of Eastwick* (1987) proves strong enough to awaken a demon, Daryl Van Horn (Jack Nicholson). The young witches enjoy the sexual liberation provided by the middle-aged but charming devil, until they realize just how dangerous he is. Then they forgo their dalliances and unite their magic to "bind" the demon.

The two sets of sisters in *Practical Magic* (1998) have inherited their magical ability from an ancestor witch along with a curse: their husbands die following the chirp of the deathwatch beetle. While the aunts (Dianne Wiest and Stockard Channing) display a blend of fairy-tale and New Age magic, the younger witches, Gillian Owens (Nicole Kidman) and Sally (Sandra Bullock), are clearly enchantresses looking for love and attempting to control it through magic. Sally marries and loses her husband to the curse, while Gillian goes from man to man, until an abusive lover threatens to overpower her. The sisters kill Gillian's boyfriend in self-defense, then use magic to bring him back to life, and out of necessity must kill him again. With exasperation, Sally tells her sister, "You have the worst taste in men." Though the romance of the enchantress is the strongest theme in the film, there are also several New Age references: a strong sense of female bonding, a knowledge of herbs used to make face creams and to open a storefront for herbal goods, and finally, a magic ritual in which the sisters call on "Mighty Hectate" to "make it right." There are no references to the Devil, but there are to the rebirth of an ancient goddess in a modern household. However, the enchantress is the strongest character type of the witches in this film. For example, when Officer Gary Hallett (Aidan Quinn) comes to investigate a possible murder, his lawman's sense of duty is overpowered by his feelings for Sally Owens.

In *Black Magic Woman* (1991), the enchantress uses the focused powers of a coven of middle-aged women to tame a Casanova. Brad Travis (Mark Hamill) is a playboy who refuses to be loyal to his lover and business partner, Diane (Amanda Wyss). Travis wakes one morning—with yet a different lover—to find a dead chicken hanging over his bed and bloody eggs by the pillows. When Travis becomes ill, his maid Carlita (Abidah Viera) suggests he is cursed. The plot of this film demonstrates the ruthlessness of the enchantress who wishes to bind a faithless lover, making him her prisoner.

The skeptical character Larry (Larry Poindexter) in *Sorceress* (1994) initially ridicules his wife's witchcraft paraphernalia, her black outfit, candle-laden alter, and ceremonial knife. "What is all this? What's it supposed to accomplish?" he asks Erica (Julie Strain) irritably. Later, as he packs his clothes to leave her, she suggests that it was her witchcraft that forced Larry from the arms of his old girlfriend into hers. He replies with contempt, "You put a spell on me, right? Well, guess what. It's worn off." However, the power of an enchantress isn't cast aside so easily. Erica's desires are clearly evil, and her witchcraft obviously potent. Here the theme of an enchantress provides justification for gratuitous nudity and sexual exploits. Similarly, in *The Serpent's Lair*, the satanic succubus Lilith (Lisa Barbuscia) has an insatiable sexual appetite.[27] Lilith appears as a black cat, causing Tom's wife, Alex (heather Medway), to fall down the stairs, an accident damaging enough to put her in the hospital. This gives Lilith the freedom she needs to seduce Tom (Jeff Fahey), which she does, sapping him of his will and his health with her sexual demands.

The enchantress may use her seductive powers to dupe or misdirect male characters, but she is just as likely to be fulfilling her own sexual desires or seeking true love and happiness. Like Adam in the Garden of Eden, male protagonists can be temporarily thwarted, even conquered by the seductive powers of witches, whose magic principally consists of youth, a shapely figure, a beautiful face, and a bold conduct. Where the witch is the protagonist, her beauty and magnetism become additional magical tools in an arsenal against evil or for securing love and domestic bliss.

Though male witches can have magnetic charms, the predominant portrait of the enchantress is female. Even the powerful Bruho Cerio (John Vargas) in the television movie *Seduced by Evil* (1994) is not as successful at seduction as his female counterparts in other films. Spurned by his consort in the seventeenth century, Cerio must resort to drugged tea in order to have his way with her reincarnation, Lee (Suzanne Sommers), only to be rejected by her again.

The New Age Witch

In the 1980s, a new, more sympathetic portrait of witchcraft emerged, stressing magical healing, feminism, reverence for nature, and mediumship between the spirit world and everyday life. Though the New Age witch portrayed in popular media frequently called herself a Wiccan, this is really too specific to describe the character. The New Age witch uses a mixture of customs and ceremonies newly invented by the witch herself or adopted from a variety of magical traditions. She will frequently express concern for the earth and the environment, veneration of a female goddess, rejection of patriarchal authority, regard for physical and spiritual healing, and interest in personal growth and empowerment. She believes cosmic forces surround us all and is often portrayed as a benevolent character, dedicated to the healing and service of others.

Narratives tend to portray the "magic" used by New Age witches more subtly than the magic used by fairy-tale, satanic, or even shamanic witches. Films may emphasize the personal experience and intuition of the New Age witch over the on-screen special effects of overt magical powers. Her magic may be a special awareness, sometimes inherited from a mother or grandmother, or a knowledge of nature so profound that it allows communication with the elements and some limited influence over them. She may use herbal or crystal healing, mediumship, channeling, or projecting an astral body as part of her craft. She is likely to call on female spirits or goddesses in her rituals. Her magic pales in comparison to the on-screen special effects of satanic or fairy-tale witches.

The character of Pa'u Zotoh Zhaan (Virginia Hey) from the science fiction series *Farscape* (1999–2004) may be the best example of a New Age witch on television. (See fig. 4.9.) Zhaan is a holy woman from an alien race. When astronaut John Crichton (Ben Browder) accidentally pilots his ship through a wormhole to an alien galaxy, Zhaan is one of the exotic aliens who befriend him. A bald, blue-skinned, gentle healer who wears priestly robes, meditates naked, and mixes herbal medicines, Zhaan exhibits a mixture of Eastern philosophy, goddess worship, and concern for nature that defines the New Age witch. However, she doesn't represent the exotic "other" of the shamanic witch. Though Zhaan may appear exotic and foreign to Crichton, she isn't exotic in the context of the series, which is populated with exotic characters. Crichton quickly accepts and turns to Zhaan as a respected adviser, as do his alien comrades. Moreover, Zhaan seems respected by the other aliens as a priestess with healing gifts. She venerates nature and late in the series is revealed to be a highly evolved "plant" with all the attributes of a human being. Finally, Zhaan sacrifices herself for the good of her shipmates, revealing the full substance of her character.

Another strong example of the ecofeminism of the New Age witch comes in the family television drama *The Witching of Ben Wagner* (1987), a film intended for young audiences. In the story, a preteen boy, Ben Wagner (Justin Gocke), moves with his family to a new town. Here Ben

Fig. 4.9. Virginia Hey as the New Age witch Pa'u Zotoh Zhaan in the television series *Farscape* (1999–2004) prepares herbal medicines and calls on the goddess to help fellow space travelers.

becomes convinced that a girl at his school, Regina Radford (Bettina Rae), is a witch, that she is able to turn herself into a black kitten, and that she possesses other powerful magic. He follows the girl to her home by the lake to meet the girl's grandmother, Grammy (Sylvia Sidney), a woman with a knowledge of herbs and healing. Grammy has a deep concern for the lake near her home, which is threatened by a real-estate development. As the story unfolds, Ben learns to overcome his superstitions and proceeds to help the women in their crusade against the development. Though the film injects doubt about the women's magical power, New Age concerns for protecting the earth, natural healing, and female strength are more central to the story than skepticism about magic.

With its "once upon a time" opening, the film *Chocolat* (2000) seems to evoke a fairy-tale magic, but its sentiments are largely New Age. A single mother, Avienne (Juliette Binoche), arrives in a small French village to open her chocolate shop during Lent, a season of soul-searching, repentance, and self-denial. Avienne uses an ancient Mayan recipe (unrefined cacao with a pinch of chili) to unlock hidden yearnings and reveal the destinies of the customers bold enough to enter a chocolate shop during Lent. We learn that Avienne's father was a French pharmacist who visited Central America, where he met Avienne's mother, one of a group of mysterious wanderers. These nomadic people moved with the north wind from village to village, dispensing remedies and healing the sick but never settling down. Avienne has inherited her mother's gentle magic and restlessness. She dispenses chocolate, advice, and friendship, and she fulfills the healing and advisory roles of the New Age witch. She makes friends with a mistreated woman, helping this woman to find the confidence to leave her abusive husband. Avienne's wish to host a fertility festival that features a naked goddess made from chocolate is a further clue that she is a New Age witch. The rigid morality of the town's leader, the Comte de Reynaud (Alfred Molina), won't let him accept this strange woman who defies the patriarchal order, refuses invitations to go to church, is unashamed of having a bastard daughter, encourages a woman to leave her husband, and befriends outcast gypsies. It becomes Avienne's task to cure this man of his rigid nature, open his mind, and help him to discover that joy in life is neither wicked nor wrong.

One of the earlier films depicting New Age witchcraft, *Resurrection* (1980), is a moving portrait of a woman with healing powers. Directed by Danile Petrie, the film stars Ellen Burstyn as Edna McCauley, a woman who recovers from a near-death experience with amazing powers to cure both illness and injury. Edna is able to stop the bleeding of Cal Carpenter (Sam Shepard), who later accuses her of dark witchcraft. Finally, Edna must reject the patriarchy that mistreats her and withdraw to an isolated life, where she can bestow her healing gifts in secret. Similarly, the character of Annie Wilson (Cate Blanchett) in *The Gift* (2000) is another example of the New Age witch, though like Edna, this character would consider herself an ordinary woman. Annie is a widow with three kids, a government check, and the ability to "see" things, a talent inherited from her grandmother. To help make ends meet, Annie dispenses psychic advice to clients who come to her house for readings. She bonds with and attempts to rescue a battered wife and a mentally disturbed man and later uses her special talent to try to solve a murder. Like Edna and Avienne, what makes Annie's character a portrait of the New Age witch is the depiction of a self-reliant woman who must depend on her own wits and her "gift" in a hostile environment full of men who try to belittle her, threaten her, seduce her, or kill her. And like Edna's healing gift, Annie's special awareness is as much a danger to her own well-being as it is a benefit to others.

Based on a popular book by Marion Zimmer Bradley, the two-part television miniseries *The Mists of Avalon* (2001) has clear feminist messages that produce an image of New Age ideology set in ancient times. The series retells the story of King Arthur from the point of view of its principal female characters: Arthur's mother, Igraine; his half sister, Morgaine; his Aunt Viviane, the Lady of the Lake; his Aunt Morgause; and his wife, Guinevere. The series unambiguously extends the idea that male-dominated Christianity supplanted an ancient pagan goddess worship. The story is told from the point of view of Morgaine (or the evil Morgan le Fey in the fairy-tale renderings of the story found in *Merlin* and *Excalibur*). Morgaine explains that she, her mother, and her aunts are followers of the old religion of the mother goddess but that Christianity is already driving the old religion underground. Worried about the status of the old religion, Aunt Viviane, the high priestess of Avalon, wants to see a king on the throne who will be sympathetic to the goddess and the ancient ways. She wants a leader who will unite both Christians and followers of the old religion against the barbarism of Saxon invaders. Viviane demands that Morgaine's mother, Igraine, betray her husband to become the mother of the next high king. Under the influence of powerful magic, Igraine does fall in love with Uther and gives birth to Arthur.

The series makes it clear that neither Viviane nor Morgaine is a fairy. They are witches. The women are human but have developed power over the elements. In this version of the story, Merlin is Viviane's associate and subordinate. Trained in the old ways by gentle Merlin, Arthur envisions his Camelot to be something like the American ideal, a free world where people "shall worship as they choose." However, Arthur marries a devout Christian woman, Guinevere. Viviane's own son, Lancelot, rejects a universe embraced by a goddess for "a man's world, where men wait for no woman's bidding." Still hoping to ensure a line of succession sympathetic to the old beliefs, Viviane arranges for Arthur to impregnate his half sister, Morgaine, during the fertility rites on the Night of Belthane. The fertility rites pictured in this scene include the burning of wicker figurines, suggesting the ancient Celtic traditions of human sacrifice. The result of this night of masked ecstasy is Mordred, a young man who will be sympathetic only to his own ambition and vengeance. Propelled by her jealousy and selfish aspirations, Viviane's other sister, Morgause, perverts the ancient magic as she perverts Arthur and Morgaine's son, turning both into instruments of evil. In this way, the series shows how a gentle New Age witchcraft of an old goddess-centered religion became corrupted, deteriorating into a satanic witchcraft bent on serving an evil resolve. Christianity appears triumphant in the end, though Morgaine observes that the idea of the goddess survives, adapted to a new religion in the form of the Virgin Mary.

A lesser-known film, *Drawing Down the Moon* (1997), presents a clearly sympathetic portrait of New Age witchcraft. Witch Gwynyth McBride (Karina Krepp) is called by the goddess to a small, economically depressed community, where she opens a homeless shelter, a day care center, and a summer tutoring program. She also feeds the hungry, heals the sick with her rituals, and organizes an economic development committee and community watch program. Gwynyth uses a combination of martial arts and Wiccan magic to defeat the dark forces of corrupt corporate greed that enslave citizens with drugs, economic depression, and despair. In another sympathetic portrait, Rose (Rae Dawn Chong) in *Hideaway* (1995) uses tarot readings to help clients, but unlike Gwynyth, Rose is overpowered by an evil stronger than New Age ritual.

Hello Again (1987) is a comedy that portrays the New Age witch not as a discerning healer but as a wacky character who dabbles unwisely with forces beyond her understanding or control. Zelda (Judith Ivey) is the cliché of mainstream backlash to New Age rhetoric. Zelda dresses like an eclectic gypsy, owns an occult bookstore, and lives in a befuddled swirl of incense and candles. When her sister Lucy (Shelley Long) squishes an insect, Zelda reacts with horror, "Are you crazy? You just killed a transmigrating soul. I mean, that could have been Beethoven . . . Botticelli . . . Jack Benny." Later, Lucy chokes to death on Zelda's exotic cuisine. In a dusty book of magic, Zelda finds the incantation that will bring her sister back to life. Obeying this resurrection recipe, which involves waiting exactly one year after the death, Zelda sits in the graveyard surrounded by candles and reads aloud the incantation. Though her magic works, Zelda emerges as an inept character, dangerously playing with forces she cannot understand.

Control, Determination, and the "Other"

Magic is a search for power over those forces that regulate life. Whatever people in early cultures couldn't control physically, they tried to control symbolically through ritual. As human beings gained more command over their environment through science, government, and technology, magic lost influence, emerging only in those areas where people had no answers and no control. Thus, magic has always been the refuge of the powerless and of people who stumble outside the borders of mainstream culture, a message clearly reinforced in media stories. Magic is presented as something laughably unreal or a dangerous weapon that might subvert the status quo. When magic genuinely operates in the world created by a media narrative, such a magical world is rarely depicted as ideal. For example, even in Harry Potter's wizardly world, magic is often treated as illegitimate and somewhat off-limits. The witches and wizards who seek to use magic must adhere to strict laws designed to protect powerless muggles and the whole of a wizardly society against the potent will of the individual witch. Again and again, movies and television remind us that the use of magic is an illicit exercise, a practice to be kept hidden or secret. This is perhaps why the character wielding magic in moving-image media, the witch, is most often portrayed as a woman, working her spells in the isolation of her domestic domain.

Scholars have noticed a demarcation between the physical attributes of men's abstract, public world of political life and those of women's private, domestic life. The recognition that women consume a significant part of adulthood with the physical activities of giving birth, raising children, and providing home care led to a natural association of women with domestic life and men with such activities as politics and military service (Rosaldo and Lamphere 21; Nicholson 73; Saxonhouse 5). Men are the usual proprietors of politics, ritual, and religion, which are public domains (Ortner; Mattelart). Western culture came to regard the domestic life of women, confined to the body and its needs and emotions, as inferior to the public world of men, drawing on what grew to be considered men's higher capabilities: their daring minds, brute strength, and aggressive courage. Male reactions to female power in political, social, economic, and religious spheres contain an element of sincere horror as well as a conscious attempt to control and diminish that power by defining it as illegitimate and unnatural, making it seem ridiculous or atrocious (Gottner-Abendroth; Press; Dixon and Wetherell; Wessinger). Some scholars believe that misogyny, gender politics, and the unorthodoxy of female participation in religious ritual resulted in the witch craze of the sixteenth century (Klaits; Barstow). In later centuries, magic and the occult continued to be associated with feminine attributes and the oral traditions of folklore, which are sometimes given the pejorative label of superstitious "old wives' tales."

The unflattering stereotypes of women using magic to manipulate their private worlds may seem outdated, but they continue to be a significant aspect of film and television portraits up to the present. And cultural propaganda that attempts to suppress this feminine "magic" as ridiculous, inconsequential, or dangerous is a significant part of the discourse. When female characters use occult powers, it is often with petty or personal motives. They are frequently driven by vanity, trivial desire, and small-minded vengeance. Female witches use magic to enhance their own beauty and desirability or to escape aging (*The Craft*; *Death Becomes Her*; *Excalibur*; *She*); to cast love spells (*The Wide Sargasso Sea* [1993]; *Black Magic*; *I Married a Witch*; *The Serpent's Lair*; *Sexual Magic* [2001]); to get private vengeance on those who have wronged them (*Carrie*; *Medea*; *Sleepy Hollow*; *The Trance* [1998]; *Bell, Book and Candle*); or to further other private domestic goals (*Bewitched*; *The Juniper Tree*). Many times, the media witch is motivated by simple jealousy. In *Virgin Spring* (1960), for example, the character Ingeri uses witchcraft against Karin simply because she is jealous of Karin's nice clothes and devoted family.

Some films mock women's functions within alternative religions, reducing the spirituality of female characters to the dangerously absurd (*Hello Again*; *Practical Magic*) or the evil (*Little Witches*; *The Haunting of Morella*; *The Witching* [1993]), contributing to persistent stereotypes of women as chaotic, confused, manipulative, and in strong need of male discipline to keep them in control. In particular, portraits of satanic witches whose implicit goals are to serve a male demon contradict more affirmative images of independent, self-reliant women. However, this message isn't absolute. Some female witches may also be involved in the larger struggle to keep the world safe from evil (*Charmed*; *Witchblade* [2000; 2001]) or bring joy and healing to their friends and communities (*The Gift*; *Chocolat*; *Farscape*; *The Butcher's Wife*; *Drawing Down the Moon*).

Media help create a culture where many girls and women believe they are trivialized, where they feel economically, politically, and socially powerless. But media can also provide an escape for some by offering narratives in which girls and women possess powerful supernatural abilities. Though films and television programs frequently portray witches as cruel, corrupt, ugly, or evil, they do hold out the possibility that the powerless female can take control of her life, if not within the legitimate public sphere of men, at least through the occult power of magic. These portrayals draw on anachronistic characterizations of women as subjects of the private realm and of magic as a private, woman's craft, that is, as "domesticated and feminine an art as embroidery" (Oppenheim 9).

In contrast, male witches and wizards in the media more often deploy their magic for superior purposes. Even though their ultimate intentions may be evil, as are the those of the character Eric Stark in *Bless the Child* or the character Boris Balkan in *The Ninth Gate*, their ambitions reside in the public sphere of men. Rather than concern for personal beauty and domestic comfort, male witches more often have world domination as the object of their magic. Their goals may be political and strategic, such as when Dargent Peytraud in *The Serpent and the Rainbow* uses his magic for the benefit of the Haitian dictator Papa Doc Duvalier. Similarly, wizards like Faust and Merlin tend to seek the power with which to govern or advise their empires. In the 1981 film *Excalibur*, Merlin the magician (Nicol Williamson) spies Arthur's evil half sister Morgana (Helen Mirren) surrounded by the stereotypical tools of witchcraft and is horrified. Morgana uses magic for her own purposes, whereas Merlin uses his magic in the noble cause of serving Arthur and the kingdom. The wizard and his young male apprentice in *Dragonslayer* (1981) undergo a dangerous journey and use powerful magic to save young women from being sacrificed to a horrible beast. The wizard Melanthius in *Sinbad and the Eye of the Tiger* attempts to help Sinbad defeat the powerful and selfish magic of the witch Zenobia.

Even the ingenue Harry Potter differs from his female counterparts in other film and television programs. For example, in *The Worst Witch* (1986), young Mildred's magic will not extend beyond the private boundaries of her school, whereas even as an inexperienced witch, Harry Potter battles the evil Lord Voldemort, a powerful adult sorcerer, for the safety of the entire world. We know that Harry Potter is destined for greatness; but in a magical universe where the most powerful positions (if not the most powerful magic) appear to be controlled by male characters, Potter's friend, Hermione Granger (Emma Watson), has a less assured destiny, though she will work twice as hard as her male counterparts on her magical studies. For male audience members who may feel marginalized or unappreciated by their communities, media narratives about powerful wizards offer stories where men and boys can use magic to claim their rightful place as leaders. Stories about male witches who resort to magic for selfish purposes, such as the sorcerer Bruho Cerio in

Seduced by Evil, stand as a warning against the use of a feminine occult for trifling personal motives.

The idea of the witch's strong, independent will is a dominant one. The witch's creed is "Do what you will," though Wiccans will add "and it harm no one." The witch has potent desires, sometimes unfathomable to the audience, but nonetheless potent enough to propel her magic, sometimes in undesirable directions. The witch's will may be so powerful that it survives her death, as in the British film *Woman in Black* (1989). Consumed in her death by a powerful hatred, the vengeful woman, Janet Goss (Pauline Moran), curses the village of Crythin Gifford. The witch's will, her desires, her hatreds, or her yearnings are her most powerful instruments. The belief that accidents don't just happen follows from this presentation of the witch's powerful will. Some person or soul must be responsible for events in a universe alive with spirits. Be they good or evil, the coincidences of life have to have intention; they are the consequence of someone's resolve.

Perhaps the one element that unites all portraits of the witch is not magic, or even will, but *otherness*. The witch is someone strange, a curious "other" who stands outside legitimate territories to intimidate the status quo. This otherness comes in the mutinous values of the satanic witch, the exotic foreignness of the shamanic witch, the aloof peculiarities of the fairy-tale witch, and the artistic nature of the New Age witch. For the ingenue witch, that other is the adult threatening to emerge from within the child with scary, grown-up power. The other resides in the feminine qualities of the enchantress that threaten men and in the erotic desires that threaten her own well-being. Media portraits of the historical witch and the dubious witch show us people on the fringes of a community, people who in some way challenge social groups, recognized authority, and timeworn assumptions.

However categorized, the witch remains unconventional. All media witches exhibit some significant divergence from the dominant social conditions through gender, race, economic power, ideology, social status, or maturity. If not a woman, the witch is another character relegated to the fringes of a society: foreigner, child, outcast, or member of a hidden community. Even the male wizards who are the advisers to kings in a public and political sphere will often be regarded by other characters in media stories as illegitimate and suspect. More than discourse about the occult and the paranormal, media narratives about witches endure as meditations on "otherness" and on fear of the "illegitimate" power and enormous resolve this other might possess.

Filmography: A Century of Witches in Film and Television

This filmography is intended as a reference for the media directly cited in chapter 4. This list also includes films and television programs not directly cited but considered significant in helping to inform the categories and discussion in the chapter.

Addams Family, The. TV series. Dir. Stanley Z. Cherry and Arthur Hiller. ABC, 1964–66.

Addams Family, The. Dir. Barry Sonnenfeld. Paramount Pictures, 1991.

Ancient Modern Witch: The Halloween Lecture. Documentary. Dir. Marion Weinstein. Earth Magic Productions, 1998.

Ancient Mysteries with Leonard Nimoy. TV documentary series. Prod. Larayne Decoeur. "Witchcraft in America." Arts and Entertainment and Moonbeam Publications, 1996.

Angel Heart. Dir. Alan Parker. TriStar Pictures, 1987.

Apprentice to Murder. Dir. Ralph L. Thomas. New World Pictures, 1988.

Baba Yaga. Dir. Corrado Farina. Video Search of Miami, 1973.

Bay Coven (aka *Eye of the Demon*). Dir. Carl Schenkel. Phoenix Entertainment Group, 1987.

Because of the Cats. Dir. Fons Rademakers. Joseph Brenner Associates and Video Search of Miami, 1973.

Bedazzled. Dir. Harold Ramis. 20th Century Fox, 2000.

Bedknobs and Broomsticks. Dir. Robert Stevenson. Walt Disney Productions, 1971.

Bell, Book and Candle. Dir. Richard Quine. Columbia Pictures and RCA, 1958.

Bewitched. TV series. Dir. William Asher and Bruce Bilson. ABC, 1964–72.

Black Cats and Broomsticks. Documentary. b&w. Dir. Larry O'Reilly. RKO Radio Pictures, 1955.

Black Magic. Dir. Daniel Tapliz. MCA, 1992.

Black Magic Woman. Dir. Deryn Warren. Vidmark Entertainment, 1991.

Black Noon. TV movie. Dir. Bernard L. Kowalski. CBS, 1971.

Black Rainbow. Dir. Mike Hodges. Miramax Films, 1990.

Black Robe (*Robe Noire*). Dir. Bruce Beresford. Samuel Goldwyn and Vidmark, 1991.

Black Witch, The. b&w, silent. Pathé Frères, 1907.

Blair Witch Project, The. Dir. Daniel Myrick and Eduardo Sánchez. Artisan Entertainment, 1999.

Bless the Child. Dir. Chuck Russell. Paramount Pictures, 2000.

Blood on Satan's Claw. Dir. Piers Haggard. Cannon Releasing, 1971.

Blues Brothers 2000. Dir. John Landis. Universal Pictures, 1998.

Bob Larson Live. Documentary. Dir. Bob Larson. "Witches." Video Learning Library, 1990.

Brotherhood of Satan. Dir. Bernard McEveety. Columbia Pictures, 1971.

Buffy the Vampire Slayer. TV series. Dir. Reza Badiyi and Scott Brazil. Warner Brothers Television, 1997–2003.

Burned at the Stake. Dir. Bert I. Gordon. Alan Landsburg, 1981.

Burning Court, The. Dir. Julien Duvivier. Sinister Cinema, 1962.

Burning Times, The. Documentary. Dir. Donna Reed. National Film Board of Canada, 1993.

Burn, Witch, Burn (aka *Night of the Eagle*). b&w. Dir. Sidney Hayers. American International Pictures, 1962.

Butcher's Wife, The. Dir. Terry Hughes. Paramount Pictures, 1991.

Cannon Movie Tales: Hansel and Gretel. TV movie. Dir. Len Talan. Warner Brothers Home Video, 1987.

Carrie. Dir. Brian De Palma. United Artists, 1976.

Casper Meets Wendy. Dir. Sean McNamara. 20th Century Fox, 1998.

Cast a Deadly Spell. TV movie. Dir. Martin Campbell. HBO, 1991.

Celts: Rich Traditions and Ancient Myths, The. TV documentary series. Dir. David Richardson. BBC and CBS, 1986.

Charmed. TV series. Dir. Gilbert Adler and John Behring. Warner Brothers Television, 1998–.

Chocolat. Dir. Lasse Hallström. Miramax Films, 2000.

Circe, the Enchantress. b&w, silent. Dir. Robert Z. Leonard. MGM Distributing, 1924.

Circe the Sorceress. Dir. Len Lurcuck. Films for the Humanities, 1989.

Conan the Barbarian. Dir John Milius. Universal Pictures, 1982.

Connecticut Yankee, A. b&w. Dir. David Butler. Fox Film, 1931.

Connecticut Yankee in King Arthur's Court, A. b&w, silent. Dir. Emmett J. Flynn. Fox Film, 1921.

Connecticut Yankee in King Arthur's Court, A. Dir. Tay Garnett. Paramount Pictures, 1949.

Connecticut Yankee in King Arthur's Court, A. TV movie. Dir. Mel Damski. Consolidated Productions, 1989.

Craft, The. Dir. Andrew Fleming. Columbia Pictures, 1996.

Crucible, The. TV movie. Dir. Alex Segal. CBS, 1967.

Crucible, The. TV movie. Dir. Don Taylor. BBC, 1980.

Crucible, The. Dir. Nicholas Hytner. 20th Century Fox, 1996.

Cry of the Banshee. Dir. Gordon Hessler. HBO and MGM, 1970.

Curse of the Demon (aka *Night of the Demon*). b&w. Dir. Jacques Tourneur. Columbia Pictures, 1957.

Damnation de Faust, La (*The Damnation of Faust*). b&w, silent. Dir. Georges Méliès. Méliès, 1898.

Dance with the Devil (aka *Perdita Durango*). Dir. Álex de la Iglesia. Trimark Pictures and Unapix Entertainment, 1997.

Dark Shadows. TV series. Exec. prod. Dan Curtis. ABC, 1966–71.

Dark Shadows. TV series. Exec. prod. Dan Curtis. NBC, 1991.

Dark Wind, The. Dir. Errol Morris. New Line Home Video, 1991.

Death Becomes Her. Dir. Robert Zemeckis. Universal Pictures, 1992.

Devil Rides Out, The (aka *The Devil's Bride*). Dir. Terence Fisher. 20th Century Fox, 1968.

Devil's Advocate, The. Dir. Taylor Hackford. Warner Brothers, 1997.

Devil's Rain, The. Dir. Robert Fuest. BijouFlix Releasing and Bryanston Distributing, 1975.

Devonsville Terror, The. Dir. Ulli Lommel. Embassy Home Entertainment, 1983.

Discovering Witchcraft: A Journey Through the Elements. Dir. Janet Farrar, Stewart Farrar, and Gavin Bone. Sothis Films, 1998.

Doctor Faustus. Dir. Richard Burton and Nevill Coghill. Columbia Pictures and RCA, 1967.

Double, Double, Toil and Trouble. TV movie. Dir. Stuart Margolin. Pacific Motion Pictures, 1993.

Dragonslayer. Dir. Matthew Robbins. Paramount Pictures, 1981.

Drawing Down the Moon. Dir. Steven Patterson. Packetrat Communications and Chaos Entertainment, 1997.

Dream of Passion, A. Dir. Jules Dassin. AVCO Embassy Pictures, 1978.

Excalibur. Dir. John Boorman. Warner Brothers, 1981.

Faerie Tale Theatre. TV series. Prod. Shelley Duvall. "Rapunzel" 5 Feb. 1983. Dir. Gilbert Cates. CBS and Fox, 1982–87.

Fait Accompli (aka *Voodoo Dawn*). Dir. Andrzej Sekula. Cutting Edge Entertainment, 1998.

Farscape. TV series. Exec. prod. Rockne S. O'Bannon. Jim Henson Television and Sci-Fi Channel, 1999–2004.

Faust. b&w, silent. Dir. Edwin S. Porter. Edison Manufacturing, 1909.

Faust. b&w, silent. Dir. Bertram Phillips. Butcher Distributing, 1923.

Faust. b&w, silent. Dir. F. W. Murnau. MGM, 1926.

Faust and Mephistopheles. b&w, silent. Dir. George Albert Smith. George Albert Smith Films, 1898.

Faust and the Devil (aka *Strange Life of Dr. Faust*). Dir. Carmine Gallone. Columbia Pictures, 1950.

Faust: Love of the Damned. Dir. Brian Yuzna. Lion's Gate, 2000.

First Family of Satanism. Documentary. Dir. Bob Larson. Video Learning Library, 1990.

French Quarter. Dir. Dennis Kane. Crown International Pictures, 1977.

From Hell It Came. Dir. Dan Milner. Allied Artists Pictures, 1957.

Full Circle. Documentary. Dir. Donna Reed. National Film Board of Canada, 1993.

Gift, The. Dir. Sam Raimi. Paramount Classics, 2000.

Goddess Remembered, The. Documentary. Dir. Donna Reed. National Film Board of Canada, 1990.

Golden Voyage of Sinbad, The. Dir. Gordon Hessler. Columbia Pictures, 1974.

Goosebumps. TV anthology series. Created by R. L. Stine. "An Old Story" 4 Oct. 1997. Dir. Ron Oliver. Nickelodeon Television, 1995.

Hansel and Gretel. b&w, silent. Dir. J. Searle Dawley. Edison Manufacturing, 1909.

Hansel and Gretel. b&w, silent. Dir. Alfred J. Goulding. Universal Pictures, 1923.

Hansel and Gretel. Animation short. b&w. Dir. Frank Moser. Terrytoons and Educational Film Exchanges, 1933.

Hansel and Gretel. Dir. John Paul. RKO Radio Pictures, 1953.

Hansel and Gretel (*Hänsel und Gretel*). Dir. Walter Janssen. Childhood Productions, 1965.

Hansel and Gretel (aka *Faerie Tale Theatre*). TV movie. Dir. Tim Burton and James Frawley. Faerie Tale Theatre, 1982.

Harry Potter and the Chamber of Secrets. Dir. Chris Columbus. Warner Brothers, 2002.

Harry Potter and the Prisoner of Azkaban. Dir. Alfonso Cuarón. Warner Brothers, 2004.

Harry Potter and the Sorcerer's Stone. Dir. Chris Columbus. Warner Brothers, 2001.

Haunting of Morella, The. Dir. Jim Wynorski. Concorde–New Horizons, 1990.

Häxan (aka *Witchcraft Through the Ages*). Documentary. b&w, silent. Dir. Benjamin Christensen. Aljosha Production, 1922.

Hello Again. Dir. Frank Perry. Buena Vista and Touchstone Pictures, 1987.

Hideaway. Dir. Brett Leonard. Columbia Pictures, 1995.

Hocus Pocus. Dir. Kenny Ortega. Walt Disney, 1993.

How to Stuff a Wild Bikini. Dir. William Asher. American International Pictures, 1965.

I Married a Witch. b&w. Dir. René Clair. United Artists, 1942.

Indiana Jones and the Temple of Doom. Dir. Steven Spielberg. Paramount Pictures, 1984.

In the Days of Witchcraft. b&w, silent. Edison Manufacturing, 1909.

In the Name of Satan. Documentary. Dir. Bob Larson. Video Learning Library, 1990.

Intimate Portrait: Witches. TV documentary. Dir. Lee Grant. Lifetime, 1998.

Joan of Arc. Dir. Victor Fleming. RKO Radio Pictures, 1948.

Joan of Arc. TV movie. Dir. Christian Duguay. CBS, 1999.

Joan the Maid: The Battles. Dir. Jacques Rivette. Seven Cinema, 1994.

Joan the Woman. b&w, silent. Dir. Cecil B. DeMille. Paramount Pictures, 1916.

Jungle Goddess. Dir. Lewis D. Collins. Screen Guild Productions, 1948.

Juniper Tree, The. Dir. Nietzcha Keene. Rhino Home Video, 1987.

King Arthur. Dir. Antoine Fuqua. Buena Vista Pictures, 2004.

Kull the Conqueror. Dir. John Nicolella. MCA and Universal, 1997.

Lady of the Lake. Dir. Maurice Devereaux. Bedford Entertainment, 1998.

Lady's Not for Burning, The. TV movie. Dir. Julian Amyes. Yorkshire Television, 1987.

Last Enchantment, The. Dir. Dan Work. Havas Productions, 1995.

Last Wave, The. Dir. Peter Weir. World Northal, 1977.

Lion, the Witch, and the Wardrobe, The. Animated TV movie. Dir. Bill Melendez. Children's Television Workshop/PBS, 1979.

Lion, the Witch, and the Wardrobe, The. TV series. Dir. Marilyn Fox. BBC, 1988.

Little Witches. Dir. Jane Simpson. A-Pix Entertainment and Two Moon Releasing, 1996.

Lord of the Rings: The Fellowship of the Ring. Dir. Peter Jackson. Warner Brothers, 2001.

Lost Souls. Dir. Janusz Kaminski. New Line Cinema, 2000.

Love at Stake. Dir. John Moffitt. Hemdale Film, 1987.

Lucinda's Spell. Dir. Jon Jacobs. Golden Shadow Pictures, 1998.

Macbeth. b&w, silent. Dir. John Emerson. Triangle Film, 1916.

Macbeth. b&w. Dir. Orson Welles. Republic Pictures, 1948.

Macbeth. TV movie. Dir. Maurice Evans. Hallmark Productions, 1954.

Macbeth. TV movie. Dir. George Schaefer. Prominent Films, 1960.

Macbeth. Dir. Roman Polanski. Columbia Pictures, 1971.

Maid of Salem. b&w. Dir. Frank Lloyd. Paramount Pictures, 1937.

Mark of the Witch. Dir. Tom Moore. Lone Star Productions and AIP Home Video, 1970.

Mary Poppins. Musical with animation. Dir. Robert Stevenson. Walt Disney and Buena Vista, 1964.

Matilda. (aka *Roald Dahl's Matilda*). Dir. Danny DeVito. Columbia TriStar and Sony Pictures, 1996.

Medea. Dir. Pier Paolo Pasolini. Euro International Film and New Line Cinema, 1969.

Merlin. TV movie. Dir. Steve Barron. Hallmark Entertainment/NBC, 1998.

Messenger: The Story of Joan of Arc, The. Dir. Luc Besson. Columbia Pictures and Sony Pictures Entertainment, 1999.

Midnight in the Garden of Good and Evil. Dir. Clint Eastwood. Warner Brothers, 1997.

Mists of Avalon, The. TV miniseries. Dir. Ulrich Edel. Warner Brothers and TNT, 2001.

Necromancy (aka *The Witching*). Dir. Bert I. Gordon. Compass/Zenith International and Cinerama, 1972.

Night Gallery (aka *Rod Serling's Night Gallery*). TV series. Dir. Edward M. Abroms and John Astin. Universal TV, 1970.

Night of Dark Shadows. TV movie. Dir. Dan Curtis. ABC and MGM, 1971.

Night of the Demon. Dir. James C. Watson. Lettuce Video and VCI Home Video, 1980.

Night of the Witches. Dir. Keith Larsen. Medford Film, 1970.

Ninth Gate, The. Dir. Roman Polanski. Artisan Entertainment, 1999.

Odyssey, The. TV movie. Dir. Andrei Konchalousky. Hallmark, 1997.

Omen, The. Dir. Richard Donner. 20th Century Fox, 1976.

Omen IV: The Awakening. TV movie. Dir. Jorge Montesi and Dominique Othenin-Girard. CBS and Fox, 1991.

Others, The. TV series. Dir. Sanford Bookstaver and Bill Condon. NBC, 2000.

Paradise Lost: The Child Murders at Robin Hood Hills. TV documentary. Dir. Joe Berlinger and Bruce Sinofsky. HBO, 1996.

Paradise Lost 2: Revelations. TV documentary. Dir. Joe Berlinger and Bruce Sinofsky. HBO, 2000.

Passion of Joan of Arc (La Passion de Jeanne d'Arc). b&w, silent. Dir. Carl Theodor Dreyer. M. J. Gourland, 1928.

Practical Magic. Dir. Griffin Dunne. Warner Brothers, 1998.

Puritan Passions. b&w, silent. Dir. Frank Tuttle. W. W. Hodkinson, 1923.

Quartier Mozart. Dir. Jean-Pierre Bekolo. Kino Video, 1992.

Quest for Camelot. Animated feature. Dir. Frederik Du Chau. Warner Brothers, 1998.

Rage: Carrie 2, The. Dir. Robert Mandel. United Artists, 1999.

Rapunzel. Animated feature. Dir. Ray Harryhausen. Bailey Films, 1951.

Real Magic: The Science of Wizardry. TV documentary. Dir. Luke Campbell. Discovery, 15 Nov. 2001.

Remember the Witches. Documentary. Dir. Laurie Meeker. National Film Board of Canada, 1985.

Resurrection. Dir. Daniel Petrie. Universal Pictures, 1980.

Rosemary's Baby. Dir. Roman Polanski. Paramount Pictures, 1968.

Sabrina, Down Under. TV movie. Dir. Kenneth R. Koch. ABC, 1999.

Sabrina Goes to Rome. TV movie. Dir. Tibor Takács. ABC, 1998.

Sabrina, the Animated Series. Animated TV series. Dir. Scott Heming and David Teague. ABC, 1999–2001.

Sabrina, the Teenage Witch. Animated TV series. Prod. Dan DeCarlo and John L. Goldwater. 20th Century Fox Television, 1971.

Sabrina, the Teenage Witch. TV series. Dir. Peter Baldwin and Robby Benson. Hallmark Home Entertainment and Paramount Television, 1996–2003.

Saint, Devil and Woman. b&w, silent. Dir. Frederick Sullivan. Thanhouser, 1916.

Saint Joan. b&w. Dir. Otto Preminger. United Artists, 1957.

Satanis. Documentary. Dir. Ray Laurent and Zoltan G. Spencer. Something Weird Video, 1968.

Satan's Cheerleaders. Dir. Greydon Clark. Liberty Home Video, 1977.

Satan's Princess (aka Malediction). Dir. Bert I. Gordon. Paramount Home Video, 1990.

Satan's School for Girls. TV movie. Dir. David Lowell Rich. ABC, 1973.

Satan's School for Girls. TV movie. Dir. Christopher Leitch. ABC, 2000.

Satan Unveiled: A Spiritual Warfare. Documentary. Dir. Bob Larson. Video Learning Library, 1996.

Scariest Places on Earth, The. TV documentary series. "Rituals of Evil" 22 June 2001. Dir. Patrick Taulère. Fox Family Channel, 2001.

Scarlet Letter, The. Dir. Roland Joffé. Buena Vista Pictures, 1995.

Season of the Witch. Dir. George A. Romero. Jack H. Harris Enterprises and Vista Video, 1972.

Secrets of the Dead. TV documentary series. "Witches Curse" 12 Nov. 2001. Dir. Mark Lewis. PBS, 2001.

Secrets of the Unknown (aka *Secrets and Mysteries*). TV documentary series. Prod. Donne E. Lusitana. "Witches." 23 Oct. 1987. Dir. Graeme Whifler, Glenn Kirschbaum, and Erik Nelson. ABC, 1986–88.

Secret World of Alex Mack, The. TV series. Exec. prod. Tommy Lynch. Nickelodeon Network, 1994–98.

Seduced by Evil. TV movie. Dir. Tony Wharmby. Malofilm Group, 1994.

Serpent and the Rainbow, The. Dir. Wes Craven. MCA and Universal Pictures, 1988.

Serpent's Lair, The. Dir. Jeffrey Reiner. New City Releasing and Warner Vision Entertainment, 1995.

Seven Footprints to Satan. b&w. Dir. Benjamin Christensen. Warner Brothers, 1929.

Seventh Seal, The (*Sjunde Inseglet*). b&w. Dir. Ingmar Bergman. Embassy Home Entertainment and Janus Films, 1957.

Sex Rituals of the Occult. Documentary. Dir. Robert Caramico. Something Weird Video, 1970.

Sexual Magic. Dir. Edward Holzman. Indigo Entertainment, 2001.

Shadowhunter. TV movie. Dir. J. S. Cardone. Republic Pictures, 1993.

She. b&w. Dir. Lansing C. Holden and Irving Pichel. RKO Radio Pictures, 1934.

She. Dir. Robert Day. MGM and Hammer Films, 1965.

Simply Irresistible. Dir. Mark Tarlov. 20th Century Fox, 1999.

Sinbad and the Eye of the Tiger. Dir. Sam Wanamaker. Columbia Pictures, 1977.

Sleeping Beauty. b&w, silent. Dir. Lucien Nonguet and Ferdinand Zecca. Pathé, 1903.

Sleeping Beauty. Animated feature. Dir. Clyde Geronimi. Buena Vista Pictures, 1959.

Sleepy Hollow. Dir. Tim Burton. Paramount Pictures, 1999.

Snow White. b&w, silent. Dir. J. Searle Dawley. Paramount Pictures, 1916.

Snow White. Dir. Michael Berz. Warner Brothers Home Video, 1987.

Snow White and the Seven Dwarfs. Animated feature. Dir. David Hand. Walt Disney and RKO Radio Pictures, 1937.

Snow White: The Fairest of Them All. TV movie. Dir. Caroline Thompson. ABC, 2001.

Something Wicked This Way Comes. Dir. Jack Clayton. Buena Vista Pictures, 1983.

Sorcerer's Apprentice, The. Dir. David Lister. Peakviewing Transatlantic, 2000.

Sorcerers' Village. Documentary. Dir. Hassoldt Davis. Film Representations, 1958.

Sorceress (aka *Le Moine et la Sorcière*). Dir. Suzanne Schiffman. European Classics Video, 1987.

Sorceress (aka *Temptress*). Dir. Jim Wynorski. Triboro Entertainment Group, 1994.

Sorceress of the Strand. b&w, silent. Dir. L. T. Meade and Robert Eustace. Eclair, 1910.

Sorceress II: The Temptress. Dir. Steve Latshaw. New Horizons Home Video, 1996.

Sorcier, Le (aka *The Witch's Revenge*). b&w, silent. Dir. Georges Méliès. Méliès, 1903.

Sorcières de Salem, Les (*The Crucible*). b&w. Dir. Raymond Rouleau. Kingsley-International Pictures, 1957.

Sorrows of Satan, The. b&w, silent. Dir. D. W. Griffith. Paramount Pictures, 1926.

Speak of the Devil. Documentary. Dir. Nick Bougas. Wavelength Video, 1995.

Spell, The. TV movie. Dir. Lee Philips. NBC, 1977.

Student von Prag, Der (*Student of Prague*). b&w, silent. Dir. Stellan Rye and Paul Wegener. Deutsche Bioscop and LS Video, 1913.

Supergirl. Dir. Jeannot Szwarc. TriStar Pictures, 1984.

Superstition (aka *The Witch*). Dir. James W. Roberson. Almi Pictures, 1982.

Suspiria. Dir. Dario Argento. International Classics and Joseph Brenner Assoc., 1977.

Swept from the Sea. Dir. Beeban Kidron. TriStar Pictures, 1997.

Sword in the Stone, The. Animated feature. Dir. Wolfgang Reitherman. Walt Disney and Buena Vista Distribution, 1963.

Tabitha. TV series. Dir. William Asher and Bruce Bilson. ABC, 1977–78.

Teen Witch. Dir. Dorian Walker. Trans World Entertainment, 1989.

Tempest, The. TV movie. Dir. Jack Bender. NBC, 1998.

Three Sovereigns for Sarah. TV movie. Dir. Philip Leacock. Prism Entertainment, 1985.

Trance, The (aka *The Eternal*). Dir. Michael Almereyda. Trimark Pictures, 1998.

Trial of Joan of Arc, The (*Procès de Jeanne d'Arc*). Dir. Robert Bresson. Pathé Contemporary Films, 1965.

Tucker's Witch. TV series. Dir. Corey Allen and Rod Daniel. CBS, 1982.

Twins of Evil. Dir. John Hough. Universal Pictures, 1972.

Unnatural History. TV series. The Learning Channel, 2001.

Vali (aka *Vali—The Witch of Positano*). Documentary. b&w. Dir. Sheldon Rochlin. New Line Cinema, 1967.

Village Witch. b&w, silent. Pathé Frères, 1906.

Virgin Spring (*Jungfrukällan*). b&w. Dir. Ingmar Bergman. Janus Films, 1960.

Virgin Witch. Dir. Ray Austin. Joseph Brenner Associates, 1972.

Voodoo Woman. b&w. Dir. Edward L. Cahn. RCA and Columbia Pictures Home Video, 1957.

Warrior and the Sorceress, The. Dir. John Broderick. New Horizons, 1984.

Weird Woman (aka *Conjure Wife*). b&w. Dir. Reginald Le Borg. Universal Pictures, 1944.

Wicker Man, The. Dir. Robin Hardy. Warner Brothers, 1973.

Wide Sargasso Sea. Dir. John Duigan. New Line Cinema, 1993.

Willow. Dir. Ron Howard. MGM and Lucasfilm, 1988.

Witch (*La Fée Carabosse ou le Poignard Fatal*). b&w, silent. Dir. Georges Méliès. Star Film, 1906.

Witch, The. b&w, silent. Dir. Van Dyke Brooke. Vitagraph Co. of America, 1908.

Witch, The. b&w, silent. Dir. Frank Powell and Nance O'Neil. Fox Film, 1916.

Witch, The. Dir. Damiano Damiani. Sinister Cinema, 1966.

Witch Academy. Dir. Fred Olen Ray. American Independent Productions and USA Cable Network, 1993.

Witchblade. TV movie. Dir. Ralph Hemecker. Warner Brothers Television and TNT, 2000.

Witchblade. TV series. Exec. prod. Ralph Hemecker. TNT, 2001–02.

Witch City. TV documentary. Dir. Joe Culterec. WGBH-TV and PBS, 1999.

Witchcraft. b&w, silent. Dir. Frank Reicher. Paramount, Famous Players, and Lasky, 1916.

Witchcraft. Dir. Don Sharp. 20th Century Fox, 1964.

Witchcraft (aka *White Angel . . . Black Angel*). Dir. Luigi Scattini. Trans American Films and Video Search of Miami, 1970.

Witchcraft. Dir. Fabrizio Laurenti and Rob Spera. Vidmark Entertainment, 1988.

Witchcraft for Yesterday and Today. Documentary. Dir. Raymond Buckland. Llewellyn Publications, 1999.

Witchery. Dir. Fabrizio Laurenti and Rob Spera. Vidmark Entertainment, 1988.

Witches, The. Dir. Cyril Frankel. Hammer Film and 20th Century Fox, 1966.

Witches, The. Dir. Nicolas Roeg. Lorimar Film Entertainment and Warner Brothers, 1990.

Witches' Brew. Dir. Richard Shorr. United Artists, 1980.

Witches of Eastwick, The. Dir. George Miller. Warner Brothers, 1987.

Witches of Salem: The Horror and the Hope. Docudrama. Dir. Dennis Azzarella. Learning Corp. of America and New World Entertainment, 1972.

Witchfinder General (aka *The Conqueror Worm*). Dir. Michael Reeves. American International Pictures, HBO, Orion Home Video, and Sinister Cinema, 1968.

Witch Girl, The. b&w, silent. Dir. Walter Edwin. Universal Film Manufacturing, 1914.

Witch Hunt. TV movie. Dir. Paul Schrader. HBO, 1994.

Witch Hunt. TV movie. Dir. Scott Hartford-Davis. Golden Square Pictures, 1999.

Witching, The. Dir. Eric Black and Matthew Jason Walsh. Tempe Video, 1993.

Witching Hour, The. b&w, silent. Dir. George Irving. Frohman Amusement, 1916.

Witching Hour, The. b&w, silent. Dir. William Desmond Taylor. Paramount Pictures, 1921.

Witching Hour, The. b&w. Dir. Henry Hathaway. Paramount Pictures, 1934.

Witching Hour, The. TV documentary. Dir. Reba Merrill. Columbia Pictures Television, 1996.

Witching of Ben Wagner, The. Dir. Paul Annett. Leucadia Film, 1987.

Witch Kiss, The. b&w, silent. Pathé Frères, 1907.

Witch of Salem, The. b&w, silent. Dir. Raymond B. West. Domino Pictures, 1913.

Witch's Curse, The (aka *Maciste all'Inferno*). Dir. Riccardo Freda. Medallion Pictures and Sinister Cinema, 1963.

Witch's Daughter, The. TV movie. Dir. Alan Macmillan. Hallmark Entertainment, 1996.

Witch's Night Out. Animated feature. Dir. John Leach. Family Home Entertainment, 1978.

Witchtrap. Dir. Kevin Tenney. Highlight Video, 1989.

Wizard of Oz, The. b&w, silent. Dir. Otis Turner. Selig Polyscope, 1910.

Wizard of Oz, The. Dir. Victor Fleming. MGM, 1939.

Woman in Black, The. TV movie. Dir. Herbert Wise. Video Collectibles and BFS Video, 1989.

World's Creepiest Destinations, The. TV documentary. The Travel Channel, 25 Sept. 2000.

Worst Witch, The. TV movie. Dir. Robert Young. Central Independent Television and BBC, 1986.

Worst Witch, The. TV series. Dir. Andrew Morgan and Stefan Pleszczynski. HBO, 1998.

You Are There. TV series. Exec. prod. Walter Cronkite. "Salem Witch Trials" 28 Oct. 1955. Dir. Bernard Girard and Sidney Lumet. CBS, 1953–57.

The Divine Animal
Evolution and Atavism in Popular Media

While Darwinian Man, though well-behaved,
At best is only a monkey shaved.
— Sir William Schwenck Gilbert, *Princess Ida*, 1884

On May 21 and 22, 2001, Americans learned a curious story about a mysterious "monkey man" that created hysteria in neighborhoods surrounding New Delhi, India. In news reports, witnesses described the monkey man as short and covered in hair. He had glowing red eyes and could leap from the tops of buildings, vanishing abruptly in the sweltering night air. One panicked resident leaped to his death from a rooftop to escape an attack, and other people were reported crushed in stampedes as a result of what one psychologist called a "mass delusion." Elected officials held Hindu ceremonies to ward off the evil spirit, hired extra police to track down the creature, and posted rewards for his capture. Though hoax and hysteria were offered as explanations for the phenomenon, the story of the monkey man was a reminder of the fascination and fear people still have with the idea of a creature that is neither human nor beast but some uncanny combination of both.[1]

Legends of the Beast

Myths from many cultures deal with the boundary between animals and humans. Perhaps this is a recognition that the animal nature in human beings is an attribute to be both honored and feared. Myths of metamorphosis, the transformation from a human into an animal, or atavistic regression from human to an earlier animal ancestor, are popular among numerous cultures, suggesting a shared desire, fear, or perhaps mental illness. Coyotes, foxes, jackals, dogs, and wolves were the popular shapeshifting creatures from Native American, Chinese, Egyptian, and European mythologies. In India, the favored shapeshifters were tigers and monkeys; in parts of Africa, they were often leopards or crocodiles. The creature of metamorphosis in Russia was most often the bear. Several cultures once performed rituals designed to remove both the physical and spiritual boundaries between human and animal, encouraging the animal to materialize within a person. The ability of an ancient shaman to assume the form or disposition of a wild creature not only gave the shaman possession of that animal's physical traits—abilities such as superior strength, keener senses, and hunting prowess—but it was also meant to open a door to the animal's special wisdom and spiritual insight. In some cultures, the blend of animal and human wasn't considered sub-human, but superhuman: a god.

The shape-shifting ability of the ancient shaman, considered a blessing for the tribe and its survival, became the curse of the medieval witch in Europe, who was believed to have made a pact with the Devil in return for the power to become an animal, often a wolf. Fear of the werewolf increased in Europe during the witchcraft persecutions of the sixteenth and seventeenth centuries, when the popular belief was that witches assumed the shape of the monstrous beast to commit heinous acts of cannibalism, incest, kidnapping, and murder (Summers). During the Inquisition, people were even tried, tortured, and executed as werewolves (Singer and Singer 122–29). One of the more famous cases was that of Peter Stubbe, who confessed to being a werewolf under interrogation.[2] Stubbe claimed that the Devil gave him a magical belt of wolf skin, which allowed him to assume the form of a powerful wolf. In this form, Stubbe allegedly committed heinous acts of murder, incest, rape, cannibalism, and intercourse with a demon and finally killed his own son to eat the boy's brain (Sidky 235–34; Otten 69–76; Wilson 73; Singer and Singer 125).

By the nineteenth century, people began to turn away from magic and look to psychology, medicine, or Darwin's theory of evolution to explain the brute within the human. Some psychologists came to believe that atavism was a condition in which the traits of ancient ancestors reappeared in a contemporary individual, not summoned through ritual magic but emerging as the uninvited onslaught of bad genetics. According to this theory, after having been dormant for thousands of generations, inferior ancestral traits—which could be physical, psychological, or both—would reappear. This thinking suggested that in early human societies, certain physical characteristics and tendencies toward violence may have offered survival advantages for people, making them better hunters and warriors. However, the traits that were useful for primitive survival created criminals in more modern societies. Moreover, an animal tends to live "in the moment," perhaps hedonistically, from a Victorian perspective. The tendencies toward laziness, excessive drinking, and licentious behavior, as well as cruelty, were considered the legacies of a primitive existence that most modern men and women had transcended but that resurfaced in criminal populations. Italian physician Cesare Lombroso originated this school of thought in 1876 when he concluded that criminals of the Italian slums were feral genetic throwbacks to a vicious past. Lombroso came to this conclusion by comparing the skulls of convicted criminals to the skulls of apes, which led him to believe that both moral aberrations and physical deformities were the result of genetic degeneration. The troglodyte had returned.[3] Atavistic legacies included physical characteristics such as a brutish appearance, apelike skull, excessive hairiness, and rough stature. Lombroso linked physical and moral deformities, claiming that both could indicate a biological predisposition to crime (Lombroso-Ferrero). Interestingly, the attributes of atavism Lombroso found in nineteenth-century Italian criminals were similar to the characteristics earlier generations ascribed to gods. For example, the Greek gods Dionysus and Pan were both described as having extravagant appetites, predilections for violence, and licentiousness. They were also depicted as creatures with a mixture of human and animal features. For Lombroso, of course, such qualities would not be evidence of the divine but of an inferior atavistic monster.

Medicine found additional explanations for some of the animal characteristics that emerged in modern people. One explanation was lycanthropy, a mental illness with peculiar symptoms. Patients suffering with this disorder believe they are wolves or some other wild beast and subsequently adopt the traits and disposition of that animal, though without any actual physical transformation. An affected person may bark, effect a crouched position, walk on all fours, eat raw meat, or assume other animal behaviors. Other medical explanations for the numerous werewolf legends or similar folklore include ergot poisoning, the ingestion of a substance that causes hallucinations; rabies, a disease transmitted through the bite of a rabid animal that produces bizarre behavior; hypertrichosis, a genetic condition that promotes excessive hair growth; and porphyria, a medical disorder that can affect the nervous system, the skin, or both. A Jungian interpretation suggests that the difficulties of survival during the Ice Age forced people to become meat-eaters, to hunt in groups, and to use animal skins as protection from colder climates, situations that influenced the collective human psyche. The result of these gradual changes from warm-climate vegetarian to cold-climate meat-eater survives today in the collective unconscious and may be expressed as sadism and lycanthropy (Eisler).

Examining the ideas about atavism presented through film and television stories confirms that the media have definite statements to make about the animal in the human. Popular media tend to reflect one of two contradictory philosophies: the beast within us is noble, maybe divine; or the beast within us is a feral horror to be suppressed. The second image tends to be more frequently displayed. Even when film and television characters purposefully call out to the noble, unspoiled animal soul of the ancestor, what emerges is often not the Apollonian potential that has been crushed and subverted by modern bureaucracy and corrupt civilization but an evil, Dionysian primitive with few, if any, redeeming features. The optimistic romanticism of the "noble savage" favored by philosophers such as Locke and Rousseau appears to have received less emphasis in popular culture than the more pessimistic notion of the vicious savage lurking within the human psyche. This beast, media stories tell us, is easily released through drugs, the bite of werewolves, faulty genetics, or paranormal curses, to haunt civil society with ancient depravity.

The Lost Animal Soul

Feminist and New Age movements have attempted to resurrect appreciation for the beast within humanity, but sympathy for the "animal soul" in popular culture is not widespread. Perhaps human concern with the "beast" comes with admiration and envy as well as fear. We respect the physical capabilities animals have that humans do not: their ability to fly or to breathe under water, their greater strength, or their keener senses. Human beings must rely on superior minds and technology to compensate for, and achieve mastery over, the innate abilities of animals.

Some media narratives express the suspicion that as human beings developed mind, language, technology, and civilization, we dulled some senses and lost others completely. The suggestion is that these missing senses, which might include such wondrous abilities as astral projection, psychokinesis, and telepathy, were the very senses that connected our animal natures more intimately to a spirit world. For example, there are those who believe that telepathy is an atavistic instinct from an era when human beings had no language. Early humans and other animals are believed to have used telepathy as a principal means of communication within and among the various species. The weekly television series *Pet Psychic* (2002–) with Sonja Fitzpatrick suggests that the atavistic trait of telepathy might reappear in some contemporary individuals. In the series,

Fitzpatrick claims to have this ability to receive "telepathic communication" from animals in the form of mental images. She demonstrates her ability to telepathically communicate with all kinds of animals and then reports these communications to the owners of the pets and the television audience. Her telepathy isn't limited to living animals but also extends to those who have died. She will offer comforting greetings to grieving pet owners from their deceased animals, sometimes suggesting that the spirit of the dead animal will return to the owner in the body of another pet. Other programs have also suggested that animals have psychic abilities and sensitivities most humans lack. For example, the television documentary *Animal Telepathy* (2002) claims that dogs have the ability to smell out melanomas in humans and have the capacity to predict natural disasters, such as earthquakes.

A made-for-television movie, *Evolution's Child* (1999), makes the similar suggestion that primitive individuals had special faculties that are lost to modern people. These include abilities to heal and to make a deep connection to the earth, which allowed ancient people to commune with nature and understand the intentions and emotions of animals. In the plot of *Evolution's Child*, a fertility doctor removes sperm from the frozen corpse of a three-thousand-year-old man. The doctor intends to study the ancient specimen, but by accident a lab assistant uses this sperm for the in vitro fertilization of one of the doctor's patients. The child, Adam (Jacob Smith), is born healthy and with no obvious deformity or physical indications of his atavistic nature. However, he has inherited an instinctual knowledge of the ancient way of life, a natural skill to heal others, and the ability to telepathically communicate with animals. Adam is obviously a gentle soul, wise beyond his years, and there is nothing criminal about him. The ancient shaman who was Adam's biological father supplied him with many genetic gifts, except for an immunity to modern-day viruses and bacteria, which prove fatal. The story implies that if Adam could have survived into adulthood, he would likely have become a great healer or leader.

Predating media discourse by many centuries is a belief that animals are deeply linked to supernatural forces. Primitive peoples apparently did not make clear distinctions among humans, animals, spirits, and gods. For the pagan, everything has a soul or spirit, including animals. Like the human spirit, the animal spirit survives death. Gods are predominantly spirit but may take on human or animal form and characteristics. Humans are also capable of interacting with, and even outwitting or becoming, gods. This lack of obvious demarcation survives in myths, fairy tales, and fables, which are populated with animal characters that can talk and interact with people as equals.[4] In these stories, animals are not soulless "things" to be exploited for human benefit, but fellow citizens in life's journey. It is interesting that a belief in the animal soul has survived throughout the centuries, though orthodox religions may not support the idea. Across America, pet memorials and cemeteries are not uncommon features, suggesting that many people are unwilling to believe in an afterlife that is spiritually isolated from animals.[5]

For children especially, a heaven without animals may not seem a very joyful prospect. An episode from the television comedy series *Everybody Loves Raymond* (1996–) provides an illustration of the predicament for parents on the question of the animal soul, when the Barone family must deal with a child's grief over the death of a pet hamster, Pumpernickel.[6] Grandfather Frank (Peter Boyle) represents a more orthodox, though humorously convoluted view, of what might happen to Pumpernickel's soul, insisting that "there's a whole separate heaven for animals." Grandmother Marie (Doris Roberts) counters that there is only one heaven that accepts all souls. Despite the grandparents' conflicting theologies, the entire family participates in a backyard funeral for the hamster.

Some beliefs not only endorse the idea of an animal soul but position animals closer to gods than humans are. For some Native Americans, nature is deeply revered, and animals are eternally connected to a spirit world.[7] These are ideas that may be commandeered in modern media to associate new concerns with old mythologies. For example, a contemporary children's film, *Legend of the Spirit Dog* (1997), appropriates and colors Native American legends about the trickster coyote to create a narrative that warns about the dangers of soulless American businesses. In a modern world of encroaching development, annoying computer games, and arguing families, this same "spirit dog" seeks out a fatherless boy to save nature from the evil of a greedy American industry, which has no head and no heart but "only big, swollen bellies."[8] The film portrays gluttonous industrialists as unconcerned about the long-term effects of polluting the environment with toxic wastes in exchange for short-term, personal profit.

A different concept of the animal soul emerged as human beings domesticated nature and built cities. People began to emphasize the differences among categories of beings, creating hierarchies with the animals on bottom and the gods on top. For living things, spiritual immortality became the prerogative of humans, the chosen creatures. Lower on the hierarchy, animals were to be exploited for their strength, hunted, eaten, and used for clothing. These more modern concepts no longer recognized a world of interconnected spirits but stressed separate classifications for animals and humans, to the point that some contemporary religious beliefs deny that an animal can have a soul. For a believer in one of these religious faiths, an atavistic regression to an earlier animal ancestor without a soul would be a truly horrific proposition.

Evolution, Atavism, and Altered States

In 1888, Robert Louis Stevenson presented the public with *The Strange Case of Dr. Jekyll and Mr. Hyde*, a story that would come to have more than thirty film and television interpretations. The story is not a tale of witchcraft or shamanism, but it suggests that science or drugs might trigger horrible, yet wondrous, atavistic episodes. Considered by some to be a strong case in support of Victorian-age prohibition because of the suggestion that liquor turns reasonable men into raving animals (Reed and Slagle), or a study in the psychology of addiction (Wright), the narrative has also been interpreted as an indictment against an immoral leisure class whose money and superficial respectability could mask atavistic degeneracy (Arata). The original story preceded Sigmund Freud's ideas of id and ego, yet many believe Dr. Jekyll's struggle with his atavistic transformation to Mr. Hyde parallels the ego's struggle to balance the demands for dominance between the id, that impulse of the unconscious that is unable to delay gratification of desires, and the superego, that internalized moral authority that requires conformity to social rules. The ego must stabilize the internal pressures from the id and the superego with the external pressures of real life. Because infants are born with id but must develop ego and superego, the id can be considered the primitive emotional state, wanting complete pleasure without constraints. Stevenson's Hyde is all id, as are many of the atavistic characters in popular culture.

Nearly every decade in the last century had at least one film or television adaptation under the title *Dr. Jekyll and Mr. Hyde* (1912; 1913; 1920; 1931; 1941; 1968; 1973; 1981; 1990; 1999), and there are many other versions more loosely based on the story with variant titles. One film adaptation won Fredric March an Oscar for his performance of the tortured Dr. Jekyll and id-driven Mr. Hyde in 1932 and clearly shows the beast in the man; March's makeup is distinctly apelike. In Spencer Tracy's version of Hyde (1941), the metamorphosis is revealed less through makeup and more through behavior.

Michael Caine's exploration of Hyde (1990) presents a creature that looks more deformed than animal, though the movie makes the clear case that this is an atavistic transformation. In this made-for-television rendering of the story, professional envy and grief cause a split between Dr. Harry Jekyll and his father-in-law, Dr. Lanyon, who believes Jekyll caused his daughter's death by using experimental treatments for the illness that ultimately killed her. Jekyll and Lanyon are both respected doctors, socializing in the most elite circles. However, Jekyll is something of a medical maverick. He tells his students that chemicals control the human mind and that "the mind controls the body; alter the mind, and you alter the man." Jekyll predicts that one day science will control human shapes and human intelligence and will "even create new breeds of men. Violent men to fight our wars, docile men to do our work."

Seeking to rediscover the strength of the human ancestor, Dr. Jekyll experiments with a drug of his own invention, "Reflux," or as Jekyll calls it, a "flowing backward." However, Jekyll's backward journey turns him from a handsome, literate man into a homely sadist who commits acts of arson, assault, and murder. The violent Mr. Hyde finds a haven in the slums, where residents avoid calling in the law because the police will only disrupt their illegal businesses. A greedy madam, Mrs. Hackett, for example, protects Hyde from the police even though he brutalizes her prostitutes. Yet when a police inspector questions Mrs. Hackett about Hyde's identity, even she admits, "He is the Devil." Soon Hyde doesn't need the drug Reflux to take control of Jekyll. The atavistic monster returns unbidden to rape Jekyll's sister-in-law and murder his own father. The film ends by suggesting that the worst parts of humanity have the more dominant genetic makeup.

Another film scientist, Dr. Moreau, embarks upon similar experiments with the boundary between human and animal, hoping to create special breeds of people with the physical characteristics to do specific kinds of work, in *The Island of Lost Souls* (1933). Unlike Dr. Jekyll, Dr. Moreau (Charles Laughton) won't experiment on himself but happily experiments on others. Moreau is something of a sadist, conducting medical tests on animals without the benefit of anesthetics, in a laboratory called the "House of Pain." Moreau's goal is to manipulate evolution through plastic surgery, among other processes. "Man is the present climax of a long process of organic evolution. All animal life is tending toward the human form," he tells Edward Parker (Richard Arlen), his reluctant guest. Moreau's better creations become his servants, performing menial tasks. The others roam the island, trying—often unsuccessfully—to follow Moreau's "law." Moreau's supreme creation is Lota (Kathleen Burke), a beautiful woman whose animal qualities return when she is sexually aroused. Curious about whether his creation is capable of loving, mating, and having children, Moreau hopes to pair her with Parker. However, the beast in Lota can't be suppressed, causing physical reversions to her earlier animal form. Eventually, wild nature defeats the human elements in all of Moreau's creations, causing them to completely reject human civilization and law.

The character of Dr. Moreau remains consistent in the two remakes (*The Island of Dr. Moreau*, 1977; 1996). (See fig. 5.1.) In both remakes and in the original, animal nature conquers civilization, though the "civilization" represented by Moreau is clearly insane and perhaps more savage than his creations' animal world. The story raises questions about the direction of human evolution and the role of an evolved, perhaps lunatic, human intelligence and a correspondingly arrogant human science in attempting to lay out or disrupt that evolutionary path.

Mary Reilly (1996) is more a discourse about social class, about the violence of humanity confined to slums and slaughterhouses, than a statement about evolution. A later version of the Jekyll-and-Hyde story, this film develops from the perspective of a woman confined to the lower

Fig. 5.1. Dr. Moreau's experiments to speed up evolution and turn animals into human beings in *The Island of Dr. Moreau* (1977). American International Pictures. Photo provided by Larry Edmunds Collection.

classes, where atavism supposedly runs rampant. Julia Roberts plays Mary Reilly, a servant who has spent most of her life on the lowest rung in the hierarchy of servitude. As a child, she had been severely beaten and molested by her own abusive and alcoholic father. Dr. Jekyll (John Malkovich) takes an interest in his servant's scars, and Mary tells him her sad history. "The drinking turned him into a different person," she explains. "It was like he carried a different person inside him and the drinking brought it out." To which Jekyll replies, "Or set him free." Jekyll seems to despise the responsibilities and constraints of the elite social class. He supposes the lower classes are freer, because they have nothing to lose. Reilly doesn't believe in the possibility of action without consequences. From her point of view, there is always something to lose, worse pain to endure, and situations even more miserable than her own. If the film makes a statement about evolution, it is about the human ability to endure and adapt under the worst socioeconomic deprivation. Reilly accepts and copes with whatever hardship is dealt to her. Unlike Jekyll, Reilly manages the darkest legacy and survives.

Nearly a century after the original Jekyll-and-Hyde story appeared, the film *Altered States* (1980) added a rendering of the scientist discovering his atavistic self not during an era of Victorian restraint but during the 1970s, a period alive with countercultural movements.[9] The movie reflects the era's burgeoning curiosity about expanding consciousness through music, drugs, and alternative religions. William Hurt plays Eddie Jessup, a scientist exploring different states of consciousness with the help of drugs and an isolation chamber. Like Dr. Jekyll, Jessup is his own subject, researching altered mental states through a variety of methods, which include sensory deprivation and travels to Mexico to participate in a sacred mushroom ceremony. By bringing in the mushroom ceremony, *Altered States* combines the science of Dr. Jekyll's laboratory with occult ritual. The Native American shaman even adds drops of Jessup's blood to a cauldron of bubbling hallucinogens. Through an interpreter, the shaman tells Jessup that during the ceremony his soul will return to the "first soul." The mushroom ceremony triggers a state of altered consciousness in Jessup, which the film depicts as surrealistic religious imagery.

Later, Jessup begins to endure physical changes similar to those experienced by Dr. Jekyll or characters bitten by werewolves. Jessup explains his atavism: "I entered another consciousness. I became another self, a more primitive self." Later, he insists to colleagues that altered states of consciousness are real and can trigger physical changes. "We've got millions of years stored away in that computer bank we call our minds. We have trillions of dormant genes in us—our whole evolutionary past. Perhaps I've tapped into that." Jessup embraces these dormant characteristics, complaining to his wife Emily (Blair Brown) that the social constructs of modern life have separated men and women from God and expelled them from Eden. He believes society and culture have perverted the noble savage, crushing what is sublime in humanity. Primitive human beings were docile souls resting in paradise, not vicious souls surviving in a cruel jungle. Yet when Jessup begins his regression to a more primal form, it is hardly a docile or sublime one. He savagely attacks a security guard, intimidates zoo animals, and mutilates sheep, providing support for the argument that the noble savage of a primitive era would become a criminal in a modern context. Jessup's regression doesn't stop with the savage man but reverts further to the stage of cells and electrical impulses. The film doesn't portray Jessup's return to the cellular state as a happy reversion to a more noble condition, but as a dark, horrific journey. Finally, the film tells us that it is love that defies the horror of complete atavism, redeeming the contemporary man and saving him from the dread of his primitive "first soul."

There are numerous media stories that explore the evolutionary paths that segregated human beings from our animal cousins. The *Planet of the Apes* (1968) and its sequels (1970; 1971; 1972; 1973; 2001) pose questions about how our own violent natures might change the flow of evolution, selecting another intelligent creature for domination and demonstrating how that dominant position can corrupt. Films like *Man Beast* (1956), *The Snow Creature* (1954), *The Abominable Snowman* (1957), *Snowbeast* (1977), and *Night of the Demon* (1980) exploit folklore based on such legendary creatures as the Yeti, Bigfoot, Sasquatch, and the Abominable Snowman. Media portraits suggest that these elusive but fierce creatures share a common ancestor with humans but took a different evolutionary path that will likely lead them to extinction. Such movies offer a warning about the prehistoric violence we may have inherited.[10]

Lycanthropy, Red Riding Hood, and the Beast

Similar to stories of the tormented Dr. Jekyll, stories about the werewolf are generally warnings about the beast inside the human being. The folktales that provided the foundation for werewolf stories were the oral vehicles that took the values and prejudices of early periods and brought them to succeeding generations, and more recently, to film and video. One of the earliest and best known of the werewolf stories is "Little Red Riding Hood," originally a morality tale showing how moral order is violated and restored. In the earliest versions of the story, the grandmother and Red Riding Hood flirt with the Devil, who appears in the form of the were- wolf. This version may be seen as a caution about the threat women bring to the social order through witchcraft and prostitution (Chase and Teasley). When Charles Perrault published the first printed version of the folktale in 1697, he modified the violence of the story to satisfy emerging bour- geois tastes. More than a century later, the Grimm brothers would popu- larize a version that includes a hero in the form of a hunter who hap- pens upon the scene in time to save the girl and her grandmother from the wolf.

In the century following the Grimm brothers' version, more than twenty films distributed under the title *Little Red Riding Hood* would personify the wolf for children. Rather than a warning about the unruly nature of the female, most of these films became cautions about the dangers of a bru- tal world for naive girls. The fairy tale has been interpreted as an effort to frighten girls as they come of sexual age with a moral lesson about venturing beyond the protection of the family and stepping off the ap- proved cultural path to consort with strange men. Movies faithful to the Grimm brothers' fairy tale are usually meant as children's fare, while the more violent werewolf films became the horror movies meant for older teens and adults. Yet, several werewolf films also pay homage to the popu- lar fairy tale. The contemporary werewolf in films and television provides obvious lessons about the savage natures in both men and women.

Clearly intended for an adult audience, *The Company of Wolves* (1984) makes one of the strongest film statements about the connection between "Little Red Riding Hood" and folklore about the werewolf. Composed of a series of stories and dreams-within-a-dream, much of the film is nar- rated by an old granny (Angela Lansbury) or retold by her granddaugh- ter, Rosaleen (Sarah Patterson). The film begins with a contemporary family returning from a shopping trip. Isolated from her family, a moody preadolescent Rosaleen dreams that her older sister is attacked and killed by wolves. The dreamer then enters as a character in her own dream, a displaced daughter who goes to stay with her granny in a medieval fairy- tale village. Granny treats her granddaughter to disturbing stories about werewolves. "The wolf may be more than he seems. . . . He may come in many disguises," granny explains. "The wolf that ate your sister was hairy on the outside, but when she [your sister] died, she went straight to heaven. The worst kind of wolves are hairy on the inside, and when they bite you, they drag you straight to Hell." Granny warns Rosaleen to never trust a man whose eyebrows meet in the middle and tells her the story of a young woman who marries a traveling man with those eyebrows characteristic of the werewolf. On their wedding night, the groom tells his bride that he must go into the yard for a moment to answer "a call of nature." When he doesn't return, the young wife becomes convinced that a wolf has killed her husband while he was "making water." Years later, after the young wife has remarried, her first husband returns as the werewolf, accuses her of faithlessness for having another man's children, and attacks her. The rescuing woodcutter in this version is the wife's second husband, who arrives home in time to lop off the werewolf's head. After the werewolf's head falls into a pot of milk and reverts into the likeness of the woman's first husband, the woodcutter slaps his wife, blaming her for inviting the attack. At the end of the story, Rosaleen tells granny, "I'd never let a man strike me." To which granny replies, "Oh, they're nice as pie until they've had their way with you, but once the bloom is gone, the beast comes out." Finally, the film suggests that women are as capable of enjoying their own wild natures as are men, when Rosaleen herself transforms.

Folklore suggests several possibilities for the origin of the werewolf: the unfortunate person was conceived under a full moon, drank from the same water source as wolves, was bitten by another werewolf, was the returned soul of an offensive person, or invited the affliction with magic rituals. Looking at the historical cases, such as that of Peter Stubbe, the history of the werewolf is very closely associated with the idea of satanic witchcraft. However, folklore tends to make stronger connections between witchcraft and atavistic transformation than does popular culture, where the relationship may be more loosely suggested, if at all. In film and television stories, the association of witchcraft with werewolves may be the mere mention of a "curse," which can be presented as a genetic malady inherited from an ancestor or an affliction like rabies, transmitted by the bite of an infected individual. In such stories, the witch's bargain with the Devil for shape-shifting power isn't as overtly drawn as might be expected. Like Dr. Jekyll's science, the witch's magic is primarily a mechanism for the more important element of human transformation.

One of the earliest films about shape changing, *The Werewolf* (1913), which is supposed to have made a connection between a Navajo shaman and a werewolf, is no longer available to screen. A later film, *Werewolf of London* (1935), is still available and has received contemporary distribution on television and video. Rather than connect the werewolf legend to witchcraft, this film makes strong statements about the infectious violence of primitive cultures, the beastly behaviors of the lower class, and misguided science. A single-minded botanist, Dr. Wilfred Glendon (Henry

Hull), is on an expedition in the wilds of Tibet to find a rare flower that blooms only in moonlight. He ignores warnings to stay away from a cursed area and proceeds with his mission, only to be attacked and bitten by a werewolf. It's important to note that this worst case of bestial behavior gets imported to England from a country where, many characters tell us, the civilized white man is scarce. Glendon brings the unusual orchid home to add to his odd collection of exotic and carnivorous plants. At a reception for the botanical society in Glendon's home, a guest suggests of Glendon's carnivorous plant that it was wrong to bring "a beastly thing like that into Christian England." The mysterious Dr. Yogami (Warner Oland) replies, "Nature is very tolerant, sir. She has no creed." But he later comments that "evolution was in a strange mood" when that creation emerged.

Like stories about Dr. Jekyll and Dr. Moreau, this film also makes a strong statement about the obsessive nature of the scientist. Glendon ignores all advice in the unwholesome pursuit of his studies and neglects his wife, who complains, "I expect you to divorce me and marry a laboratory." He is self-absorbed and single-minded, morally atavistic even before being bitten by the werewolf. This film also echoes statements made in several versions of the Jekyll-and-Hyde story: atavistic deportment is a common feature of the slum, where murder and drunkenness are typical and expected behaviors. Glendon's werewolfism drives him to rent an apartment in the low-income district from a landlady who complains about the beastly behavior of her former husband. When Glendon asks her, "What would you say if I were to tell you it was possible for a man to turn into a werewolf," her flirtatious, thick Cockney reply is, "I'd say I was Little Red Riding Hood."

Like Glendon, Larry Talbot (Lon Chaney Jr.) in *The Wolf Man* (1941) becomes a werewolf after having been bitten by one. Unlike the obsessed Glendon, Talbot is a likable fellow, returning to his father's estate to take up his responsibilities and learn the family business. He meets Gwen Conliffe (Evelyn Ankers), who helps her father run an antique shop in the village, and begins a flirtation with her. A little put off by Talbot's aggressive friendliness, Gwen references the "Little Red Riding Hood" story, which she also claims is a werewolf story. Talbot buys a cane with a silver wolf's head on it from Gwen's store and convinces her to go with him that evening to the gypsy camp to have their fortunes told. It is here that a werewolf bites Talbot, cursing him with the lunar blood-lust. The movie puts forward a "logical" theory of the werewolf as "an ancient explanation for the dual personality" or "schizophrenia . . . the good and evil in every man's soul. . . . In this case the evil takes the shape of an animal. . . . Most anything can happen to a man in his own mind." Talbot's father, Sir John Talbot (Claude Rains) tells us that even a good man can fall victim to the curse: "Even a man who is pure in heart and says his prayers by night may become a wolf when the wolfsbane blooms. And the autumn moon is bright." He further suggests that "fighting superstition is as hard as fighting against Satan himself."

Another atavistic horror of the period, *Leopard Man* (1943), shows the vulnerability of civilized man to ancient and bestial depravity, this time in the form of a leopard. The movie explains that there are "men with kinks in their brains. Men who kill for pleasure." This film makes a brief link between ancient religious rites and the atavistic metamorphosis of a respected museum curator into a murderous beast.

The film *An American Werewolf in London* (1981) mixes shocking dream imagery, gore, and startling special effects to poke fun at horror-movie archetypes. Yet, this mixture of comedy and horror also reiterates the problem presented in *The Wolf Man*. Both victims of the werewolf, David Kessler (David Naughton) and Larry Talbot are nice guys. Neither wants to sadistically hunt down and murder victims but are devoured by the spirit of the werewolf into becoming monsters. In a similar way, the character of Ted (Michael Paré) in *Bad Moon* (1996) is basically a nice guy on assignment in a jungle in Nepal, when a werewolf mauls him. Ted tries unsuccessfully to resist the blood-lust passed along to him like an infectious disease. He shackles himself to trees to keep from hurting people. Clearly, even nice guys can be cursed, and as a result, be driven to do beastly things.

Reverend Lowe (Everett McGill) rationalizes the violence he commits while a werewolf in *Silver Bullet* (1985). Lowe excuses the murder of a young woman, explaining that she had been planning to commit suicide. By killing her, the preacher as werewolf prevented her suicide and saved her soul. However, the movie makes it clear that this werewolf is not a sympathetic creature, roaming the town to commit good deeds. Lowe serves as a warning that even a man of God can succumb to the atavistic beast within and will use his civilized mind to excuse his violence. It takes the keen insight of children not blinded by the biases of civilization to discover the werewolf and destroy him.

The connection between witchcraft and the transformation of human into animal is more clearly drawn in *Cat People* (1942). The movie opens with the quote from a book, *The Anatomy of Atavism*, supposedly written by one of the characters in the film, Dr. Louis Judd: "Even as fog continues to lie in the valleys, so does ancient sin cling to the low places, the depressions in the world consciousness." A decent, all-American guy, Oliver Reed (Kent Smith), becomes attracted to a mysterious and beautiful Serbian-born artist, Irena Dubrovna (Simone Simon). She tells him the dark history of her people:

> When King John . . . came to our village, he found dreadful things. People bowed down to Satan and said their masses to him. They had become witches and were evil. King John put some of them to the sword, but some, the wisest and most wicked, escaped into the mountain.

Reed is captivated by the exotic girl and marries her, but the marriage is a troubled one. Irena longs for a happy relationship with her new husband but can't seem to manage it. Reed promises to be patient, waiting to consummate the marriage when Irena is ready, but he turns to psychiatry and Dr. Louis Judd (Tom Conway) for help. Under hypnosis, Irena reveals to Judd that cat women change into violent beasts when aroused to any passion: jealousy, anger, or desire. She tells the doctor, "You are very wise and know a great deal. Yet, when you speak of the soul you mean the mind. And it is not my mind that is troubled." The corrupt and foolish doctor attempts to take advantage of his patient and finds himself in trouble when she becomes aroused. One of the earliest films to associate female sexuality with violent, bestial horror, *Cat People* would be remade in 1982. In the remake, sexual relations trigger the transformation of Irena (Nastassja Kinski) into a panther, a permanent condition unless the creature is satisfied with violence. In this version, sexuality awakens the beast, and violence restores the character's human appearance.

A more recent movie, *Ginger Snaps* (2000), also uses the werewolf as a metaphor for the dangers of blossoming female sexuality in a manner somewhat similar to the use of telekinesis in *Carrie* (1976).[11] Two sisters, Ginger (Katharine Isabelle) and Brigitte (Emily Perkins), reject mainstream values, which they view as insipid and hypocritical. They are obsessed with images of bizarre death, staging and photographing scenes of faked violence for a school project to "gross out" their teacher and classmates. However, their obsession with death runs deeper than shock value. The sisters make a suicide pact, believing their suicide would be the ultimate insult to family and community.

On the night of her first period, which also happens to be a full moon, Ginger is bitten by a werewolf. Her body begins to undergo changes that eclipse those of a normal adolescence. She becomes sexually aggressive with Jason (Jesse Moss), a high-school classmate, and infects him with werewolfism, as if shape-shifting were a sexually transmitted disease.[12] Soon the violence escalates. Ginger viciously attacks and mutilates animals. For help, Brigitte turns to the local drug dealer, Sam (Kris Lemche), who grows marijuana in a large greenhouse and seems to have some esoteric knowledge of plants. Sam suggests monkshood as an herbal cure, which the pair cook in a manner similar to preparing heroin or cocaine for injection. The monkshood works on Jason, but Ginger never gets her dose.[13]

The werewolf as a metaphor for female sexuality was also central to the British television series *Wilderness* (1996), in which the character Alice White (Amanda Ooms) turns to a psychologist for help to rid herself of her inner wolf. Young men coming of age are just as troubled by their inner beasts as young women are. For example, in *I Was a Teenage Werewolf* (1957), Tony Rivers (Michael Landon) becomes the victim of Dr. Alfred Brandon's (Whitt Bissell) hypnotic regression experiments, which turn him into the true delinquent, a werewolf.

Like most werewolf films, *The Howling* (1980) refutes the idea that stifling civilization creates the conditions of human violence. The film's ultimate message seems to be that civilization redeems humanity, distinguishing us from animals. However, the film opens with a contradictory statement by a television psychiatrist, Dr. George Waggner (Patrick Macnee), who insists that "repression is the father of neuroses." Waggner suggests that the misunderstood wild nature within humanity has been inhibited by culture to the point that some people are made crazy with self-restraint and must eventually explode into violence. He mourns the loss of the noble savage, unfettered by civilization. Yet, the savages Waggner admires and seeks to protect are neither noble nor natural. *The Howling* frames the conflict between savage and civil from the perspective of newswoman Karen White (Dee Wallace-Stone), who agrees to be the decoy for a serial killer as part of an investigative report. She survives an attack but is traumatized by the event, which presumably takes the life of the serial killer, an artistic drifter named Eddie Quest. Dr. Waggner recommends that Karen visit his mental health resort, the Colony, to relax and recover from the trauma.

The main activity of the Colony, however, turns out to be group therapy for werewolves. Dr. Waggner's ambition is to redirect the violence of the werewolves so that they might coexist with people undetected. But he is not successful. As one Colony member tells him, "You can't tame what was meant to be wild, Doc. It ain't natural." Connections to witchcraft in the movie come in the character of Marsha (Elizabeth Brooks), described as a very "elemental person" and a "nymphomaniac." Marsha appears to be a key member of the group, seducing Karen's husband Bill (Christopher Stone) and making him a member of her werewolf pack. Meanwhile, Karen's colleagues, investigative reporters Terry (Belinda Balaski) and Chris (Dennis Dugan), become involved in research for a special television feature about the "Mind of Eddie Quest," an investigation into the motives of a serial killer, "guaranteed to make ratings history." Their inquiry leads them to the subject of lycanthropy, and eventually the reporters watch the 1941 film *Wolf Man* as part of their research. *The Howling* also references the wolf from children's cartoons, crosscutting the comedy violence of animation with a werewolf's attack on Terry. Finally, Karen uncovers the "truth" of the serial violence and makes a heroic effort to put an end to the werewolf colony, even sacrificing herself. She tells her viewing audience, "From the day we're born there is a battle we must fight, a struggle between what is kind and good in our natures and what is cruel and violent. That choice is our birthright as human beings and separates us from the animals."

A fundamental supposition behind the stories of Jekyll and Hyde and many of the werewolf or shape-shifting narratives is the idea that atavistic savagery remains a constant threat to Western civilization. Though a progressive Western culture destroys or assimilates primitive ones, attempting to control whatever is wild or aggressive in people, these films imply that exotic, older, and more savage cultures continue to seduce and pollute contemporary civilization with their unrepressed violence and sexuality.

Divine Regressions and Noble Savages

In most media accounts of atavistic transformations, the primitive is savage and undesirable. However, there are important exceptions. The film *Wolfen* (1981) has the violence of a typical horror movie about werewolves, however, it excuses the violence and expresses sympathy, even admiration, for the creatures behind it. A city cop, Dewey Wilson (Albert Finney), is assigned to solve a bizarre set of terrible murders in which it appears that the victims were killed by animals or madmen. The mortician Whittington (Gregory Hines) tells him, "Something out there might be eating people." In his pursuit, Wilson learns about Native American legends of shapeshifters and wolf spirits. The wolfen are shapeshifters, creatures that adapted to human domination and population explosion by going underground and preying on sick, abandoned people who will not be missed. An old Indian explains:

> Twenty thousand years the skins [humans] and wolves, the two great hunting nations, lived together. Nature in balance. Then the slaughter came. The

smart ones went underground into the new wilderness, the slums. They became the scavengers. Not animals, . . . they might be gods.

The movie expresses compassion for the werewolves, depicted as supremely
intelligent creatures, perhaps divine. Unlike the wolfen, we humans may
have technology, but according to this film, we have lost our senses.

The real-life story of Julia Pastrana (1834–60) was so extraordinary that
in 1963 Italian director Marco Ferreri made a movie based on her life, *The
Ape Woman* (or *La Donna Scimmia*, 1963). Like Tod Browning's *Freaks*
(1932), this film asserts that the atavistic criminal is more likely to be
hiding under a normal, even beautiful, physique, and the physical atavism that appears so monstrous to us may conceal a gentle and highly
principled spirit and is not always the physical indication of a vicious,
criminal soul, as Lombroso implied. In fact, the normal-looking husband
who exhibited Julia Pastrana was more of a moral criminal than his unfortunate wife, who was described as a gentle and talented lady. Likely a
victim of hypertrichosis, a rare genetic disorder that causes the growth
of long hair all over the body and face, Pastrana was described in her time
as a hybrid, the cross between a human and either a bear, an orangutan,
or a gorilla (Bondeson 218–44). Her husband, who was also her impre-
sario, dressed her in elaborate feminine attire and had her perform for
audiences. "La femme-gorille," as she was known, toured both Europe
and America in the 1850s, dancing, singing, and playing the guitar and
the harmonica. Her performances were very profitable, even though
many venues considered her exhibition an outrage to public decency
and morals. According to Jan Bondeson, "Some German obstetricians
strongly objected to the public exhibition of Julia Pastrana, for fear pregnant women might miscarry at the sight of her, or even have children
exactly like her through maternal impression" (225). When Julia died
giving birth to a son who also died, her husband had the bodies of both
his wife and his similarly afflicted child embalmed and continued to
exhibit the mummies.

The fictional character of Tara Talbot (Victoria Sanchez) in the television film *Wolf Girl* (2001) suffers from the same hypertrichosis that
made the real Julia Pastrana a human curiosity: she is covered from head
to toe in hair. Tara's parents were from Romania. The father, ashamed of
his freak daughter, abandons his family. The mother finally leaves the
child in the care of Harley Dune (Tim Curry) to become one of several
human oddities exhibited in a traveling sideshow. Arriving in a small
town, Tara becomes the object of ridicule and torment by local teens but
is befriended by the son of a scientist involved in cosmetic research. This

boy attempts to help Tara become a normal girl. Using drugs developed by his mother, the teenager tries to induce a gradual transformation in Tara from hairy beast to a beautiful girl with clear, hairless skin. However, clear skin may come at a price: the cost of a noble soul for savage beauty.

In some media presentations, the werewolf, or "the beast within," is introduced as the best part of humanity. For example, comedies such as *Teen Wolf* (1985) or the television series *Big Wolf on Campus* (1999–2002), *Fangface* (1978), and *The Drak Pack* (1980) present the beast inside a teenage boy as powerful but not dangerous. The beast gives the boy keener senses, helps him to be a better athlete, improves his ability to recognize and fight true evil, or makes him more attractive to girls. Even the character of Eddie (Butch Patrick) in the television series *The Munsters* (1964–66) is more precocious than dangerous.

Though an adult romance rather than a children's comedy, the film *Wolf* (1994) makes a similar statement about the benefits of being a werewolf for an aging man. At the beginning of the movie, the years seems to be overtaking Will Randall (Jack Nicholson), an editor for an aggressive New York publishing house. He seems tired, cynical, beaten, his editorial leadership no longer respected. In the normal course of events, a son will usurp the father's role, a prince will dethrone the king, and younger associates will force older ones into retirement. This is the case for Randall when his boss offers him a choice between "no job and a job no one would want." His old-fashioned style can't seem to compete with the devious charms of his younger co-worker Stewart (James Spader), who slyly filches Randall's job while also seducing Randall's wife. The bite of the werewolf changes the normal course of events for Randall; he won't be forced into early retirement. He sleeps late and wakes with new energy, a stronger sexual appetite, and senses that are incredibly acute, capable of literally sniffing out betrayal. Randall is afraid this uncanny gift of the wolf is really a curse that "will come at a price." Yet, reconnecting to the primitive self doesn't necessarily mean reconnecting to the uncivilized self in this movie. Randall does atavistically transform into a creature that prowls the grounds of an estate, killing and eating a deer. However, the movie presents this action as the natural predatory behavior of a creature that hunts to eat. In essence, Randall remains a literate, intellectual man, only now more talented, with keener physical abilities and the ruthless acumen of the beast to apply to the corporate jungle of a major publishing company. He learns that "the demon wolf is not evil, unless the man he has bitten is evil." In a culture that exalts the "edginess" of youth over the experience of age, the movie also suggests there may be a few new tricks left in an old dog.

Another example of the noble savage comes in the form of "transgenics," the part-man, part-beast characters in the television series *Dark Angel* (2000–2001). Following Dr. Moreau's ideas about manipulating human and animal genetics, the series introduces us to the resulting human mutants. These are creatures designed to be smarter and more athletic than ordinary human beings. Some transgenics even possess highly developed psychokinetic powers. The main character in the series is Max (Jessica Alba), a genetically enhanced woman designed to possess the superhuman cunning, strength, and reflexes needed to be the perfect soldier. Max is a transgenic but doesn't have the look of an animal. She does have an animal's superior strength and agility. She escapes her military handlers and must continue to elude them in a decaying twenty-first-century civilization. She must also help protect her genetically manipulated "siblings" from mistreatment by a "genetically average" population that feels threatened by the transgenics. Joshua (Kevin Durand) is Max's older brother, the prototype of the genetically manipulated human. He is a creature with features similar to those of a fierce animal. Yet, Joshua is gentle, faithful, and artistic. Like the character Vincent from the earlier television series *Beauty and the Beast* (1987–90), or the beast from movie renderings of the fairy tale (1947; 1991), Joshua reminds audiences to look beyond superficial appearances for what is truly bestial in human nature. Other transgenics in the series, like Max, don't have an animal appearance but have animal traits such as great physical strength and intuition. Some transgenics have atavistic traits, such as psychic abilities, that reconnect humans to the divine animal, though the series questions whether the transgenics have reconnected to the wisdom that will help them judiciously use such divine gifts.

Nature and Atavistic Violence

In the *Werewolf Complex*, author Denis Duclos argues that a contemporary American society that traps an autonomous individual within a repressive social order creates a situation in which the serial killer, or his fictional counterpart, the werewolf, can thrive. Though America is a cultural amalgam, Duclos believes Americans are wedded to the Anglo-Saxon mythology of a beast within us all that must be kept under control. This "werewolf complex" is a distinct malady of Anglo-American culture, "an obsessive oscillation between uncontrolled savagery and political correctness, compulsive aggressiveness and hysterical expostulating" (13). Duclos claims the violent energy of the werewolf cannot be exterminated, for that is the energy of nature.

However, the violence of the werewolf in popular culture is not always depicted as the violence of nature, which is the ferocity necessary to fight for survival: to hunt, forage, reproduce, and protect offspring. In this respect, the werewolf is clearly unnatural. The animal that kills to eat or survive is innocent, obeying only the law of nature. The werewolf that kills viciously and repetitively without motive has rejected any version of law. Eddie Quest in *The Howling* doesn't kill for food or protection; he kills for the fun of it. Ted's blood-lust in *Bad Moon* causes him to turn on his own family in a dysfunctional violence that—if it were the predominant characteristic in nature—might lead to the extinction of the species. In *An American Werewolf in London*, David Kessler savagely murders his best friend, behavior that has no survival value at all. If the violence of the werewolf is meant to be the atavistic violence of an animal, it is an animal gone mad. The crimes of werewolves, cat women, leopard men, and Mr. Hyde are the motiveless violence of boredom, not the imperative tooth and claw of nature. In this sense, the violence displayed in many media stories is not truly atavistic, not the reappearance of an ancient characteristic, but the emergence of a new one. It is the existential dilemma of a mind that has examined life and can find no purpose in it, a mind that has rejected the protective fiction of culture for the resulting infection of nihilism.

It is significant that werewolf stories tend to have either science or magic as the mechanism of metamorphosis, because both can lead to the rejection of social fictions: magic, because it can reduce human activity to ineffectual or pointless mystery; science, because the requisites of logic frequently lead to more and more questions and to ultimate, unsolved enigmas. It is also worth noting that many of the shape-changing characters of popular media are members of a privileged class, characters with the opportunity for boredom. Glendon (*Werewolf of London*), Jekyll (*Dr. Jekyll and Mr. Hyde*), Kessler (*An American Werewolf in London*), Ginger (*Ginger Snaps*), and Larry Talbot (*The Wolf Man*) are not overly preoccupied with the labors of everyday life. They have the leisure of intellectual curiosity and the freedom to venture into foreign cultures or alternative conditions that raise doubts about the validity of civilization. For example, in *Altered States*, Eddie Jessup is obviously questing. For him, the dominant cultural fiction in which he lives is a farce. He searches for meaning and a new reality through altered mental states and alternative cultures. Orthodox religious belief might have saved Jessup, but he chooses science instead. Science leads him to face a brutal reality—the futility and ultimate chaos of life. Jessup declares, "I was in that ultimate moment of terror that is the beginning of life . . . and it is nothing. Simple, hideous nothing. The final truth of all things is that there is no final truth."

Potential werewolves in media stories often express a desire to be completely free from the repression of civilization. Yet, complete freedom is difficult to achieve because people internalize the cultural norms of a civilization, norms that create the illusions of nonviolence, civility, and beauty, among others. For example, contemporary Americans can buy meat at a grocery store far removed from the slaughter of the animal that provided it: an illusion of nonviolence. Cultural scripts help mask raw emotion with polite behaviors: an illusion of courtesy. Clothes, cosmetics, and deodorants disguise the smells and blemishes of the human body: an illusion of beauty. A Jekyll rejects these illusions in his search for the freedom Hyde offers. For example, John Malkovich's Jekyll is the portrayal of a man who has recognized the fictions of beauty, nonviolence, and courtesy in civilization as absurd social fantasies. He wants to be released from them. In the movie *Ginger Snaps*, the potential werewolf Ginger has already rejected the dominant social fiction for the dark, often violent aesthetic of the Goth subculture. Kessler has left the protection of home to backpack in a remote section of England, where primitive pubs and primitive ideas can taint an impressionable mind. Looking for diversions, the privileged Larry Talbot leaves the protection of his estate and ventures into the exotic gypsy camp. Rejecting the dominant civilization for the exotic one, even temporarily, allows the questing, restless character to become polluted with doubt. Irena Dubrovna (*Cat People*) wants to hide in the illusion of a civilized marriage but can't. She is already infected with the savage perspective she inherited from the "wisest and most wicked" of her people, the exotic attitude that won't allow her inside the cultural fictions that come with marriage to a decent American guy.

By rejecting civilization, a character may also eliminate the defenses that help create self-esteem and meaning for the human condition. In order to become contaminated, to be bitten, the potential werewolf must venture beyond the peripheries of civilization and then spurn all its illusions. Without protective fictions, life might seem to have no inherent meaning, or no meaning that can be comprehended. The werewolf rediscovers the vitality missing in a meaningless life by turning to motiveless violence.[14] When Ginger begins to welcome the bloody ferocity of her transformation into a wolf, her sister Brigitte becomes appalled by the "real" violence she once adored as a fabricated plaything. Faced with all the implications of a sincerely valueless life, Brigitte realizes that the existential dilemma is not just an adolescent game. But there is no turning back for the werewolf. Having rejected the collaborative fiction, Ginger, Irena, Glendon, Jekyll, Ted (*Bad Moon*), and Reverend Lowe (*Silver Bullet*) are aware of their miserable destinies and almost seem relieved when the end finally arrives. No life is valuable, not even their own.[15] Their stories remind audiences that rejecting all the comfortable delusions of civilization can lead to the horror of absolute chaos, the darkness of the soul.

Not all stories about the beast within the human are tragic stories of violence. Will Randall in *Wolf* doesn't fully reject the protective mirage of culture and the significance that cultural values can bring to human life. As a werewolf, he has the energy to choose his own meanings and destiny rather than have those choices thrust upon him. Randall is a werewolf in control. Young Rosaleen in *The Company of Wolves* can appreciate what is elemental without becoming a spiritual corpse. Even Eddie Jessup can be saved from the pointless, stark, primordial realities of life by Emily's love.

Rather than succumb to chaos, some atavistic creatures presented in popular media do triumph, questioning elements of civilization without dismissing all of its protective values.[16] Perhaps the more compelling atavistic stories in film and television are those in which searches for the divine animal involve a civilized character who rediscovers respect for nature, physical prowess, and animal intuition and in which the viewing audience can experience a return to older concepts of a spiritually interconnected world. Finally, stories like those of Joshua (*Dark Angel*), Tara Talbot (*Wolf Girl*), and Julia Pastrana (*The Ape Woman*) remind audiences that savage features are not necessarily the signs of atavistic regression and a criminal nature but may conceal a gentle, civil, principled character.

Filmography: Atavistic Media

Though not a list of all popular films and television programs relevant to the topic of atavism, this filmography is intended to serve as a reference for the media that inform the discussion and that are cited in this chapter.

The Abominable Snowman, The. Dir. Val Guest. Warner Brothers, 1957.
Altered States. Dir. Ken Russell. Warner Brothers, 1980.
American Werewolf in London, An. Dir. John Landis. Universal Pictures, 1981.
Animal Telepathy. TV documentary. Dir. Kris Denton. TLC, 2002.
Ape Woman, The (La Donna Scimmia). Dir. Marco Ferreri. Embassy Pictures and Something Weird Video, 1963.
Bad Moon. Dir. Eric Red. Warner Brothers, 1996.

Beast Must Die, The. Dir. Paul Annett. Lara Classics, 1974.

Beauty and the Beast (La Belle et la Bête). Dir. Jean Cocteau. Leper Pictures, 1947.

Beauty and the Beast. TV series. Exec. prod. Ron Koslow. CBS, 1987–90.

Beauty and the Beast. Dir. Gary Trousdale and Kirk Wise. Buena Vista, 1991.

Big Wolf on Campus. TV series. Dir. Carl Goldstein, Jim Kaufman, Peter D. Marshall, Peter Svatek, Adam Weissman, Eric Canuel, and Carl Goldberg. Fox Family Channel, 1999–2002.

Blue Moon. Dir. Brian Garton. D. G. Ltd., 1998.

Boy Who Cried Werewolf, The. Dir. Nathan Juran. Universal Pictures, 1973.

Cat People. b&w. Dir. Jacques Tourneur. RKO Radio Pictures, 1942.

Cat People. Dir. Paul Schrader. MCA, Universal Pictures, 1982.

Company of Wolves, The. Dir. Neil Jordan. Cannon Films, 1984.

Conquest of the Planet of the Apes. Dir. J. Lee Thompson. 20th Century Fox, 1972.

Creature from the Black Lagoon. Dir. Jack Arnold. Universal Pictures, 1954.

Cry of the Werewolf. b&w. Dir. Henry Levin. Columbia Pictures, 1944.

Curse, The. Dir. Jacqueline Garry. Arrow Releasing, 1999.

Dark Angel. TV series. Exec. prod. James Cameron. Fox Network, 2000–2001.

Daughter of Dr. Jekyll. b&w. Dir. Edgar G. Ulmer. Allied Artists Pictures, 1957.

Death Moon. TV movie. Dir. Bruce Kessler. CBS, 1978.

Drak Pack. TV series. Exec. prod. William Hannah and Joseph Barbera. Hannah Barbera and CBS, 1980.

Dr. Jekyll and Mr. Hyde. b&w, silent. Dir. Lucius Henderson. Kino Video, Thanhouser Film, 1912.

Dr. Jekyll and Mr. Hyde. b&w, silent. Dir. Herbert Brenon. Sinister Cinema, Universal Pictures, 1913.

Dr. Jekyll and Mr. Hyde. b&w, silent. Dir. John S. Robertson. Paramount Pictures, 1920.

Dr. Jekyll and Mr. Hyde. b&w. Dir. Rouben Mamoulian. MGM, United Artists, Paramount Pictures, 1931.

Dr. Jekyll and Mr. Hyde. b&w. Dir. Victor Fleming. MGM, 1941.

Dr. Jekyll and Mr. Hyde. TV movie. Dir. Charles Jarrott. ABC, 1968.

Dr. Jekyll and Mr. Hyde. TV movie. Dir. David Winters. NBC, 1973.

Dr. Jekyll and Mr. Hyde. TV movie. Dir. Alastair Reid. PBS, 1981.

Dr. Jekyll and Mr. Hyde. TV movie. Dir. David Wickes. King Phoenix Entertainment, 1990.

Dr. Jekyll and Mr. Hyde. Dir. Collin Buds. EuroVideo, 1999.

Evolution's Child. TV movie. Dir. Jeffrey Reiner. USA Network, 1999.

Face of the Screaming Werewolf. Dir. Gilberto Martínez Solares, Rafael Portillo, and Jerry Warren. A. D. P. Pictures, 1964.

Fangface. Animated TV series. Dir. Rudy Larriva. ABC, 1978.

Freaks. Dir. Tod Browning. MGM, 1932.

Ginger Snaps. Dir. John Fawcett. Unapix Entertainment, 2000.

Ginger Snaps Back: The Beginning. Dir. Grant Harvey. Lions Gate Films, 2004.

Ginger Snaps 2: Unleashed. Dir. Brett Sullivan. Lions Gate Films, 2004.

Half Human: The Story of the Abominable Snowman. Dir. Kenneth G. Crane and Ishir Honda. Sinister Cinema, 1957.

Howling, The. Dir. Joe Dante. MGM, 1980.

Howling: New Moon Rising, The. Dir. Clive Turner. New Line Cinema, 1995.

Huntress: Spirit of the Night. Dir. Mark S. Manos. Torchlight Entertainment, 1991.

Island of Dr. Moreau, The. Dir. Don Taylor. American International Pictures, 1977.

Island of Dr. Moreau, The. Dir. John Frankenheimer. New Line Cinema, 1996.

Island of Lost Souls. Dir. Erle C. Kenton. Universal Pictures, 1933.

I Was a Teenage Werewolf. Dir. Gene Fowler Jr. American International Pictures, 1957.

Leopard Man. Dir. Jacques Tourneur. RKO Radio Pictures, 1943.

Mad at the Moon. Dir. Martin Donovan. Republic Pictures, 1992.

Man Beast. Dir. Jerry Warren. Associated Producers, 1956.

Mary Reilly. Dir. Stephen Frears. TriStar Pictures, 1996.

Monster on Campus. Dir. Jack Arnold. Universal Pictures, 1958.

Munsters, The. TV series. Dir. Norman Abbott and David Alexander. CBS, 1964–66.

My Mom's a Werewolf. Dir. Michael Fischa. Crown International Pictures, Prism
   Pictures, 1998.

Night of the Demon. Dir. James C. Wasson. VCI Home Video, 1980.

Pet Psychic. TV series. Dir. R. A. Fernandez. Animal Planet, Discovery Communications, 2002–.

Planet of the Apes (aka *Monkey Planet*). Dir. Franklin J. Schaffner. 20th Century Fox,
   1968.

Planet of the Apes. Dir. Tim Burton. 20th Century Fox, 2001.

Silver Bullet. Dir. Daniel Attias. Paramount Pictures, 1985.

Snowbeast. TV movie. Dir. Herb Wallerstein. NBC, 1977.

Snow Creature. Dir. W. Lee Wilder. United Artists, 1954.

Son of Dr. Jekyll. b&w. Dir. Seymour Friedman. Columbia Pictures, 1951.

Teen Wolf. Dir. Rod Daniel. Atlantic, 1985.

Two Faces of Dr. Jekyll, The. Dir. Terence Fisher. American International Pictures,
   1960.

Werewolf, The. b&w, silent. Dir. Henry McRae. Bison/Universal, 1913. (No longer
   available for screening.)

Werewolf, The. Dir. Fred F. Sears. Columbia Pictures, 1956.

Werewolf. TV series. Exec. prod. Frank Lupo. TriStar Television, 1987–88.

Werewolf of London. b&w. Dir. Stuart Walker. MCA, Universal Pictures, 1935.

Wilderness. TV series. Dir. Ben Bolt. BBC, 1996.

Wolf. Dir. Mike Nichols. Columbia Pictures, 1994.

Wolfen. Dir. Michael Wadleigh. Warner Brothers, 1981.

Wolf Girl. TV movie. Dir. Thom Fitzgerald. USA Network, 2001.

Wolf Man, The. Dir. George Waggner. Universal Pictures, 1941.

The Recycled Soul
What Movies and Television Tell Us about Reincarnation

Immortality is a terrible curse.
—Simone de Beauvoir, *All Men Are Mortal* (1955)

*W*hen film critics speak of movie "reincarnations," they usually mean remakes of older films or updated versions of familiar stories. When political analysts use the term, they are usually referring to leaders who remake their images or policies to create a better fit with a current political climate. In the plot of the American film *Audrey Rose* (1977), when an Englishman tries to convince a New York couple that their young daughter is really the reincarnation of his, the character isn't implying a resemblance between the two girls. He means that his daughter's soul has literally been reborn into the body of another child. Throughout the last century, popular media have presented the idea of reincarnation to an American public, often adapting the concept to fit with Western thinking that treasures the idea of a unique and eternal human psyche, a value in contrast to the original Buddhist concept. In addition to stories about reincarnation, media narratives flirt with the idea of the transmigration of an indestructible human soul from one body to the next. What emerges from our popular media is a concept of reincarnation that may be uniquely American.

Reincarnation: Ego Escaped or Ego Preserved?

Reincarnation is a feature of Indian philosophy, Hinduism, Jainism, Sikhism, and Mahayana Buddhism, among others. Similar concepts include metempsychosis, the passing of the soul, spirit, or personality upon death into another body; and transmigration, the release of the soul into a new form of being.

The idea of reincarnation is that the soul becomes incarnate in a succession of bodies, carrying into each new life the burden of past-life deeds. The situation into which the soul will be reborn may be predetermined by actions—good or bad—done in the former incarnation, the karma that becomes the soul's baggage. Souls of evil people may be reborn in lower life forms, such as animals, insects, even plants. However, some (largely Western) beliefs segregate life forms such that a human soul will always reside in a human body. If the soul has a good character in several existences, or if upon the death of the body the soul was properly centered with appropriate thoughts, it may finally return to a state of pure being, or nirvana. The soul has been formed, enriched, perhaps even perverted by previous lives but may not remember them, just as an adult rarely remembers learning first words, taking first steps, or experiencing other events of infancy.

In the Eastern concept of reincarnation, the soul's struggle is to achieve complete purification and become free from the continuous cycle of suffering. While experiencing life in the body, a soul can become impure through association with bodily passion, which will prolong the soul's endeavor to become enlightened and escape the painful and infinite orbit of death and rebirth. However, there are varying ways the doctrines of karma and rebirth have been interpreted. In the Hindu concept, which is comparable to modern Buddhist thought, the same individual performs and suffers in different lives. Traditional Buddhism denies there is a permanent, fundamental self. In this interpretation, there is no fixed core that darts from body to body, rather what becomes reincarnated is a flow of spirit, an appetite for life and emotions that might influence a future individual. In this view, karmic energy is just as responsible for conscious life as the physical contributions of parents.

In the book *Breaking the Circle: Death and the Afterlife in Buddhism*, Carl Becker recognizes that Buddhist philosophy has been modified by every culture it has entered or influenced. Original Buddhism does not accept the idea of a temporal or eternal soul but rather a psychic process that neither exists nor ceases to exist. Becker characterizes the idea of reincarnation as one based on both psychic influence and psychic continuity. The philosophy of reincarnation has the core assumptions that cause and effect may be distance from one another but still linked, that psychic forces exist independent of physical bodies, and that realms other than the material one reside in this universe (22). As Becker notes, the idea of reincarnation is an ancient one, predating Buddha. The philosophy has also crossed the globe in various configurations, influencing beliefs from Asia to Africa and from Australia to the Americas. Among some African groups, such as the Ukwuani people of Nigeria, physical similarities within a family from generation to generation are considered to be the uncanny influence of a reincarnated ancestor's soul on a baby's body, rather than the effect of inherited genetics.

Islam, Christianity, and Judaism generally consider the idea of reincarnation a heresy, though some occult sects of these religions might endorse it. For example, there are references to the ideas of dualism and rebirth in the Jewish Cabala. Among early Christians, the only group to embrace reincarnation was the Cathari, a group that would be condemned to death for heresy by the Roman Catholic Church in the thirteenth century. Orthodox Judaism and Christianity never embraced the concept of reincarnation.[1] Yet, survey research shows that a substantial number of contemporary Westerners coming from Judeo-Christian traditions have accepted some variation of the idea (Ashford and Timms). The American counterculture and youth movements of the 1960s promoted an idealized image of Asian culture, imagining it to be the reverse of everything they disliked about America. The American counterculture retooled Asian philosophy to reflect countercultural ideals (Diem and Lewis 56), and these paraphrased versions of reincarnation gained a following. Western converts tended to adopt a simplified account, ignoring difficult questions such as the concept of an infinite past and the ultimate fate of the soul. "Their main concern seems to be that death, i.e., the death of the present life, should not end, and a few additional lives would probably be quite sufficient to appease their longings" (P. Edwards 12).

The idea of reincarnation began to influence Western film narratives even as early as the silent era. For example, in *What Happened to Rosa* (1920), a fortune-teller, Madame O'Donnelly (Eugenie Besserer), convinces a young woman (Mabel Normand) that she is the reborn spirit of Rosa, a beautiful Spanish dancer. However, the real surge of movies and television programs influenced by the concept of reincarnation followed the sensation of a best-selling book, *The Search for Bridey Murphy*, and the movie based on it (1956). Most of the media narratives with ideas about reincarnation as a central theme would predictably come in the following decades.

Reincarnation and the Cherished Self

In a study of Western attitudes toward reincarnation, Tony Walter suggests that Americans and Europeans use the idea of rebirth as a way of clinging to personal identity or self (21). This differs from the Hindu or

Buddhist concept, in which the ultimate goal is to dissolve individual identity and return to a state of pure being. Because the modern Western world is rooted in the idea of individualism, the doctrine of rebirth seems bonded to the idea of a permanent core of the individual human spirit and personality, a unique soul that resumes from life to life.

The film *Being Human* (1994) presents an example of how the Western mind conceives reincarnation. The film follows the character of Hector (Robin Williams) through several lifetimes, beginning with that of a prehistoric man; then as the slave of a bankrupt Roman businessman; then a traveler in medieval Europe; then a shipwrecked Renaissance merchant; and finally, a divorced American, living the rootless life of modern capitalism. The character remains essentially the same, struggling with similar themes from lifetime to lifetime. Through circumstance and choice, Hector forfeits wives, lovers, and children as history progresses, until as a contemporary man, he reconnects with his lost children and finds personal satisfaction, though probably not enlightenment.

In addition to the idea of a single soul journeying through history and various lifetimes, *Being Human* takes opportunities to question metaphysical beliefs and the meaning of a person's life circumstances. When the slave Hector learns that his Roman master, Lucinnius (John Turturro), expects Hector to die with him in a suicide pact, Hector questions his master: "Do we go anywhere when we die?" Lucinnius replies, "I hope not. I just want it to stop, just stop." Hector then wonders, "If I die a slave, will I be a slave forever?" Lucinnius believes so and agrees to free Hector so his soul won't be enslaved for eternity. In subsequent lives, Hector is not a slave but rather seems to progress upward in economic power, becoming a slave owner himself in one lifetime. The film also comments on the hypocrisy of medieval Christian dogma, which denies the position of reincarnation that the film seems to support. A priest (Vincent D'Onofrio) lectures Hector and fellow travelers:

> If we cease carnal union entirely, then in fifty or so years, we'll all be rid of our earthly lives, and God can proceed with his reign over his heavenly kingdom ... that same paradise that God gave to man before, but that man was so unfit to inhabit that within seven hours, Eve was already tempting her master.

In contradiction to his lecture, this same priest later asserts that if anyone "dallies" with the attractive, young widow traveling with the group, it will be himself.

Being Human doesn't make an overt attempt to explain the concept of reincarnation but just presents its possibility. Hector's character changes as history and circumstances change, but his personality is similar in each story. He maintains the same gender and physical characteristics, even the same name, so that the continuity of his character and personality throughout history is clear. Though Hector seems to have found some peace in the last life the film presents, there is no indication that he has a desire to escape the wheel of suffering. Quite the opposite, *Being Human* presents life as a precious and satisfying challenge, with constantly shifting delights and sorrows. The only character who seems to desire escape is the slave owner Lucinnius, whose financial troubles lead him to suicide.

Film Interpretations of a Complex Concept

Little Buddha (1993), *Kundun* (1997), and *Audrey Rose* (1977) are examples of popular-film attempts to explain to American audiences the concept of reincarnation in its Eastern context.

Bernardo Bertolucci's 1993 film *Little Buddha* provides a limited history of the Buddha and the spiritual principles of Buddhism, while confronting a fictional American family with the possibility that their beloved son might "belong" to another culture and another religion.[2] The film opens with the "tale of the goat and the priest," told as a voice-over with illustrations. The priest intends to kill the goat as a sacrifice to the gods. As he raises the ritual knife to cut the goat's throat, the goat begins to laugh. The priest asks why the goat is laughing. "After 499 times dying and being reborn as a goat, I will be reborn as a human being." Then the goat begins to cry, and the priest asks him why he is now crying. "For you, poor priest. Five hundred years ago, I, too, was a priest and sacrificed goats to the gods." The lesson to be learned from the story is a basic principle in the idea of reincarnation: one must respect other lives, even the lives of animals. The fable sets the tone for the remainder of the film, which has the similar quality of an ancient fable, even in its contemporary settings.

Little Buddha follows the quest of Lama Norbu (Ruocheng Ying) and others from the Paromon Monastery in Bhutan to Seattle as they look for the reincarnated soul of their highest monk, Lama Dorje. The search will lead them to an American boy, Jesse Conrad (Alex Wiesendanger). Jesse's father (Chris Isaak) initially resists the priests and their notion that his son may be their spiritual leader. He tells Norbu, "I don't believe in reincarnation and neither does my wife." Norbu illustrates the idea of reincarnation, explaining it to Jesse's father as the relationship between container and contents. He breaks a cup of tea. "The cup is no longer a cup, but what is the tea?" The father replies, "still tea." "Exactly," Norbu explains, "in the cup, on the table, or on the floor. It moves from one container to another, but it's still tea. Even in the towel, it's still tea. The same tea."

The American family's understandable resistance to foreign ideas and foreign theology quickly gives way to acceptance and sympathy for the Buddhist religion. Jesse's mother (Bridget Fonda) says, "I like the idea of reincarnation." To which her husband replies, "Suppose you come back as an ant?" The mother isn't disturbed by the idea of life as an insect. "So what's wrong with an ant?" "You can get squished," her husband complains. "People can get squished, too," she replies, something her husband reluctantly admits is true. All creatures, large or small, are subject to misfortune and suffering.

In addition to young Jesse, Lama Norbu's search discovers two other possibilities for the reincarnation of his spiritual leader: a boy from Katmandu and a Indian girl. All three children return with Norbu to Bhutan where they undergo tests to determine who is the true reincarnation. The priests believe the child carrying the reincarnated soul will recognize objects from his past life. As it turns out, the soul of Lama Dorje has been reincarnated into three separate children, a rare event, but one, the film tells us, that can happen, especially when the teacher has much work to do. With this development, the film is consistent with the Buddhist theory that the essence of a dying person "might influence more than one fetal organism at a time," which helps keep the idea of reincarnation in harmony with the increasing population (Becker 19).

The movie weaves the search for the soul of Lama Dorje with the spiritual journey of Prince Siddhartha (Keanu Reeves) from the bliss of ignorance as a pampered prince to enlightenment as the Buddha. Lama Norbu begins narrating Siddhartha's story to the children, which becomes dramatically presented flashbacks to Siddhartha's life. Scenes show how Siddhartha escapes his father's palace one day only to be shocked by the sight of old, sick men. He learns that age, infirmity, and death are the fate of all humankind. Looking for a way to save the world from sickness and death, Siddhartha leaves the luxury of riches and the comforts of family to follow a band of ascetics, but he soon learns that the path to enlightenment is the "middle way." Even the middle path is not without temptations, as Mara, Lord of Darkness (Anupam Shyam), sends his daughters and other visions to confuse Siddhartha. In his confrontations with Mara, Siddhartha learns to look beyond form: "Lord of my own ego, you are pure illusion. You do not exist." Siddhartha's task is to lift the curse of reincarnation and bring enlightenment to others.

Like *Little Buddha*, Martin Scorsese's *Kundun* also opens with a legend: Centuries ago, a baby was born in Tibet, but robbers came to the child's home, and his family had to run away to save their lives. When the family returned, they found the infant they had left behind was still alive, guarded by a pair of black crows. He was then given the name "Kundun," which means "the Presence." This film differs from *Little Buddha* in that it is a dramatic account of the fourteenth Dalai Lama, a child chosen to come back to life to love all living things, to care for them, and to have compassion for them. The movie presents the faith that the child born to a rural family in 1935 is the reincarnation of a spiritual leader who died four years before. While the blessed destiny for an enlightened soul with all karma erased is nirvana, an advanced soul, a bodhisattva, might choose to delay nirvana in order to help other souls (Becker 48–50). This is the case with the Dalai Lama, who is believed to be the incarnation of Avalokitesvara, the bodhisattva of compassion. As with Jesse in *Little Buddha*, the authenticity of the reincarnation must be tested. Because the bodhisattva who chooses rebirth retains the memory of past lives, the boy should be able to select from a collection of objects those that had belonged to his former incarnation. The film shows how the Dalai Lama is found and tested but also presents the predicament of a young boy expected to have the wisdom collected from many lives as a great teacher, while his people and his faith come under the attack of a hostile enemy.

Audrey Rose is another example of a film attempting to explain the idea of reincarnation to Western audiences, even bringing in the character of an Indian guru and segments with documentary-like footage designed to be instructive. However, like many films featuring reincarnation as a theme, *Audrey Rose* gives the concept a definite Western spin. The film is most often classified as a horror film, though it doesn't have the typical sequence of brutal deaths or gory special effects that were already requisites for most horror movies when the film was made. The movie does open with a fatal car accident but quickly shifts to the happy home life of a New York family: Janice (Marsha Mason), Bill (John Beck), and their young daughter Ivy (Susan Swift). Ivy has been troubled with bad dreams. Janice is worried about her daughter, but more worried about a mysterious man (Anthony Hopkins) who appears to be stalking her family and taking a special interest in Ivy. Finally, the man introduces himself as Elliot Hoover, the father of a young girl killed in a car accident on the very day Ivy was born. He claims that Ivy is his own daughter reincarnated: "I could recognize all the subtle qualities that once belonged to Audrey Rose."

Like Jesse's father in *Little Buddha*, Bill is at once appalled by the idea that his child might also be someone else's child. His reaction becomes even more negative as the movie progresses. Elliot is no Tibetan monk, so Bill is certain his family has been set upon by a psychotic or an extortionist. He will not accept the possibility of reincarnation, even when events seem to suggest it as a potential explanation for Ivy's nightmares and strange behavior. Bill tells his wife:

> When I die, it's going to be the end of me. No wings, no harps, no pitchforks, nothing. It's done. It's the end. It's finished. I don't see myself floating around some maternity ward waiting to sneak into the body of some poor unsuspecting infant. I think he'd resent it.

Ivy, too, resists the idea of reincarnation, telling her mother, "I'm my own self, not somebody else."

The most horrific action elements in the film come in Ivy's nightmares, when she remembers her past life as Audrey Rose and relives her final, painful moments in a burning car. As the nightmares turn more violent, Elliot becomes concerned that the intrusion of Ivy's past life as Audrey may prove fatal to her. He desperately tries to sway Janice, a Catholic, to consider the possibility of reincarnation, telling her about his own spiritual quest in India, where he became a believer: "Life is one act in a vast cosmic drama. . . . Our bodies die, our aged vessels crack, releasing the ensnared soul yet again on its vast journey homeward through many lifetimes, many lifetimes." Janice seems to concede the possibility of reincarnation, but her husband Bill will never be won over. Attempting to help Ivy through an especially intense nightmare, Elliot takes the girl to his own apartment, but Bill has him arrested for kidnapping. At his trial, Elliot's defense is that he was only taking care of his own child reincarnated as Ivy. This is in direct conflict with the idea of the biological parent's rights and "ownership" of a child. The defense calls an Indian guru, Maharishi Gupta Pradesh, to explain the concept to the jury:

> Reincarnation inspires us to love all people, for in the course of our numerous rebirths, we have been parents, children, friend to one another. . . . Death is not the end to life but a momentary separation. . . . As a man casts off worn out garments and takes new ones, so the soul casts off old bodies and enters into ones that are new.[3]

In an unprecedented move, the judge allows the prosecution to introduce hypnotic regression as a method of proving that Ivy cannot be Audrey Rose. The session won't have a happy outcome.

Though at times the film seems sympathetic to the idea of reincarnation, the principal message seems to be that a past life can traumatize and extinguish a current one. This film reveals some particular problems with the idea of reincarnation for Americans: the possibility of compounded suffering from multiple lives, and the knowledge that your family does not truly belong to you. It also questions the idea of self to which most Americans cling. Ivy insists to her mother that she is not somebody else, yet the film tells us she is: a little girl named Audrey Rose and perhaps other "selves" as well. There is no indication in the film that a bad karma causes Ivy's misery. Audrey Rose is reborn into an equivalent, upper-middle-class circumstance. Here, the horror comes in the memory of those last moments for Audrey, when she was painfully burning to death in a wrecked car. Buddhist thought suggests that the focus of consciousness at the moment of death will have particular importance for the nature of rebirth (Becker 69). However, the implication is that these thoughts have more to do with the situation for rebirth than with memories tormenting a soul in its new life, as interpreted by the film. If Ivy is suffering because of bad deeds committed in a past life, the movie doesn't reveal this. Finally, the movie acknowledges the growing popularity of the practice of psychotherapy in the 1970s. One of the New Age treatments for mental or emotional disorders was regression therapy, which undertakes to solve a patient's problems by revealing their root causes in the wounds of childhood and even further back, in the traumas of past lives. By the time this film was released, hypnotic regression had become a controversial therapy for treating psychiatric patients as well as a method for acknowledging the possibility of reincarnation.

Hypnotic regression is not the preferred research methodology for investigating past lives, though movies may make it seem so. Real-life researchers involved in this type of study prefer to investigate cases in which young children seem to spontaneously remember another identity. They interview the child and family members about these past-life memories and then see if things the child remembers can be corroborated.[4] In addition to memories, some researchers consider birthmarks, mannerisms, and phobias connected to the manner of death in a previous life as potential evidence for claims of reincarnation. Considered authoritative evidence for these cases is "xenoglossy," which is when subjects spontaneously speak in languages they do not currently know or have not studied but supposedly spoke in a past life. Studies investigating the claims of children to remember previous lives have given the concept of reincarnation credibility for some. It was hypnotic regression, however, that caught the public imagination. The apparent ability of one housewife to recall details, elements of language, and specific customs from a past life under hypnotic regression helped to make the Bridey Murphy case one of the most compelling.

Bridey Murphy and Hypnotic Regression

Reincarnation and hypnotic regression became familiar concepts in America when Morey Bernstein's book and a narrative film based on it, both titled *The Search for Bridey Murphy* (1956), sparked a national interest in the idea of past lives and the methodology of hypnotic regression as a way to expose those lives. (See fig. 6.1.) Both the book and the film are predicated on the real case of a Colorado housewife who claimed to remember her past life as Bridey Murphy, an eighteenth-century Irish woman. In 1952, Bernstein began experimenting with hypnotic regression on Virginia Burns Tighe (called "Ruth Simmons" in both the book and the film). Under hypnosis, Tighe remembered previous lives, including a short life as the infant daughter of John and Vera Jamieson (Bernstein 118–19) and her death as the elderly Bridey Murphy. The book reports that Tighe claimed not to have gone to purgatory but to have remained like a ghost for a short while in her house. She also claimed to have stayed for a time in the spirit world, a place she liked, though it wasn't better than life on earth: "It wasn't full enough. It wasn't . . . just . . . couldn't do all the things . . . couldn't accomplish anything and . . . couldn't talk to anybody very long. They'd go away . . . didn't stay very long" (123). In the film, Louis Hayward plays Bernstein, who uses hypnosis to guide Ruth Simmons (Teresa Wright) into a trance and then—through hypnotic regression—back to her former life. Reconnected with the memory of her life as Bridey Murphy, Simmons begins to speak and sing in a thick brogue, telling detailed stories about her life in Ireland.

Following *The Search for Bridey Murphy*, media producers became intrigued by the ideas of reincarnation and hypnotic regression as a means of uncovering those former lives. Several movies would explore both themes. In *The Undead* (1957), a woman regresses mentally and physically under the influence of hypnosis, to the point that she slips time and can alter history in her past life. Another hypnotic regression has a therapist learning that his fiancée is the reincarnation of an Aztec maiden in *The Aztec Mummy* (1957). In *Hold That Hypnotist* (1957), hypnotic regression takes a man back to the seventeenth century and an encounter with Blackbeard, the pirate. In *Face of the Screaming Werewolf* (1964), a hypnotist (Ramón Gay) learns that Ann Taylor (Rosa Arenas) is the reincar-

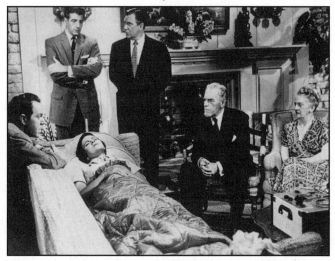

Fig. 6.1. Under hypnotic regression, an American housewife (Teresa Wright) reveals a prior life as a nineteenth-century Irish lady who lived in Belfast in *The Search for Bridey Murphy* (1956). Paramount Pictures. Photo provided by Larry Edmunds Collection.

nation of an Aztec woman. She leads researchers to the mummified remains of a werewolf, who is then resuscitated, to the misfortune of all. *Attack of the Mayan Mummy* (1964) is a very similar story with the same characters, showing how hypnotic regression leads to past lives and horrific finds. Hypnotic regression experiments also go astray in *I Was a Teenage Werewolf* (1957), this time causing atavistic reversions in a teenage boy.[5] In ridicule of the popularity of reincarnation, some entertainments continued to push the concept to even more ridiculous extremes. For example, the NBC sitcom *My Mother the Car* (1965–66) toyed with the idea of reincarnation of a human soul into an inanimate object, in this case, the soul of a man's dead mother into his classic 1928 Porter automobile.

Some narratives of the period paired the idea of reincarnation with evolution. On an elementary level, both concepts seem to deal with progress over time. In the case of evolution, it is the "survival of the fit" that causes the physical adaptations as a species develops from generation to generation. In the case of reincarnation, it is the "survival," or evolution, of the soul as it adapts to the various conditions of karma from one life to the next. However, in the Eastern sense, the more "fit" soul would depart the cycle rather than survive to suffer. Mixing the idea of evolution with the ideas of reincarnation and hypnotic regression, some producers wondered whether hypnosis might take souls back to memories of lives as creatures that are now extinct. The blend of these concepts created humorous and horrific stories. For example, in *The She Creature* (1956), hypnotist Dr. Carlo Lombardi (Chester Morris) causes his assistant (Marla English) to regress to the form of a prehistoric monster. In the remake, *Creature of Destruction* (1967), another hypnotist, Dr. John Basso (Les Tremayne), also causes his assistant, Doreena (Pat Delaney), to transform into the prehistoric sea monster she was in a past life. A film produced by Ed Wood, *The Bride and the Beast* (1958), suggests that if a past life could be that of an animal, then the memory of a past life as a gorilla might make a young woman prefer the amorous advances of another gorilla over those of her husband.

Hypnotic regression was also the key to discovering reincarnation in the musical *On a Clear Day You Can See Forever* (1970). Dr. Marc Chabot (Yves Montand) is a professor of psychiatry at a private medical school. When Daisy Gamble (Barbra Streisand) wants him to use hypnosis to cure her smoking addiction, he inadvertently regresses her to a former life. Daisy turns out to be an exceptional subject for Dr. Chabot. Not only is she easily hypnotized, she has psychic abilities that allow her to locate lost objects and predict when the phone will ring. Dr. Chabot becomes fascinated by Daisy and the character she becomes under hypnosis. When the local press reports his controversial research, Dr. Chabot's colleagues at the medical school want him to deny that reincarnation is the explanation for his findings. The president of the college, Dr. Mason Hume (Bob Newhart), declares, "reincarnation is appalling. It kills ambition, perpetuates human misery, and propagates false hopes. . . . And is obviously a pack of lies." However, when a rich beneficiary wants to fund research on reincarnation, Dr. Hume becomes more open-minded. The movie ends with the suggestion that the guarantee of rebirth is not a punishment, but a reward. The love Dr. Chabot feels for Daisy Gamble will be realized in a future life.

The Horrors of Past Lives

Though the idea of reincarnation may be reinterpreted by Western culture as a way of clinging to self and identity, producers were quick to see the horrific potential of a recycled soul, putting a Hollywood spin on the idea of life as suffering. Like the horror of *Audrey Rose*, the neo-noir film *Dead Again* (1991) shows the negative impact of past lives on present ones, though its explanations about reincarnation come from an interpretation that makes no attempt to correctly portray Eastern philosophy. The film follows detective Mike Church (Kenneth Branagh) as he tries to assist a mysterious woman (Emma Thompson) to recover her memory. On the pretext of trying to help them, a dishonest hypnotist (Derek Jacobi) tells the woman to "picture yourself walking down a flight of stairs . . . to a door. . . . Just beyond the door is a time or place you'll wish to visit." When regression therapy reveals events from 1948 rather than the woman's current identity, Church goes to see a disbarred psychiatrist, Dr. Cozy Carlisle (Robin Williams), for advice. Carlisle explains that he has also used regression therapy with patients and found that they sometimes remembered past lives under hypnosis. He tells Church, "Sometimes a trauma in a present life can lead you back to a trauma in a past life. . . . You take what you learn in this life, and you use it in the next. That's karma." Church replies, "I thought karma was, I do something bad in this life and I'm a termite in the next." Carlisle doesn't consider karma to be the influences that determine the situation in which a soul will be reborn. According to him, karma becomes a cosmic cycle of outrage and retribution, the "karmic credit plan" through which souls are yoked together, continuing to interact from lifetime to lifetime. "You burn someone in this life, they get to burn you in the next. . . . Buy now, pay forever." Hypnotic regression reveals that Church and the woman with amnesia are psychically connected, the reincarnated victim and suspect in a murder that happened more than forty years before.

An earlier film, *Déjà Vu* (1985), provides another illustration of psychic outrage and retribution as a troubled soul repeats tragedy, like a damaged vinyl record repeating the same musical phrase in a persisting cycle. Writer Greg Thomas (Nigel Terry) attends the screening of an old dance film with his girlfriend, Maggie (Jaclyn Smith), and becomes obsessed with the prima ballerina, Brooke Ashley (also played by Jaclyn Smith). As the couple leave the theater, Greg remarks on the uncanny resemblance between Maggie and Brooke. Later, he discovers that Brooke died in 1935 in a mysterious fire that killed her mother, Eleanor Harvey (Claire Bloom), as well as her lover and choreographer, Michael Richardson (also played by Nigel Terry). He decides to write a screenplay that will feature Brooke as the central character. In the process of conducting his research, he uncovers a spiritualist, Olga Nabocov (Shelley Winters), who had been a close friend and adviser to Brooke. Olga tells him, "there was a strong spiritual side to Brooke's nature. . . . Her dreams were very vivid and left her with a strange sense of foreboding." She begins to suspect that Greg is really the reincarnation of Brooke's lover. Using hypnotic regression, Olga helps him recover memories of his life as Michael and his love affair with Brooke. When Greg tries to explain his experiences to Maggie, she tells him about the prominent American medium Edgar Cayce as a way of interpreting and legitimizing the events. The reference to Cayce slows the action of the film but links the plot to a celebrated American spiritualist.[6] Like *Dead Again*, this film also suggests that the same souls continue to interact from lifetime to lifetime, and the same forces of jealousy and vengeance resume in each incarnation. This film literally supports Dr. Carlisle's observation that "you burn someone in this life, they get to burn you in the next." *Déjà Vu* does offer the hope that love cruelly thwarted in one life may have a chance for success in another.

Several horror movies play out variations on this idea of irrevocably connected souls, allowing a nefarious predator to stalk its victims throughout eternity. One variant on this theme is the plot of an undying monster who thinks a beautiful young woman is the reincarnation of a lost love. What usually sparks this sentiment is the uncanny likeness between the young woman and the monster's former lover, many centuries deceased. Films with this plot reflect the belief among some Africans, such as the Yoruba, that physical similarities within a family from one generation to the next result from the spirit of an ancestor returning to enter the body of a newly born child. In the movies, it is this physical resemblance that causes a monster to recognize and menace a reincarnated lover. This idea became central to the plot of such films as *The Mummy* (1932); the remake more than twenty years later, *The Mummy* (1959); *Fright* (1956); *Curse of the Faceless Man* (1958); the vampire film *Bram Stoker's Dracula* (1992); and a film about an evil sorcerer, *Seduced by Evil* (1994), discussed in chapter 4. The plot of *Bram Stoker's Dracula* provides an illustration. The story begins with the tragic love of Vlad the Impaler (Gary Oldman) and his wife, Elisabeta (Winona Ryder). When Elisabeta hears the false report that Vlad has been killed in the Crusades, she commits suicide, jumping off a parapet of the castle. Upon returning from the Crusades and learning about his wife's death, Vlad curses God, vowing to wait for the return of his love. He seems certain that Elisabeta will be reincarnated; in the meantime, he accepts the eternal life offered by vampirism and waits for her rebirth. Centuries later, when Jonathan Harker (Keanu Reeves) comes to his castle, Vlad Dracula notices that a photograph of the man's fiancée, Mina Murray, is the exact image of his beloved wife Elisabeta. He realizes that Mina must be Elisabeta's reincarnation.

Another aspect of reincarnation exploited by horror films is the notion that the world can never be safe from the truly evil soul. Like every other soul (except for the ones blessed enough to find nirvana), the evil soul recycles, looking for an appropriate vessel through which to continue its offensive work. Often, in the Hollywood interpretation, the evil soul is strong enough to choose its physical destiny, to escape the burden of karma and be reborn into privileged life circumstances. Evil souls in horror films never seem to return as gnats, but as creatures with the power and opportunity to hurt others. For example, in *The Awakening* (1980), an American archaeologist, Matthew Corbeck (Charlton Heston), is in Egypt with his pregnant wife (Jill Townsend) searching for the long-lost tomb of an Egyptian queen. At the same moment he discovers and opens the cursed tomb of Queen Kara, his wife gives birth to a baby girl. The malevolent soul of the Egyptian queen is released from the tomb and becomes reincarnated in the body of the Corbecks' daughter (Stephanie Zimbalist). In another example of how the evil soul is reborn, *Demonsoul* (1994) portrays hypnotic regression therapy being used to reveal that a woman (Kerry Norton) was a vampire in a past life, though the vampire can only take control when her current reincarnation is in a state of hypnotic trance.

Fluke and the Dilemma of Karma

The idea of karma arises from a human longing to believe that we live in a just universe. It provides a cosmic explanation for why some people are born to comfort and others are born to sorrow. If this life seems unfair, it is due to the bad karma of a prior one. In film and television narratives, the role of karma may be more implied than directly discussed. The cosmic law of karma doesn't always apply in horror movies, where some evil characters seem exempt from the justice of karma and must be put down by the film's hero.

The movie *Fluke* (1995) provides an appreciably American illustration of the concept of karma. As the fable of the "priest and the goat" from *Little Buddha* explains, the soul of a person who commits an offense may be reborn in a lower life form or in more disagreeable circumstances. In *Fluke*, greed and ambition cause a man to move down the hierarchy of life conditions in order to learn some hard lessons. The film begins with a voice-over asking audiences to listen with an open mind, "forgetting for a moment what you believe and don't believe." The film tells the story of a hardworking businessman, Thomas Johnson (Matthew Modine), who dies in an auto accident during a sinister race down a rain-soaked highway. The car flips off the road, and Thomas dies. His soul travels down a corridor of pulsing red lights, and he is reborn as a mongrel puppy. A homeless woman, Bella (Collin Wilcox Paxton), befriends the puppy and names him Fluke. When Bella dies, Fluke is befriended by another homeless soul, Rumbo (Samuel L. Jackson), an older dog who teaches him how to score free meals from restaurants and dodge the dogcatchers. Fluke begins to have dreams of his prior life and asks Rumbo if he was always a dog. We learn that Rumbo's special friendship with the owner of a restaurant that feeds the dogs is due in part to a relationship with this man in a previous life.

When Fluke gets caught and sold for animal testing in a laboratory, Rumbo comes to the rescue. Rumbo manages to free all the animals in the lab but is shot and killed in the process. After Rumbo dies, Fluke's memories of his previous life as a husband and father become clearer, driving him to return to his old hometown and to wait outside a school for his son, Brian (Max Pomeranc). When his wife, Carol (Nancy Travis), comes to pick up her son at school, naturally enough, she doesn't recognize the soul of her husband in the body of a dog. Her reaction to the large, grimy animal is to drive away, leaving Fluke to follow the car to his old home. But he is persistent and pathetic, first appealing to Brian and finally winning Carol's sympathy. They eventually adopt him.

As a dog, Fluke can spend "quality time" with his family, realizing that he neglected them while he was a man. His life as a dog might be blissful, but his vivid memories of life as Thomas Johnson intrude. Fluke believes his former business partner, Jeff Newman (Eric Stoltz), is a ruthless man, responsible for his death. He believes he must protect his family from this villain. When Jeff, who is attracted to Carol, comes to the house to take her on a date, Fluke attacks him. But Fluke's reincarnation wasn't meant to make him into the family guard dog. His memories must fully return for him to realize that his own behavior is responsible for his current life position. "I didn't know how to live life as a man, and I don't know how to live as a dog. . . . Life is to be cherished in all forms." Of course, the lessons of Fluke's past life are most useful when he can recall the complete memory. Only then is he able to understand the lessons of karma, in this case, how to arrange the priorities of life and how to behave toward the people who love him. Like most Americans, Fluke cherishes memories as a prime part of the distinctive stuff of self. Reincarnation without memory is like being an Alzheimer's patient, living in the current moment, incapable of planning for the future from an understanding of the past, perhaps not even able to recognize the people one loves or recall favorite times together; perhaps not even able to recognize oneself.

At the movie's end, we learn that Rumbo has been reincarnated as a squirrel. If good deeds influenced Rumbo's karma, audiences must conclude that his life circumstances as a squirrel are an improvement over those as a dog. An alternate interpretation suggests that Rumbo's heroic rescue—

though well-intentioned—interfered with the ability of the animals in the testing lab to suffer and atone for some horrendous deeds of a past life. This would justify Rumbo's death and rebirth in a lower life form. Yet another interpretation of the film hints that human life, with its self-awareness and problems of ego, may not be the pinnacle of the cosmic hierarchy. It's interesting that the animals in this film retain such distinct memories of prior lives, abilities that should be the province of a bodhisattva.

Another example of lowered life circumstances as punishment for wickedness occurs in the children's television series *100 Deeds for Eddie McDowd* (1999–2002). The premise of the series involves a malicious kid, Eddie McDowd (Seth Green and Jason Hervey), who must be taught a lesson about how to treat others. Eddie doesn't literally die and become reincarnated but instead is cursed with a magical transformation: his soul is trapped in the body of a dog. Like the priest suffering 499 lives as a goat in order to be reincarnated as a human, Eddie has to perform a hundred good deeds as a dog in order to return to human form. He finds himself in the animal shelter, where he is adopted and befriended by a young boy he once bullied. Although his penitence is presented as a hundred deeds rather than a hundred lives, Eddie knows what it means to suffer the "bad karma" from being a bully. With the knowledge of each deed, he has some idea about his progress, unlike the soul without memory or knowledge of its place on the cosmic hierarchy or the lifetimes it must endure before nirvana.

An earlier film, *You Never Can Tell* (1951), suggests that animals that bring shame upon themselves are reincarnated, returned to earth not as humans, not as animals, but as "humanimals," and must "expiate their sins." Humanimals have the bodies of humans but the souls of animals. The film presents a segregated afterlife. The soul of a good dog will advance to the "beastatory," a heaven for animals governed by a ghostly lion spirit. Here, the spirit of a dog named King asks to be returned to earth in order to solve his own murder and protect his faithful trustee, Ellen Hathaway (Peggy Dow). The lion spirit grants King's request, and the dog's soul is reincarnated as private investigator Rex Shepard (Dick Powell). As the humanimal Shepard, King retains the memory of his past life as a dog, unlike other humanimals, who have no such awareness of a former existence. Like a good police dog, he sniffs out the murderer, who is also plotting to steal the inheritance an eccentric millionaire had willed to King. After he solves the murder case, he discovers that his beloved Ellen is also a humanimal and decides to remain on earth with her rather than return to the beastatory. Because life on earth is not segregated in the manner of the film's afterlife, that raises the possibility of a human soul falling in love with a humanimal. Though the film is a comedy sympathetic to the innocent and simpleminded humanimals, it also gives expression to the idea that burgeoning violence, stupidity, or lack of civility in humankind might be taken as evidence of an ever-increasing number of animal souls becoming reincarnated in human bodies.

In a similar vein, *Oh, Heavenly Dog!* (1980) tells the story of Browning (Chevy Chase), a private investigator who meets an untimely death while investigating a case. Because his character was neither truly good nor truly bad, divine judgment, in the Christian sense, can't be rendered. Browning is given one last assignment to determine his soul's fate. He is returned to earth as a dog to solve his own murder and possibly rescue his soul.

Though the idea of reincarnation seems to teach respect for all creatures, karma can suggest that the suffering of the poor and diseased is the deserved punishment for wickedness in a prior life. Perhaps the bodies of animals carry souls that merit punishment. As Paul Edwards notes in the book *Reincarnation: A Critical Examination*, the concept of karma can provide a backhanded justification for such wrongs as caste systems, slavery, and other inequities, which become not human inventions but divine punishments. However, Edwards notes that some interpretations of karma suggest that it is not something "administered" by God, or if it is, the full impact of God's justice may never be understood by observing the apparent inequities of life (35–47). This criticism of karma does not appear in movie narratives, which cater more to a human need to see evil punished and goodness rewarded. In the movies, guilt is generally obvious, punishment deserved, and the two directly connected.

The Processing of Souls

Though only minimally suggesting the idea of reincarnation, the horror film *The Seventh Sign* (1988) does provide quite a bit of discourse on the intermediate states of the soul. In a mix of philosophies, the film presents the idea of a finite number of disembodied souls contained in an ethereal place but also suggests that an old soul can be recycled and given a second chance to do the righteous thing.

As the movie opens, the first of the seven signs that foreshadow the end of the world are in progress. Abby Quinn (Demi Moore), a young American woman in yet another difficult pregnancy, begins to suspect that odd occurrences happening around the world are really signs of the Apocalypse. She also has flashes of her prior life in Roman times. A mysterious man, David Banner (Jürgen Prochnow), is the ancient-languages expert renting the room over her garage. Making polite yet ominous dinner conversation, Banner relates a Hebrew story about God's mansion in heaven and a particular room, called the "Guf," or hall of souls, where spirits wait to be born into bodies. He tells Abby that when the last soul is used and the Guf is empty, the world will end. The first baby born without a soul will be the seventh and final sign of God's wrath. Abby becomes fearful that the baby she carries is intended to be that last sign. As her visions of a prior life become stronger, Abby learns that she was present at Christ's crucifixion and recognizes that David is really Christ come back to earth. She also learns that Father Lucci (Peter Friedman) is really the Roman soldier cursed by God to live forever with "no escape from the misery of life." In that prior life, Abby had been offered the opportunity to die for Christ but had refused. Given a second chance, Abby makes the sacrifice and by doing so refills the Guf with souls, "saving the world." A more Eastern spin on the story might suggest that rather than save the world, Abby only condemned souls to the misery of physical life.

The comedy *Chances Are* (1989) uses the idea of reincarnation as a key element. The film presents the intermediate state between death and rebirth as a wait in a bureaucratic processing station, where angels in suits reassign the soul to a new body and then inoculate it with a serum of forgetfulness. Corinne Jeffries (Cybill Shepherd) starts out happily married and pregnant but is then widowed on her first anniversary. She is so in love with her husband, Louie (Christopher McDonald), that she won't remarry but raises her daughter Miranda (Mary Stuart Masterson) alone. At the heavenly processing station, Louie cuts in line, demanding to be returned to life immediately. He is reincarnated as Alex Finch (Robert Downey Jr.), but angels neglect to give him his inoculation. Alex does manage to forget his former life as Louie, until twenty years later in college when destiny brings Alex and Louie's daughter together. When Miranda invites Alex home to meet her mom, he begins to remember his former life as Louie and realizes that he is attracted to his own daughter. The movie tells us that from lifetime to lifetime, we keep meeting the souls we are attracted to: "You never know who is lurking in what body." This movie also suggests that when it comes to the spiritual self, there really is no such thing as incest. An earlier film, *The Reincarnation of Peter Proud* (1975), raises the problem of psychic incest as one for serious moral concern.

Since the concept of reincarnation relies on a dualism that considers the soul to be independent from the body, producers have tinkered with the idea that a soul wouldn't need to be recycled into that of a newborn but could enter any body, even a vintage body that has been vacated or one that is currently in use by another soul. This idea of the metempsychosis of the soul would get rehashed repeatedly in narrative plots.

The romantic comedy *Heaven Can Wait* (1978) is a remake of an earlier film, *Here Comes Mr. Jordan* (1941), both dealing with a bureaucratic mix-up in the afterlife that allows a soul to be temporarily replaced in another adult body. The afterlives in both films are similar to the one presented in *Chances Are*: a vaporous place where souls wait to be sorted and reprocessed. Not wishing the man to suffer when he is hit by a car, an angel whisks pro quarterback Joe Pendleton (Warren Beatty) to this heavenly reprocessing center prematurely in *Heaven Can Wait*. But this was not Pendleton's destiny; he was supposed to lead his team to a win in the Superbowl. Because he wasn't supposed to die, and because his body has already been cremated, angels temporarily reassign Pendleton's soul to the body of a millionaire, Leo Farnsworth (also Beatty), recently murdered by his wife and her accountant lover. As Farnsworth, Pendleton buys his old team and trains to become their quarterback again. He also enhances Farnsworth's reputation by donating to charities and doing other good works. His selflessness wins the heart of Betty Logan (Julie Christie), an activist who had been prepared to dislike the millionaire. When Farnsworth is murdered a second time, Pendleton is reassigned to the body of a teammate, Tom Jarrett (Beatty again), the moment that player is killed by an especially ferocious tackle. With this last switch, Pendleton loses the memories of his prior lives. However, Betty is still able to recognize the spirit of her lover in the body of another man. In the original version, *Here Comes Mr. Jordan*, Joe Pendleton (Robert Montgomery) is a boxer also given a new life as a millionaire due to a divine mistake.

In another version of the same story, *Down to Earth* (2001), Chris Rock plays Lance Barton, a talented but failed comedian, who gets booed off the famous Apollo Theater stage. Like Joe Pendleton, Lance is ushered to heaven too soon, when a truck runs over him. This heaven is an exclusive nightclub, where souls wait in line to be admitted to eternal dancing in a misty discotheque. The manager of the club, Mr. King (Chazz Palminteri), says of his heaven, "It's happening, baby. The food is great, the women are beautiful, the music is hot.... The fun never stops." But Lance is determined to be a successful comedian on earth, and Mr. King agrees to arrange for this. Lance returns to life in the body of a middle-aged, white millionaire, Charles Wellington (Brian Rhodes). Lance finds it difficult to perform black comedy in a white man's body and even more difficult to woo Sontee Jenkins (Regina King), an activist determined to save a community hospital from Wellington's corporate machine. Like

Joe Pendleton as Leo Farnsworth, Lance impresses the woman he loves by being generous with Wellington's money and performing charitable works. When Wellington is murdered a second time, Lance's soul has a less temporary stay in the body of another African American comedian, Joe Guy (Chris Rock again). Lance is ecstatic to be young and black again, even if it means being poor. This time, King tells Lance he will "become" Joe Guy, without retaining the memories of Lance Barton. Lance complains that King is taking away his soul. King tells him, "Lance, I can't take your soul. Nobody can do that. Where you're from, what you look like . . . that's just clothing. The funny thing about reincarnation, kid, even when you're not you, you're still you." Like many reincarnation comedies, this one reminds audiences to respect all people regardless of race or status and to appreciate the conditions (even the miseries) into which we are born. Finally, the comedy reiterates the sweet myth that true love will find its "soul mate," regardless of the body it possesses.

Transmigrations and Filmic Body-Swapping

The romantic comedy *All of Me* (1984) provides another expression of the idea of transmigration, in which a soul with personality and identity intact moves from one body to another. Like *Here Comes Mr. Jordan*, *Heaven Can Wait*, and *Down to Earth*, souls aren't reborn into infant bodies but exercise a psychic trade of adult bodies. In *All of Me*, a dying millionaire intends to have her soul transferred into the body of a younger, willing woman in order to live the life of health and happiness that had been denied to her. Lawyer Roger Cobb (Steve Martin) visits the bedridden millionaire, Edwina Cutwater (Lilly Tomlin), in order to write her will. Edwina wishes to leave her inheritance to Terry Hoskins (Victoria Tennent), her stableman's daughter. She explains to Roger that upon her death, her Hindu guru, Prahka Lasa (Richard Libertini), will remove her soul and transfer it into Terry's body. She tells Roger, "If my wealth can't help me in this life, then, by god, it's going to buy me a new one."

Terry seems complacent, explaining to Roger, "my soul will leave my body forever and become one with the universe." The lawyer believes the ritual is a scam to swindle a sick and desperate woman out of her fortune. However, Prahka Lasa—described and presented in the film as a "cosmic weirdo"—successfully catches Edwina's soul as her body dies, accommodating her soul temporarily in a sacred bowl. Rather than move into Terry's body, Edwina's soul is then transferred into Roger, when the sacred bowl is accidentally dropped out the window and onto Roger's head. Roger regains consciousness and finds Edwina's spirit sharing his body. A fight for physical control ensues. The two souls eventually agree to a truce, working together to find Edwina's soul a more satisfying fit inside Terry's body. A prime obstacle is that Terry, now heir to Edwina's riches, has no intention of relinquishing her own body or her newfound fortune. With complex slapstick, Edwina's soul transmigrates to a variety of vessels before finding its destined home in Terry's body. Terry's soul ends up in the body of a horse, a lower life circumstance befitting Terry's criminal nature. No mention is made of the horse's soul, though audiences might imagine it has become "one with the universe" or transmigrated elsewhere.

Prelude to a Kiss (1992) is one of several films that portray the transmigration of souls in a body swap that doesn't involve a character's death. On her wedding day, Rita (Meg Ryan) is kissed by an elderly wedding guest (Sydney Walker), and they swap souls: Rita, because she is pessimistic about life and wonders what it would be like on the finishing end of it; and the elderly man, because he is terminally ill with a failing liver and would like the chance to experience life healthy again, "from the other side of the bed." The movie implies that any soul that wants to transmigrate bad enough can do so if there is another soul willing to make the swap. Caught in the middle of this exchange is the bridegroom, Peter (Alec Baldwin), who recognizes and loves his wife in spite of the fact that her soul is trapped in the decrepit body of a dying man. A reversal becomes possible when the elderly man decides that "the idea of living forever—it's not so good," and Rita discovers how precious life and love can be. Other films that present the idea of souls leaping from body to body include *Summer Switch* (1986), *Vice Versa* (1988), *Freaky Friday* (1995), and *Like Father, Like Son* (1987). In addition to providing fish-out-of-water comedy, such plots allow characters to swap perspectives in order to become less egocentric, to learn to respect the troubles of others, or to better appreciate qualities of their own lives that had been taken for granted.

Not all stories of transmigration are comedies. For example, in *The Mephisto Waltz* (1971), Myles Clarkson (Alan Alda) is a classical piano player with a brilliant career. He befriends another pianist, not knowing that the dying man plans to have their souls switch places at his death, allowing the evil pianist to live on in the younger man's body. Similarly, in *Blood from the Mummy's Tomb* (1971), the spirit of an ancient Egyptian queen (Valeria Leon) transmigrates into the body of a young woman, the daughter of an archaeologist, who had the audacity to tamper with her tomb. Stories like these more clearly connect the idea of transmigration to possession.

The television series *Quantum Leap* (1989–93) illustrates transmigration from episode to episode when scientist Sam Beckett (Scott Bacula) tests his theory of time travel with his own invention. During the experiment, his accelerator goes out of control, causing him to travel forward and backward in time but also to leap from body to body and from life to life. This causes Beckett to experience the troubles of many different characters, and he helps them to solve their problems, though his constant wish is to repair the accelerator and return to his own life. Unlike souls reborn to a new life, characters who swap bodies usually return to their own bodies before the film is over. Beckett provides the exception, transmigrating continually from body to body, season after season, and is still transmigrating in syndicated reruns.

In media stories where characters must die for transmigration to occur, the moment of death seems critical. For example, the "Lazarus" episode from the first season of the television series *The X-Files* (1993–2002) suggests that an FBI agent and a criminal—both critically wounded in a shoot-out—have swapped bodies. During the near-death experience of FBI Agent Jack Willis (Christopher Allport), a dying criminal, Warren James Dupree (Jason Schombing), is able to take possession of the agent's body when his own body expires. The motivating force behind Dupree's psychic transference to the FBI agent's body is a fierce love for his girlfriend and partner in crime. Agent Fox Mulder (David Duchovny) suspects that a psychic transference has occurred, but there is also the possibility that it is a psychological rather than a paranormal possession. We learn that Agent Willis had pursued the criminal pair for nearly a year and had admitted his envy of the couple's self-absorbed union, a turbulent love affair in which criminal violence became an aphrodisiac. However, the final events of the episode support Mulder's explanation.

A Mediated Philosophy of Reincarnation

As with stories of magic and witchcraft and narratives about atavistic transformations, media present the idea of reincarnation in a variety of ways, from the ridiculous (*My Mother the Car*; *The Bride and the Beast*; *You Never Can Tell*) to the serious (*Little Buddha*; *Siddhartha* [1972]; *Kundun*). The manner in which narratives express the concept is varied as well. Sometimes reincarnation comes mixed in narratives along with Judeo-Christian lore about heaven and hell (*The Seventh Sign*; *Here Comes Mr. Jordan*; *Heaven Can Wait*; *Down to Earth*; *Chances Are*; *Oh, Heavenly Dog!*). Many media narratives feature hypnotic regression as the tool that validates reincarnation (*The Search for Bridey Murphy*; *On a Clear Day*

You Can See Forever; *Audrey Rose*; *Dead Again*). The tendency for the concept to be used to supply the suspense in thriller and horror films or to be exploited for humor in comedies indicates some resistance to the more difficult questions reincarnation presents, as well as perhaps some opposition to it. Regardless of genre, the media narratives tend to support the idea of an unsophisticated dualism, a separation of soul and body that insists the human soul survives its cadaver and can influence its own spiritual destiny.

Though the concept might be trivialized, Western narratives frequently show reincarnation as an idea with advantages. Sometimes there is choice and purpose in the transmigration. Souls can return to earth for another chance, to seek retribution for some wrong, to complete work left undone, to reconnect with loved ones. Rather than submit that rebirth is the miserable lot in a "wheel of suffering" that the soul should desire to escape, media narratives suggest that life is precious, and even its sorrows are to be valued for the lessons they teach and the diversions they bring. For most American audiences, life may not be miserable enough to desire a permanent escape. Buddhist teachings indicate that suffering is not only due to the material and physical conditions of life but comes from the ego's self-awareness, the illusion of difference between self and others. However, that distinction of self is an unquestionable value for Americans, one that can be seen reflected over and over again in American media. The American ideal is not to merge with the oneness, the mass, but to rise above it. To be chosen on *American Idol*, revered above all others; to come out of nowhere and be recognized for greatness, rather than join the oblivious mass in a cosmic oneness.[7] On the other hand, if death is inevitable, the idea of a fresh, new body can be made palatable. As Maharishi Gupta Pradesh, the Indian guru in *Audrey Rose*, suggests, the old body is cast off like a garment, a fashion out of date. This reduces the physical body to a disposable commodity, a concept that seems in tune with the American lifestyle.

Films and television programs do seem to suggest there is a permanent core of the individual human personality, a unique soul that repossesses life with each new birth or body swap. This is something Lance Barton (*Down to Earth*) needs to know when he relinquishes his memory; he will be himself regardless of the circumstances or stories in which karma places him. However, clear distinctions between mind and soul are not always expressed in media narratives, with some narratives suggesting that one is a critical aspect of the other.

The context of viewing film and television narratives may be more powerful than the stories themselves for providing a naive understanding and perhaps acceptance of reincarnation. The media-viewing situation becomes a paradigm for dualism, framing the concept as a natural one. As discussed in chapter 2, audiences are familiar with the experience of emotional disembodiment while watching film or television, being emotionally in one environment while physically in another. Media use for many Americans is a varied succession of vicarious experiences. Disappointing stories might be followed by more satisfying ones, just as unfulfilled longings of this life might be satisfied in the next one. Unlike real life, which often seems unfair, media stories generally support a sense of cosmic justice. Characters tend to get what they deserve. Karma works.

Perhaps one of the things that most makes reincarnation appealing in film and television presentations is the problem producers have of conceiving and creating an afterlife that would seem perpetually desirable or satisfying. Cloudy bureaucracies, beastatories, Gufs, and heavenly discotheques would certainly seem dreary for an eternity. Media stories tell us that the really interesting stuff is happening on earth among physical bodies with material substance. This is where the intrigues are, where conflicts happen, where challenges are met and overcome. Given the option between heaven and reincarnation, Joe Pendleton (*Heaven Can Wait*), Edwina Cutwater (*All of Me*), Louie Jeffries (*Chances Are*), and Rex Shepard (*You Never Can Tell*) choose a physical life with all its unique travails and disappointments over anonymous bliss. If conflict is the essence of drama, nirvana wouldn't make for gripping film or television. Finally, media stories suggest that the problems of life are where human beings can apply their creativity, which may be what brings us closest to God.

Filmography: Recycled Souls

Not a comprehensive list of all relevant media on this topic, this list is intended as a reference for those media that inform the discussion in this chapter.

All of Me. Dir. Carl Reiner. Universal Pictures, 1984.
Attack of the Mayan Mummy. Dir. Rafael Portillo and Jerry Warren. Rhino Video, 1964.
Audrey Rose. Dir. Robert Wise. MGM, 1977.
Awakening, The. Dir. Mike Newell. Orion Pictures, Warner Brothers, 1980.
Aztec Mummy, The. Dir. Rafael Portillo. Azteca Films, 1957.
Being Human. Dir. Bill Forsyth. Warner Brothers, 1994.
Blood from the Mummy's Tomb. Dir. Seth Holt. Hammer Films and American International Pictures, 1971.
Bram Stoker's Dracula (aka *Dracula*). Dir. Francis Ford Coppola. Columbia Pictures, 1992.
Bride and the Beast, The. Dir. Adrian Weiss. Allied Artists Pictures, 1958.

Chances Are. Dir. Emile Ardolino. TriStar Pictures, 1989.

Cleo/Leo. Dir. Chuck Vincent. New World Pictures, 1989.

Creature of Destruction. Dir. Larry Buchanan. American-International Television, 1967.

Curse of the Faceless Man. Dir. Edward L. Cahn. United Artists, 1958.

Dead Again. Dir. Kenneth Branagh. Paramount Pictures, 1991.

Déjà Vu. Dir. Anthony B. Richmond. MGM, 1985.

Demonsoul. Dir. Elisar Cabrera. Vista Street Entertainment, 1994.

Down to Earth. Dir. Chris Weitz and Paul Weitz. Paramount Pictures, 2001.

Dying to Remember. TV movie. Dir. Arthur Allan Seidelman. Paramount Home Video, 1993.

Fluke. Dir. Carlo Carlei. MGM, 1995.

Freaky Friday. Dir. Gary Nelson. Buena Vista Pictures, 1976.

Freaky Friday. TV movie. Dir. Melanie Mayron. Walt Disney Television, 1995.

Fright (aka *Spell of the Hypnotist*). Dir. W. Lee Wilder. Budd Rogers Releasing and Sinister Cinema, 1956.

Heaven Can Wait. Dir. Warren Beatty and Buck Henry. Paramount Pictures, 1978.

Here Comes Mr. Jordan. Dir. Alexander Hall. Columbia Pictures, 1941.

Hold That Hypnotist. Dir. Autin Jewel. Allied Artist Pictures, 1957.

Ice Angel. TV movie. Dir. George Erschbamer. Fox Family Channel, 2000.

I've Lived Before. Dir. Richard Bartlett. Universal Pictures, 1956.

Kundun. Dir. Martin Scorsese. Buena Vista Pictures, 1997.

Like Father, Like Son. Dir. Rod Daniel. TriStar Pictures, 1987.

Little Buddha. Dir. Bernardo Bertolucci. Miramax, 1993.

Mephisto Waltz, The. Dir. Paul Wendkos. 20th Century Fox, 1971.

Mummy, The. b&w. Dir. Karl Freund. Universal Pictures, 1932.

Mummy, The. Dir. Terence Fisher. Hammer Films and Universal International Pictures, 1959.

Mummy Returns, The. Dir. Stephen Sommers. MCA, Universal Pictures, 2001.

Mummy's Ghost, The. b&w. Dir. Reginald Le Borg. Universal Pictures, 1944.

My Blood Runs Cold. Dir. William Conrad. Warner Brothers, 1965.

My Mother the Car. TV series. Dir. Rodney Amateau, David Davis, Sidney Miller, Tom Montgomery, and James Sheldon. NBC, 1965–66.

Naked Souls. Dir. Lyndon Chubbuck. Warner Vision Entertainment, 1995.

Oh, Heavenly Dog! Dir. Joe Camp. 20th Century Fox, 1980.

On a Clear Day You Can See Forever. Dir. Vincente Minnelli. Paramount Pictures, 1970.

100 Deeds for Eddie McDowd. TV series. Dir. Mitchel Katlin. Nickelodeon Network, 1999–2002.

Out on a Limb. TV series. Dir. Robert Butler. ABC, 1987.

Prelude to a Kiss. Dir. Norman René. 20th Century Fox, 1992.

Quantum Leap. TV series. Exec. prod. Donald P. Bellisario. NBC, 1989–93.

Reincarnation of Peter Proud, The. Dir. J. Lee Thompson. American International Pictures, 1975.

Return. Dir. Andrew Silver. Silver Pictures, 1986.

Search for Bridey Murphy, The. Dir. Noel Langley. Paramount Pictures, 1956.

Seventh Sign, The. Dir. Carl Schultz. TriStar Pictures, 1988.

She Creature, The. Dir. Edward L. Cahn. American International Pictures, 1956.

Siddhartha. Dir. Conrad Rooks. Columbia Pictures, 1972.

Summer Switch. Dir. Ken Kwapis. Learning Corp. of America, 1986.

Switch. Dir. Blake Edwards. Warner Brothers, 1991.

Undead, The. Dir. Roger Corman. American International Pictures, 1957.

Vice Versa. Dir. Brian Gilbert. Columbia Pictures, 1988.

What Happened to Rosa? b&w, silent. Dir. Victor Schertzinger. Goldwyn Distributing, Grapevine Video, 1920.

While I Live. b&w. Dir. John Harlow. Sinister Cinema, 1947.

Wish Upon a Star. Dir. Blair Treu. Leucadia Film, Warner Brothers Home Video, 1996.

X Change. Dir. Allan Moyle. Trimark Pictures, 2000.

X-Files. TV series. Exec. prod. Chris Carter. "Lazarus" 4 Feb. 1994. Dir. David Nutter. Fox Television, 1993–2002.

You Never Can Tell. b&w. Dir. Lou Breslow. Universal International Pictures, 1951.

conclusion

Marketing the Metaphysical

Conclusion
Marketing the Metaphysical

It's a great art to know how to sell wind.
—Baltasar Gracián, *The Art of Worldly Wisdom* (1647)

*T*he process of creating media texts has become big business in America. Yet, for some producers, the process still sympathizes with the artist's desire for transformation and connection to "cult value." The producer's yearning to reconnect to the artist's ancient discourse with the divine and to the shaman's control over time, space, matter, and human action can be accommodated somewhat through the creative aspects of media production. Media artists unite their skills, sometimes forming a temporary tribe, sometimes finding personal transformation in the practice of their craft. We still tell stories—if not to influence a god, then to influence each other.

Likewise, the desire to engage in the imaginative process of media interpretation also connects media audiences to cult value. Media experiences extend human senses beyond biological limits, demonstrating how our physical self can be in one location while our emotional self travels unfettered by physical limitations. For this transformation to occur, audience members must suspend disbelief, engaging emotionally with the mediated material. When this happens, media stories can reconnect audiences to that tribal world of cosmic cycles and primordial archetypes. Mediated experiences let audiences "live" in many cultures and many time periods, "hear" many conflicting voices. When audiences involve their own imaginations in the production of meaning for the narratives they see, they experience something of the media wizard's control over story.

While the processes of production and viewing (encoding and decoding) can have cult value, the stories American media systems deliver provide audiences with an array of explanations for the human condition.

Many of these stories suggest that our physical world is not the limit of human existence. Though it appears that American movie and television stories frequently reject skeptical interpretations and ask audiences to accept paranormal readings for events within narratives, the discourse is not one-sided. Overt and serious expressions of skepticism may not predominate, but they do exist in popular media. Though television does air series featuring psychics such as John Edward and James Van Praagh to serve as intermediaries between the deceased and their living families and friends,[1] elsewhere on television, audiences can hear skeptical comments and scientific explanations from debunkers. For example, a segment on ABC's *Primetime Live* provided a demonstration of "cold reading," which showed that psychic powers are not necessary to convince gullible audiences that someone is "channeling" spirits of the dead.[2] In the segment, a man who has studied the techniques of cold reading, Ian Rowland, puts on a show similar to the psychic readings in popular television programs. Members of the volunteer audience seemed tearfully convinced that Rowland had successfully contacted deceased relatives. Rowland later explained that his technique of cold reading consists of carefully crafted questions and alert attention to audience reactions, but not contact with the dead. Even with this disclaimer following the demonstration, participants seemed reluctant to give up the belief that communication might be channeled from beyond.

As discussed in chapter 4, dramas and documentaries about historical and dubious witches maintain a skeptical position regarding the accused witches' supernatural abilities. A classic Hollywood plotline involves human fraud as the explanation for supernatural events. The skeptical view may get additional support from comedies with overblown portrayals of the paranormal that make the likelihood of the supernatural seem ridiculous. Weak production values, poor special effects, and bad aesthetics combine to help demystify the "occult" process of media production as well as any paranormal subject matter they may present.

Media documentaries and narratives about the supernatural do not cause paranormal belief or disbelief in audiences. However, media use and media stories about the supernatural do oblige a human need. Through the media narrative, audience members can escape everyday tensions, lose their egos within the narrative, and yet know a rush of control. Through media use, they experience the power to travel out of their bodies to other worlds and return. Through media use, they gain ultimate power over the paranormal: they can engage it as a vicarious experience, decide what it means, deny it as a bit of trifling entertainment, or turn it off altogether.

As we've seen in previous chapters, there has been no shortage of media stories about the supernatural or occult ritual. These stories have always had a potent presence, whether we acknowledge them or not. Perhaps when it comes to the supernatural and the occult, media power may be best described as marketing and publicity. Audiences may not buy into the supernatural, but they know about it.

Media Stories and Supernatural Tourism

Like several old cities rich with folk tradition, Charleston, South Carolina, has a booming business in ghost tours. Guides takes visitors for a walk around the old parts of town to examine local sites believed to be haunted. During the stroll, the conductors of these tours will recite ghostly stories of haunted inns, Gullah superstitions, and assorted other stories about spooks and voodoo from Charleston's exuberant folklore. The prime validating force behind the ghost walk in a number of cities, including Charleston, is that some of the supernatural stories have been featured in books, newspaper accounts, and—most important—on television programs. The implication is that if programs on the Learning Channel, the History Channel, the Travel Channel, USA Today, or Home and Garden Television (HGTV) feature these stories, they must be important, intriguing, perhaps even true. The authenticating energy of these media is something publicized on the many brochures and discount coupons offered to tourists. For example, one Charleston brochure proudly declares of its tour, "seen on CNN."

Paranormal tourism is a relatively new industry that has learned to capitalize on the defects of history rather than attempt to hide them. A location is no longer marred by its past tragedies, nor is there any need to gag the inevitable folklore associated with dire stories, if they can draw in curious and paying customers. A haunted hotel becomes enhanced by the presence of its ghosts; apparitions and poltergeists become publicity features. The phenomenon is so widespread that travel guides and web pages that list hotels, restaurants, bed-and-breakfasts, gardens, and other tourist attractions across the country will advertise their reputation for being haunted when they are lucky enough to have one.[3] For example, the reportedly haunted Winchester Mansion, built with the fortune from the Winchester repeating rifle, has been featured on such television programs as Fox Family Channel's *Scariest Places on Earth* (2001–), the History Channel's *Haunted History* (1999–2000), Arts and Entertainment's *America's Castles* (2001), and the Discovery Channel's *America's Haunted Houses* (2002) and was even the "mystery house" on HGTV's *Dream Builders*

(2001). Also reported to be the inspiration for Stephen King's television miniseries *Rose Red* (2002),[4] the Winchester Mansion is now a popular tourist attraction, serving as an example of media breederism, a feature of news and infotainment media in which a "top story" claims the attention of multiple media outlets and concentrated public attention.[5] That negotiating synergy among folklore, media marketing, and individuals attempting to apply occult knowledge creates a dynamic that can be playful as well as serious.

The Ghost Walk

On March 15, 2001, I chose to experience "Dr. Harry Spectre's Ghost and Voodoo Walk," a tour that advertised the use of an electromagnetic-field (EMF) detector, or "ghost finder."[6] According to our guide, this was "the very same equipment used by professional paranormal investigators." The idea is that ghosts disturb electromagnetic fields, and the EMF scanner will pick up the disruptions, providing a reading of how strong the ghostly presence is in a particular location.[7] The brochure for the tour states that this is "Charleston's only Ghost Walking Tour where each party is equipped with the GhostFinder. The same electro-magnetic field detector used by professional paranormal investigators. . . . So if you're serious about ghosts . . . who ya gonna call?"—an obvious reference to the comedy film *Ghost Busters* (1984). The brochure was a clue that association with popular television and film narratives had become an important aspect in both the marketing and interpretation of Charleston folklore. (See fig. 7.1.) I was surprised by the degree to which movies and television would play a role in what I previously imagined would be an adventure in oral storytelling. On the spring night that I made the circuit with Dr. Harry Spectre's Ghost and Voodoo Walk, the streets were particularly thick with tour groups. Each tour had a special feature, such as candlelight, historical costumes, or—in the case of my group—EMF detectors. As we passed one of the "Candlelight Tours" guided by a picturesque young woman wearing a long hooded cape and holding an antique lantern, our guide said quite contemptuously, "They have lanterns, *we* have EMF detectors."

As with several of the Charleston ghost tours, "Dr. Spectre" attributes some of the stops on his route to stories found in the books *Charleston Ghosts* and *Doctor to the Dead*.[8] However, these books were only briefly mentioned. Our tour guide's more frequent references were not to books but to popular films and television programs. The brochure for this particular tour even featured a quote from the movie *Poltergeist* (1982): "There

Fig. 7.1. Ghost walk brochures. Photo by E. D. Edwards.

is no death. It is only a transition to a different sphere of consciousness." The character of a tiny psychic healer and clairvoyant, Tangina (Zelda Rubinstein), presents this philosophy. Our guide compared several of his Charleston folklore stories to this film about the trials of a family haunted by unfriendly spirits that use the television as a portal between spheres. One story in particular, about a parking deck built over a forgotten Quaker cemetery, allegedly haunted by the spirits of those buried underneath, drew extensive comparisons to *Poltergeist*. Like the haunted subdivision in the movie, this parking deck, we were told, had "disturbed the dead and profaned their sacred resting place."

Part of our guide's explanation for why certain places seemed especially haunted involved a soul's attachment to a particular, familiar location or to the spiritual energy of the living people who remained in those locations—an opinion also reflected in *Poltergeist*. The character Tangina tells the haunted family that their kidnapped daughter, Carol Anne,

> is a living presence in their [ghosts'] spiritual, earthbound plane. They're attracted to the one thing about her that's different. . . . Her life-force . . . is strong. It gives off its own illumination. It is a light that implies life and memory of love and earthly pleasures, something they desperately desire but can't have anymore.

This idea likely heightened the haunted experience for tourists. They might imagine themselves as ghost magnets, guided into places where spirits are supposed to linger, waiting to cling to the magnetic strength of curious tourists like supernatural metal shavings.

In addition to the multiple references to *Poltergeist*, our guide felt compelled to mention a number of films with ghostly characters, including *Ghost Story* (1981), *Ghost* (1990), and *Sixth Sense* (1999).[9] He invoked *Ghost Story* to explain how a haunting might result from the ghost's desire for revenge. He used *Ghost* to explain how a spirit might become earthbound to protect a loved one. And he applied *Sixth Sense* as a familiar example of how a spirit might be confused about its own status. Interestingly, most of the people on our particular tour had seen all the movies our host referenced. It's possible our guide had observed from experience that these films were a unifying element for his guests. People who sign up for a ghost tour are apt to have seen popular movies with ghostly themes.

Sometimes the relationship between the movie illustrations and the folk stories our guide told seemed a bit thin. For example, he mentioned *Midnight in the Garden of Good and Evil* (1997) as a way of imagining how "witch doctors or conjure doctors" call on the spirits of the dead to influence the course of events. We stood in a dark alley near King Street while our guide told us the "Legend of Crook-Neck Dick." The conjure man in the Charleston folklore was "Dr." Jack Warren, who used his magic to save a man named "Rumpetty Dick Middleton" from hanging for the crime of murder. Dick was not an innocent man who deserved to be saved. He had committed a number of heinous crimes, including murder. However, Dick's evident guilt would not stop the conjure doctor from helping him. The night before the hanging, Dr. Jack asked the spirits to make it rain. The spirits obliged. Rain swelled the wood of the scaffold so that on the sheriff's first attempt to hang the man, the trap stuck. When the sheriff made a second effort to hang Dick, the lever jammed. Finally, the sheriff's men busted the trap loose and managed to hang the condemned man. The rope and fall broke Dick's neck, but the killer didn't die. The sheriff decided that even though Dick lived, the law had been satisfied with his hanging and set the man free. Dr. Jack's magic had saved him, allowing Dick "to walk away from his deserved punishment." The connection between saving a man from hanging and pouring a libation over a dead man's grave (the pivotal action of the conjure woman in *Midnight in the Garden of Good and Evil*) seems tenuous, but our guide appeared to think that a movie based on a famous Savannah trial helped to explain or enhance the considerably older Charleston folklore. My own memory of the movie plot bears slim comparison to our guide's descriptions of Charleston voodoo. The conjure woman Minerva (Irma P. Hall) is not the central figure in the film but one of many idiosyncratic characters. However, our guide seemed convinced that both the film and the folklore confirmed that voodoo was a "force to be reckoned with," and most of his guests appeared to agree.

"Dr. Spectre" also expressed—or at least assumed for the purposes of the tour—a firm belief that when spirits become earthbound, they can be discerned by devices such as film and video cameras, audio recordings, and—of course—EMF detectors. Technology can reveal the truth even when the human eye or ear perceives nothing. Part of our host's declaration was undoubtedly meant to impress upon his visitors the technological advantages of Harry Spectre's tour over its competitors. The young man appeared to have considerable faith in photography as well as EMF detectors. At one Charleston cemetery, he encouraged the group to take pictures of the graves, because "someone in the group will probably snap a picture of a ghost." He claimed that his guests had sent him photographs of this haunted cemetery that contained mysterious blurs, foggy blotches, and other unexplained imagery. He suggested that these and other anomalies on the photographs were likely due to the presence of restless spirits. I took several photographs around the cemetery, the church, and the surrounding area but spotted no anomalies on my developed film. (See fig. 7.2.) If there had been, there are explanations other than ghosts for many of these. One of the most popular is the errant finger or camera strap that strays in front of the lens to create a ghostly abnormality on the photograph.

The last stop on our Charleston tour was a house that had been converted into a popular restaurant in 1976. Named for the loyal dog that sat on its porch, Poogan's Porch is as famous for the ghost of the little dog as it is for its regional low-country cuisine. The seafood restaurant was originally an old Charleston home, the residence of an elderly woman, Zoe St. Amand, whose ghost is also supposed to have a presence in the building. According to our guide, customers and staff have seen her apparition with some frequency for years. He proudly reported to us that the house had been one of the haunted places featured on an HGTV special, *The Ghostly Homes of Charleston* (2000).[10] If that wasn't authentication enough, this house was the one place on the tour where we were guaranteed to get a reading on our EMF detectors because it was so actively haunted. We were directed to hold our EMF detectors along an outside wall under a window. As predicted, needles bounced. Everyone got a reading.

Fig. 7.2. Cemetery in Charleston, South Carolina. Light passing through branches and objects out of focus in the foreground might account for the interpretation of ghostly images in such pictures.
Photo by E. D. Edwards.

Media "Marketing" and Mutual Pretense

Paranormal tourism entangles media narratives and folklore accounts with packaged commercial experiences like the ghost walk.[11] For the planned commercial ghost tour, media narratives serve as indirect marketing as well as a means of interpretation for oral legends. More direct marketing occurs in the publicity from news, documentary, and "reality

TV" accounts. Having been referenced on CNN or featured in an HGTV segment of *Haunted Houses* (2000–) or *Real Scary Stories* (2000–) can make a particular location seem like an exceptionally desirable stop. This media connection doesn't change the story associated with a haunted location—doesn't make a particular legend scarier or more dramatic—but it does add an interest to the folklore beyond its naturally compelling story elements. This is similar to the concept of advertising's "added value," a feature of media marketing that gives a product or service additional merit for reasons not inherent in that item or application but due solely to media notoriety. Added value suggests that media promotion bestows new and desired qualities on a product that might otherwise not be as prized by the public. With folklore as a "product," publicity becomes a validating force, notifying tourists of which stories are significant. Tourists can go home and tell their friends about a visit to the haunted house featured on a television program or in a newspaper, magazine, or book. Media narratives with themes similar to local legends can serve an interpretative role where the folklore has not evolved to the stage of providing clear-cut meanings or moral lessons for audiences.

For the tourists on Dr. Harry Spectre's Ghost and Voodoo Walk, media narratives brought an added dimension of "play" by providing them with imagery as they pretended to be parapsychologists. Most people have never observed actual parapsychologists at work, but many people have seen actors assume the role for movies or have seen parapsychologists interviewed in documentaries. Both narrative and documentary depictions of parapsychologists often portray individuals equipped with infrared cameras, Geiger counters, EMF detectors, or digital thermal scanners to check for hot or cold spots, and other mysterious technology. The psychic advisers in narrative films, such as *The Entity* (1981), *Poltergeists* (1982), *Ghost Busters* (1984), and *The House That Screamed* (2001), and ghost hunters in documentaries like *The Paranormal* (1997) and in segments of television series, such as the SciFi Channel's *Sightings* (1991–97) and Fox Family Channel's *Real Scary Stories* and *Scariest Places on Earth*, use a variety of equipment in the hunt for ghosts. With EMF detectors in hand, tourists can imagine themselves as serious ghost hunters walking the haunted streets of Charleston in search of paranormal evidence. Standing on the site of a haunted cemetery, tourists can become the lead characters in their own mental movies, a prime goal of paranormal tourism. At this interpersonal level, even the determined skeptic might engage in a polite game of mutual pretense because—like the movies—the ghost walk is just for fun.

When media engage our imagination, a film or video may make us laugh, cry, think—may even lead us to believe. But as Alfred Korzybski observed, "the map is not the territory." Watching a video of a Jamaican spirit doctor dancing in the center of a circle of worshipers to rhythm of pounding drums is not the same as being in the circle or dancing ourselves. Watching might increase our heart rate or rivet our attention to the colorful scene. Our muscles might even twitch in response to the dancer's movements. Though mediated experience can engage the imagination and even be transformative, it cannot completely substitute for the transformation of the physical experience. Just seeing a video won't let us feel the heat of the Haitian night. We won't smell the burning charcoal and the fragrance of breadfruit mingled with the sharp odor of human bodies. By simply watching, we can't know the uncertain terror and fascination of being there. Mediated experience leaves some things out and alters others.

Because mediated experience is so unsatisfactory in this sense, performances in the magical tradition have revived for many contemporary people the pleasures (and terrors) of personal transformation. Tired of more passive, spectator roles in both orthodox religions and mediated re-creations, some individuals yearn to be an active player, the valued member of a tribe. With some of the more hands-on rituals offered by New Age and neopagan movements, individuals can actively participate in their own emotional transformation. Practices such as channeling, astral projection, crystal healing, drumming, keening, smudging, and dancing engage all the senses. An awakened craving for transformation produces an exploitable market for spiritual experiences outside orthodox religious establishments, an "exotification" and appropriation of sacred knowledge (Schechner).

A mechanism that helps ordinary, middle-class Americans breach logical convention and participate in activities like ghost walks and neopagan rituals is "the drama of mutual pretense," a social ritual engaged within the interpersonal context of face-to-face interaction. This is a ritual in which participants agree—if not to believe—at least to *pretend* to believe in a consensual fiction (Glaser and Straus). Participants engaging in mutual pretense create a drama in which everyone consents to play a serious role. All parties act properly to maintain the illusion. The prime example Glaser and Straus give is the instance in a hospital setting when both patient and staff know the patient is dying but pretend otherwise. The rationale for the pretense is that the patient, family, friends, and nursing staff all function better when shielded by the fiction that the patient will recover. This mutual pretense can help family members avoid overwhelming grief and protects hospital staff from raw emotional scenes. It is a dramatic exercise that can shield people from bleak realities and graceless moments. The necessity for this ritual also illustrates the tension that Americans have with the notion of dying.

A more playful example of mutual pretense occurs in the meetings of the Society for Creative Anachronisms (SCA), where members develop new names, new personal narratives, and new customs and wear costumes inventively adapted from their understanding of a historical period. During meetings, all members agree to become these characters and respond to one another according to the rules of this fictional culture, addressing one another as if they truly were the characters they pretend to be. SCA members can live within this fiction for a weekend, an entire week, or longer.

Mutual pretense can also function well in interpersonal situations where courtesy demands that participants not challenge the social fiction or embarrass other parties. To challenge the guide of a ghost walk or defy neopagan rituals after having been invited to participate would be considered impolite.

Negotiated and Mediated Magic

Supernatural adventure-seeking and cursory experimentation with the occult have definite playful qualities. Interviews with a few, particularly young, neopagan witches suggest that "tourism" may be an apt description for the playful qualities and the depth of commitment of some of them to occult practices. For some people, these excursions into the occult are part of a quest for self-actualization that may eventually lead them down more serious paths. For others, the occult is a place to play. Though these subjects appear to have a sincere belief in a universe awake with spiritual purpose, they also find that dancing, drumming, and casting spells is fun. Some rituals I have been invited to observe seem to have about them the character of performance. There is also a "commercial quality" in the paraphernalia some neopagan witches use. The talismans, tarot cards, crystals, Ouija boards, and other ritual objects are souvenirs of a New Age occult now widely available in gift shops and bookstores, rather than the esoteric items secretly passed from master to acolyte. (See fig. 7.3.) This is not a criticism but an acknowledgment that the "occult device" has become a widely available, easily procurable consumer good.[12]

In the 1990s, I interviewed several people who referred to themselves as "witches," "neopagans," or "Wiccans" interchangeably.[13] One informal

Fig. 7.3. The paraphernalia of modern witches is widely available in gift shops and on Internet sites. Photo by E. D. Edwards.

gathering I attended in 1996 at a private home began with the ritual of cleansing, or "smudging." The members of the circle were not a coven that gathered regularly but acquaintances who met by chance at a spirituality conference. All of the women seemed familiar with smudging, which involved investing each person with the smoke from incense and a smudge stick made of bound herbs. These were passed around, each person smudging the person next to her in the circle with smoke. The ceremony consisted of consecrating the group, inviting the goddess to join, saying prayers, and drumming, but there were no magical incantations intended to produce a specific outcome. On some level, there was an earnestness in the ritual, but on another level, I sensed awkwardness and even glibness. Some of this was likely due to the chance and temporary formation of the meeting.[14] Members of this gathering were loosely affiliated, with no inclination to form a more solid or lasting tribal commitment. This would be a singular event.

From later interviews with different witches, I learned that these temporary, spontaneous meetings were not uncommon. Witches I met tended to float from group to group. Several of the individuals I interviewed told me that they were usually solitary witches. The "craft" was something they learned through books or developed on their own. No one I met had a family tradition of paganism. My experiences seemed to support Kelly's observation that American witches are an antiauthoritarian group, "not inclined to accept the personal authority of any guru" (139). The unwillingness of several of my subjects to join a coven or form a lasting group with a formal set of traditions may be due to the rebellious independence that supposedly characterizes the contemporary American witch. However, it may also reflect the shallow restlessness of a media-connected era. The solitary witch, like the solitary television viewer, can always change the channel at her whim. One young woman explained to me the attractions of being a lone witch:

> I don't want to belong to a coven. I like variety. I can go where I want ... where the spirits guide me ... whenever I feel like it. I don't want someone else to tell me how to behave or what to believe. I can find my own way and my own rituals. I can write my own Book of Shadows.[15]

The solitary witch who does want direction or an example to follow can look to the media for a high priestess. While some witches scorn the publicity-seeking "media witches," others will use books written by these witches and their appearances on television programs for guidance. The young coven-scorning witch I interviewed admitted that she actively sought out and applied things she learned from books, websites, and even television. For example, a Lifetime cable channel broadcast of the series *Unsolved Mysteries* featured a segment on Laurie Cabot, known as the "Official Witch of Salem," one of several celebrity witches who have their own books and websites. The segment described Cabot as an ordained high priestess descended from Celtic ancestry. She is a middle-aged woman with the outward appearance of a traditional fairy-tale witch. In the *Unsolved Mysteries* segment, she uses her psychic abilities to help Salem police capture a criminal. She tells police the criminal is attempting to disguise himself by shaving his beard and mustache and then performs a binding spell on a straw doll to slow the man's escape.[16] The police were later successful in apprehending the man. The program suggests that Cabot's spell caused the criminal to idle needlessly at a deserted house rather than continue with his getaway. My solitary witch adapted her own version of a binding ritual after watching this segment.

Though there is still secrecy in the practice of neopagan witchcraft, one coven I observed was trying to create a more public presence. This group gathered for a very public weekly meeting at a local bookstore in Greensboro, North Carolina, though their ritual observances were held in another, undisclosed location. The "high priestess" of the group explained to me that the public meeting was necessary "to show the community that we are good people, ordinary people, and not people to be afraid of." The group seemed young, mostly in their twenties, with nearly as many men as women. The weekly meetings consisted of sharing personal stories, listening to a brief lecture, discussing craft fundamentals, and organizing charitable giving efforts. At one meeting I observed, the group was raising money to help feed and buy winter coats for an impoverished Native American tribe. The high priestess explained the similarities between the coven and the tribe they wanted to sponsor. This included a shared belief in the pervasive "nature of consciousness that connects all life." I briefly interviewed the high priestess about her perceptions of media narratives depicting witchcraft. She claimed to have very little interest in the popular-culture discourse about witchcraft, but her general assessment was that film and television portraits were too negative, too glitzy, and too unrealistic.

Other witches I interviewed were more optimistic about dramatic narratives in film and television, endorsing *The Craft* (1996), *The Mists of Avalon* (2001), and *Chocolat* (2001) as films that provided more reasonable portraits of witchcraft. Television series like *Sabrina* and *Charmed* drew complaints for being "unrealistic" and "silly." Film and television portraits of satanic witches drew complaints for being "obscene," "malicious," and "defamatory." However, one witch told me he enjoyed watching any movies or television programs about witches and magic, even negative depictions. He liked seeing magic work in a blunt or exaggerated way, which it often does in the movies:

> I think skeptics are terrified of the idea that some people might have real magical power. It's not that the skeptics are so smart and logical. They're afraid to believe. Magic makes the world unpredictable. They think that's horrible, unscientific. I think it's great. The world *is* unpredictable. I love it in the movies when the skeptics realize they're not so smart after all.

None of the witches I met would acknowledge media as the agents that led them to their current beliefs and practices. Some expressed dissatisfaction with the religion they were raised in as too political, too secular, and more interested in how people behaved rather than in what they felt.[17] Some believed neopaganism returned esteem and power to nature and to individuals. For others, witchcraft was more democratic, respecting men and women equally. The men and women I interviewed were explicit about the differences between the "Wicca way" and the satanism that appears in media stories. As one witch said:

We put emphasis on personal growth and healing, on our mystical and psychic experiences, the feminine in the divine, and our spiritual appreciation of nature. This is not what the movies tell you about us. We appreciate the sacramental aspects of sexuality. In the movies, sex is not sacred. It's pornography. It's satanic and nasty.

Like the high priestess of the public coven, this solitary witch expressed a disdain for popular media portraits of witchcraft, particularly portraits of the satanic witch. The *Blair Witch Project* (1999) ranked at the top of her list of hated movies.[18] She complained that this film was yet another in a long list of negative portraits of the witch. She worried that a production style that mimics the documentary makes it seem that there really was a historical character named Elly Kedward behind the ritual murder of young children. "The real demons of this world are all man-made," this young witch insisted, and then added, "just like the movies."

Media Appropriation of Folk Narratives

In the introduction to *British Folk Tales*, Katharine Briggs complains bitterly about the ways media appropriate and reconfigure folk stories to fit requisites of mass production and distribution:

> Folklore is being invaded and captured by the mass media for commercialization. True traditions are coarsened and falsified. This is not the legitimate, spontaneous growth which we find in stories handed down from father to son or in customs that alter as they are practiced, it is ignorant and willful debasement for the sake of money. This danger is particularly present in America and England. (3)

I would argue that this appropriation and accommodation of oral narratives is not the offense of film and television producers alone but very likely what troubadours and storytellers did long before the arrival of mass media: select the most compelling narratives and then adapt the stories to what they thought people would be intrigued to hear and happy to generously reward. I believe the more serious complaint with popular media has to do with their power to reach large audiences, to escape time and space, and to have considerable potency, even authority, in the telling. Preserved on paper, Charles Perrault's and the Brothers Grimm's versions of fairy tales continue while oral versions fade. Preserved on film and broadcast on television, Disney versions of *Cinderella* or *Snow White* become the visual definitions of these fairy stories for multiple generations in communities across the globe. Unlike the ancestors' oral versions, the media producer's version of a story will not evolve. It might get a remake, it might be reedited or colorized, but once it is fixed in a medium and kept without tampering, it can be revisited for generations.

Media adaptations of personal narratives and local stories bypass their development through generations of folklore. Re-created as film and television dramas, oral narratives lose their ragged uncertainty. Personal, intense experience becomes replaced with recognizable types and structured stories. Even the oral narratives preserved by the documentary may be modified in dramatic and structural directions by the presence of a camera and the interviewees' knowledge that their personal accounts may leave the local neighborhood to become part of the select domain of television.[19]

Because media can give their versions an authenticating power, it's easy for audiences to forget that media adaptations are simply new voices telling old stories with a more intense marketplace sensitivity. Unlike the local raconteur's kitchen-table account, the media producer's version has the potential to produce considerable income. Financially successful versions incite other producers to consider new variations of familiar plots or create new mythologies associated with the old themes. This is another criticism of mediated folklore. Not only do media adapt old stories, they create new "occult lore" or odd amalgams of old wisdom. Sometimes the fabricated "media lore" lays false claims to ancient foundations. The Ouija board offers an illustration.

First introduced to the American public in the late 1800s as a parlor game, the Ouija board quickly became a tool used by occult groups for divination and spiritualism. The game consists of a board printed with "yes," "no," numerals, and letters of the alphabet. There is also a pointing device, sometimes called a "planchette." Players put their fingers on the planchette and ask the board a question. If all goes right, the planchette will then move across the board. Supposedly guided by the force of a spirit, the planchette will point to or spell out answers to questions. Some people who seriously work the Ouija board for spirit communication believe the device has a mysterious history that dates back to ancient Greece.

Film and television narratives often support the notion that an effective tool for divination must have an ancient, esoteric history. For example, in *Witchboard* (1985), Brandon Sinclair (Stephen Nichols) explains that the Ouija board "has been around since recorded history. It was in wide use as far back as 540 BC." He later provides instructions for the board's use:

> For the best results, the Ouija board should be used by two people, preferably a man and a woman. . . . It shouldn't be sitting on a table. It should sit on our knees, so there's as much body contact as possible. Also, the two

people should have clean, pure systems, so that the energy flowing through the planchette is as strong as it might be.

Brandon concludes by telling his friends that "spirits are lousy spellers and a lot of them like to lie." After another character, Linda (Tawny Kitaen), unwisely uses the board alone, deadly poltergeist activity invades the house, and she becomes addicted to the Ouija board in a type of progressive entrapment that leads to possession. Referencing *The Exorcist* (1973), Linda's boyfriend (Todd Allen) quips, "So what you're telling me is that I'm living with Linda Blair?" The character of young Regan (Linda Blair) had also been playing with a Ouija board prior to her possession. This is just one example of a movie that self-reflexively mentions other popular movies and television programs, which is often done in a manner that initially appears to ridicule the counterfeit authority of movies and media in general. However, as is the case with *Witchboard*, many movie narratives ultimately support the supernatural expertise of the referenced film when the characters learn that the paranormal is indeed playing an active role in their misery.

Several other films and television programs, such as *Deadly Messages* (1985), *Witchboard 2* (1993), *Only You* (1994), *Witchboard 3: The Possession* (1995), *Love Games* (1998), *What Lies Beneath* (2000), and *Long Time Dead* (2002), among others, feature the Ouija board not as a harmless parlor game but as a serious occult device. For example, in an October 26, 2002, segment of the Travel Channel's *Top Ten Ghostly Getaways*, viewers learned that a Ouija board divulged the identity of a ghost haunting the Springer Opera House in Columbus, Georgia. During a seance, the Ouija board spelled out the name of an actor associated with the opera house who "lived and died for the stage." There seems to be a small segment of serious users who believe the Ouija board is a legitimate tool with which to contact spirits. A nonrandom sample of people responding to a survey about Ouija board use reveals that over 90 percent of users claim successful communication with a spirit in at least one session with the board (Palmer). Users believe the device can uncover accurate information, an idea to which media programs lend support.

Anecdotal evidence suggests that even among serious users, fundamental information about the methods for working the Ouija board initially came from popular movies and was later expanded. The "sleeper effect" in media theory suggests that over time, people may forget where they initially learned information, so that information from a source with low credibility—like a Hollywood movie—may eventually seep into the vat of acquired knowledge.[20] Though the Ouija board was developed in

America as a game, serious users believe it is not a plaything. Self-professed adepts of the Ouija board will both reference popular movies and scoff at these depictions. As one solemn user told me, "The movies get some of it right but won't show you the whole truth. . . . Because people think it's just part of the story in a horror movie, they still believe it's just a game to play at Halloween . . . and that's really scary." Serious users also appear to have developed new lore associated with the Ouija board that was not initiated through media depictions but evolved through use of the board, storytelling, and interpersonal sharing of experiences.

Among the subjects I interviewed for the documentary *Wondrous Events*, three expressed the belief that use of a Ouija board was the direct cause of a haunting or had revealed the presence of spirits. These stories, repeatedly told for friends and family, had assumed a dramatic structure with moral lessons about venturing into the taboo. For example, one subject told me that a young friend contacted the spirit of her deceased father using a Ouija board. Afterwards, the young woman's house became haunted. Doors, windows, and drawers would open and shut. Objects would mysteriously move around the house. People heard unexplained voices, footsteps, and other mystifying sounds in the house and yard. The woman believed the Ouija board had awakened the ghost of her friend's father, who was angry at not being allowed to rest in peace. The other two subjects told me that after using a Ouija board, one had experienced a deep sense of anxiety, and the other met with a chain of minor misfortunes. Unlike the relatively safe entertainment of the ghost walk, serious users consider the Ouija board to be more like an extreme sport: exotic and dangerous.

It is interesting to see the dynamic relationship between media stories and folklore. Popular media and oral narratives exist as parallel and interconnected systems of expression and statement, which mirror social meaning and value. Themes that resonate in the popular imagination are likely to be appreciated in each arena, receiving new emphasis as real-life observations and media accounts are reprised in popular culture or passed orally within a community. At each junction between narrator and public, an account receives personal, creative interpretations to reflect new concerns. Telling and shaping a narrative to fit a particular audience, both media and local raconteurs spread the subconscious anxieties and dramatic realities of American life.

The "Real" and the Mediated Occult

In its interpersonal context, events like the ghost walk or the neopagan ritual uphold a fiction many contemporary Americans may need, just as some dying patients may have an intense need to imagine that they will live. The mutual make-believe between a dying patient and staff may help create an illusion that inspires hope. In a neopagan ritual, participants agree that human beings are not limited by the physical world, by the confines of their bodies, or by the earthly laws of time and space. The ritual inspires faith and wonderment. However, each of the actors within the ritual must share the context of mutual pretense, or the drama collapses. Frequently, actors in a game of mutual pretense will comply even if they don't truly believe. Otherwise, the game is over, and where's the fun in that? If pretense becomes faith, then the transformative possibilities are fortified.

For audience transformation to occur while watching a film or video, the audience members must suspend disbelief, engaging in a ritual of mutual pretense with the mediated material. In its mediated form, mutual pretense becomes an agreement spectators makes with themselves, giving themselves permission to involve their imagination and allow mediated stories to move them toward transformation. Unlike the pretense involved in a neopagan ritual, audience members watching a fictional movie know with certainty that the mediated experience is not a real one. Yet, the feelings aroused by watching and the emotional transformation that occurs can seem very real. The audience can find empathy for mediated characters and concern for the drama. Though this relationship between mediated text and audience is more fragile than the relationship of participants involved in interpersonal mutual pretense, the audience often willingly, even eagerly, suspends disbelief, for otherwise there is no possibility of engagement, no hope of transformation. This powerful desire for transformation appears to remain constant for some people, regardless of the communication context in which that desire is expressed. The escape of the human mind may not be from boredom to titillation, as critics often characterize the motivation for media use, but from longing to the hope that the transformative experience brings.

American audiences seem as addicted to magical thinking as we are to our magical media. Both are narcotics essential for momentarily disguising bitter truths, for finding form in the anguish of an amorphous and capricious world. Both our media and our magical thinking are important ingredients in the collaborative manufacture of that master opiate: modern culture. Life is its own movie, its own episodic television show. We write our personal scripts in an improvisation that is sometimes bewildering, with events beyond our control. We cope with the absurdities, injustices, horrors, and joys, trying to make sense of them. Some of us look hopefully for the possibility of magic, some instrument to wield against the inequities of life. When life's drama is confusing or our own role is not a choice one, the media experience can help us transcend chaotic reality, enhancing it with those exquisite fictions that can bring meaning, awe, and satisfaction.

Notes

Bibliography

Index

Notes

1. Possessed and Dispossessed by Mass Media

1. Information about the British ban of the movie can be found in *Billboard* 27 Mar. 1999: 83.

2. An early concern about media effects involved the influence of mediated violence. The Payne Fund Studies examined movies over a three-year period, from 1929 to 1932. The result was a ten-volume report on the influence of movies on children by W. W. Charters in *Motion Pictures and Youth: A Summary* (New York: Macmillan, 1933). Following public pressure for some sort of restrictions, the film industry strengthened its production code and self-censorship. In 1954, Wertham voiced similar concerns about the influence of popular action-comics. Scholars quickly recognized that the problem of media influence on audiences is extremely complex. The notion of direct effects and the theory of a mass society have been attacked as simplistic. See DeFleur and Ball-Rokeach; Perry; and Lowery and DeFleur 237. For a more recent account of this concept, see James G. Webster and Patricia F. Phalen, *The Mass Audience: Rediscovering the Dominant Model* (Mahwah: Erlbaum, 1997).

3. This is frequently referred to as the "magic bullet" theory. The case most often cited in support of this view of media influence was the October 31, 1938, broadcast of *War of the Worlds*, which created a sensation because of the widespread panic it caused. See J. C. Merrill, J. Lee, and E. J. Friedlander, *Modern Mass Media* (Grand Rapids: Harper, 1990), 172–74.

4. Blatty initially developed the story as a book, *The Exorcist* (New York: Harper, 1971), before producing it as a film. The supposed authenticity of the story may be responsible for some of the power of the film. Audiences learned that the inspiration for the story was a mysterious diary kept by Father Bishop during a "real" exorcism in 1949.

5. At least two sequels were directly inspired by the 1973 film: *Exorcist II: The Heretic* (1977), and *The Exorcist III* (or *William Peter Blatty's The Exorcist III*, 1990). There have been several other films with similar themes, including *Kung Fu Exorcist* (1976), *Teenage Exorcist* (1991), and *Exorcist Master* (1993). On May 4, 1991, the ABC television documentary program *20/20* broadcast a Roman Catholic Church–approved exorcism of a little girl. In 1993, Thomas B. Allen published *Possessed: The True Story of an Exorcism* (New York: Bantam), which investigates the case on which Blatty based his story.

6. The Ouija board, first introduced to the American public in the late 1800s as a parlor game, quickly became a tool used by occult groups for divination and spiritualism.

The film *The Exorcist* reveals that twelve-year-old Regan had been playing with a Ouija board prior to her possession, talking to a presence she calls "Captain Howdy."

7. See Blatty's remarks on the Warner Brothers DVD re-release of *The Exorcist* (2000), which includes restored material and interviews with director William Friedkin, Blatty, and various actors.

8. *The Hour of Power* is Reverend Schuller's television program, first aired in 1970 and still broadcasting as of 2005. The program is produced at the Crystal Cathedral in Orange County, California.

9. Callie Khouri's remarks were part of the videotaped Writers Guild of America Conference "Words into Pictures" (Sound Images, 1999). The scene she refers to is one in which the character shoots and kills a man who attacked her friend Thelma.

10. The Pokemon phenomenon included a video game, movies, card game, television series, toys, and other merchandise. See Michele Orecklin, "Pokemon: The Cutest Obsession," *Time* 10 May 1999: 42. Some Christian critics charged that creators of the craze based Pokemon on Eastern occult religions, which could lead to dangerous obsessions.

11. In J. K. Rowling's Harry Potter series, a young wizard living with abusive relatives who are "muggles" (people not gifted in the magic arts) enrolls in the Hogwarts School of Witchcraft and Wizardry, learns magic, and confronts an evil sorcerer. The popularity of the children's fantasy trilogy caused some Christian groups to try to have the series banned in schools. See Jim Milliott, "Groups Fight Potter Banning," *Publishers Weekly* 7 Feb. 2000:10; and David Keim, "Parents Push for Wizard-Free Reading," *Christianity Today* 10 Jan. 2000: 23. The announcement that Warner Brothers would make a film based on the series created additional concern and calls to boycott the movie when it was released in 2001.

12. George Gerbner developed "cultivation theory" in response to problems of mediated violence, in particular, television violence. He argues that because television continuously shows audiences a violent world, people come to believe their neighborhoods are more violent than they actually are. See Gerbner, Gross, Morgan, and Signorelli.

13. In the television series *Glory Days* (dir. David Petrarca, Warner Brothers Television, 2002), the episode "The Devil Made Me Do It" depicts a teenage piano prodigy who claims to be possessed by a demon but is actually staging his violent outbreaks.

14. Many television series, such as *The Jerry Springer Show* (MCA Universal Television, 1991), *The Real World* (MTV, 1992), *Survivor* (CBS, 2000), and *America's Funniest Home Videos* (ABC, 1990), seemed to respond to the desire of ordinary people to be on television and the that of audiences to see the flaws of others revealed.

15. On Saturday, January 5, 2002, a Florida teenager, Charles Bishop, flew a stolen Cessna into a downtown Tampa skyscraper, killing himself in a suicide mission that echoed the hijackings by terrorists on September 11, 2001. Bishop flew his plane into the forty-two-story Bank of America building, mimicking the attacks on the World Trade Center and the Pentagon. A note found on the teen's body expressed sympathy for Osama bin Laden. See Ned Potter, "'Acted Alone' but Police Say Teen Who Crashed Plane Expressed Support for Bin Laden," *ABCnews.com*, 7 Jan. 2002, <http//www.abcnews.com>.

16. Wicca is a pagan, goddess-centered religion associated with witchcraft.

17. DeFleur and Ball-Rokeach 145–325 provides a historical overview of the ways scholars have imagined the media to influence individuals and society.

18. In 1994, Kirwan Rockefeller examined three case studies of people that revealed emotionally moving film experiences and showed how these experiences contributed

to the behavior and cognitive frameworks constructed by individuals. See "Film and Dream Imagery in Personal Mythology," *Humanistic Psychologist* 22.2 (1994): 182–202.

19. On the dilemma of the British government's 2001 census, see "The Best and Worst of Everything," *Parade* 30 Dec. 2001: 5.

2. Out of Body

1. *Captain Kangaroo*, exec. prod. Bob Calver, CBS, 1955–84.

2. When I told this story to a woman in 1998, she suggested that my child's psyche had anticipated e-mail. While I don't believe this was the case, it is interesting that a youth of the new millennium could whisk a digital letter and drawing to a contemporary children's program host.

3. The made-for-television film *Nightworld: Lost Souls* (dir. Jeff Woolnough, Fox Family, 1998) makes reference to Edison's apparatus, calling it a "Spiritual Harmonizer." It looks something like a cross between a record player and a radio but opens a frequency to the afterlife.

4. The original thinking was that such a device would allow physically handicapped individuals to fully know life, but quickly the noble intentions of the new technology become perverted by people using it for pornographic abuses and covert military operations.

5. After several years of teaching media production courses, I believe many students are attracted to the idea of media production not only because of its glamour but because they mistakenly believe their work environment will mirror their experience as audiences in archaic time. They are unprepared and sometimes overwhelmed by the tyranny of production schedules in linear time.

6. In a Gannett Foundation symposium, Morbid Curiosity and the Mass Media, April 5–6, 1984, in Knoxville, Tennessee, researcher Jack Haskins suggested the yin-yang relationship between media and social events. Not all violent or morbid themes will be avoided in times of social stress if audiences find the content to be in some way relevant. See James A. Crook, Jack B. Haskins, and Paul G. Ashdown, eds., *Morbid Curiosity and the Mass Media: Proceedings of a Symposium* (Knoxville: Gannett Foundation and the University of Tennessee, 1984).

7. For additional discussion about satanic images in the World Trade Center photos, see the Urban Legends Reference Pages, <http://www.snopes.com/rumors/wtcface.htm> (accessed 2 Oct. 2002).

8. Falwell's and Robertson's comments were made during the September 13, 2001, broadcast of the Christian Broadcast Network's *700 Club*.

9. Many news broadcasts relayed the president's comments on September 11, 2001, including an NPR news special and the CBS News special report.

10. CNN carried the press conference live on October 11, 2001, as did NBC News' "Special Report: America Strikes Back," as well as CBS and ABC.

11. The CNN program was *People in the News*, an episode titled "John Walker: American Taliban Fighter," narrated by Daryn Kagan. See Harry Stein, "How the Father Figures: Why Does the Press Ignore the Story of John Walker Lindh's Dad?" *Weekly Standard* 28 Jan. 2002: 14; and Jonah Goldberg, "Family Trouble," *National Review* 25 Jan. 2002, 28 Mar. 2002 <http://www.nationalreview.com/goldberg/goldberg012502.shtml>.

12. The quote is from a press conference given by Attorney General John Ashcroft and U.S. Attorney Paul McNulty on Tuesday, February 5, 2002, at the Justice Department in

Washington and carried live on CNN and possibly most other networks, but I saw and recorded it from CNN. I looked at moving-image media rather than transcripts, because at the time I thought it was important to also consider nonverbal messages.

13. For a discussion of miracle tickets, see the documentary *Deadheads: An American Subculture*, dir. Emily D. Edwards, Films for the Humanities, 1990.

14. The nomadic tent city that campers established at every concert site relocated in smaller groups away from the concert area in the fall of 1989, when parking lot camps were prohibited. After 1989, the tent city and its main thoroughfare, "Shake Down Street," became controlled spaces for vendors.

15. Dead TV was first produced in 1988 by Scott Wiseman and Kathleen Watkins and aired on a public-access channel in San Francisco owned by Viacom, Channel 25. I had the opportunity to speak with Wiseman several times by phone when I was finishing my documentary in 1990. He explained Dead TV as a public-access television program not affiliated with the band but developed by loyal fans. Dead Heads who attended the concerts with camcorders made videotapes of the Dead Head "scene" and sent footage back to Wiseman, Watkins, and other volunteers, who would then edit the footage into a news-magazine-style program. The show was then "bicycled," or delivered, to public-access channels in communities across the country. The Well began in 1985 as one of the early virtual communities. It became a virtual "scene" for some Dead Heads between tours of the band. On its website (<http://www.well.com>), it is self-described as a "literate watering hole for thinkers from all walks of life, be they artists, journalists, programmers, or activists."

16. This doesn't explain all of the allure of street drugs. In addition to spiritual reasons, there is also the promise of a quick-fix solution to physical and emotional problems. See Perrine 438–70.

17. Examples of critics who compare television to addiction include McIlwraith; Benjamin Lev, "Turning It Off," *NEA Today* March 1995: 27; and Marie Winn, *Unplugging the Plug-in Drug* (New York: Penguin, 1987).

18. For a discussion about Internet addiction, see Kendall Hamilton and Claudia Kalb, "They Log On, but They Can't Log Off," *Newsweek* 18 Dec. 1995: 60–62.

19. See, for example, *Up in Smoke*, dir. Lou Adler, Paramount Pictures, 1978.

20. Christopher Lloyd as "Reverend Jim" Ignatowski in "Zen and the Art of Cab Driving," *Taxi*, dir. Will Mackenzie, exec. prod. James L. Brooks, Stan Daniels, David Davis, and Ed Weinberger, ABC, 19 Mar. 1981.

3. Creating Worlds

1. For example, Peter Berger calls social life a balancing act, a fiction as contrived as any narrative. See "Society as Drama," *Drama in Life: The Uses of Communication in Society*, ed. James E. Combs and Michael W. Mansfield (New York: Hastings House, 1976), 38–45.

2. In an address to the 55th annual convention of the University Film and Video Association in Rochester, New York, July 31–August 3, 2001, the president of the International Cinematographers Guild and six-time Emmy winner George Spiro Dibie shared his insights into past and current Hollywood production practices. This included the advice Hollywood might give hopeful young producers and actors to "get a job in porno" as a way of breaking into films. During the flight of mainstream production to Canada in the 1990s, where productions were less expensive to mount because of Canadian tax rebates and cheap labor, seasoned film crews found work in pornography to pay their

bills. See Dave Chrisman, "Porn Again: Why Mainstream Film Crew Members Work on Pornography," *Los Angeles Magazine* Jan. 2000: 14.

3. Writing under the pen name of Frank Burch, Travis published a short essay about his experiences with the world of sadomasochistic film in the first issue of *Morbid Curiosity*. Travis had mentioned to me several times that he might write a full account of his years as a participant observer of the pornography subculture. However, he died on May 11, 2000, before this was possible.

4. *MOS* is a film industry term indicating that no sound was recorded on the shot. It comes from the German film directors' expression "*mit* out sound." Most film and video production textbooks provide an explanation for MOS. For example, see Wales 281.

5. *PAL* stands for "phase alternating line," a color television standard used in many countries in Europe and around the world, consisting of 625 interlaced lines and 25 frames per second. PAL was not compatible with the NTSC (National Television Systems Committee) standard used in the United States, which is 525 interlaced lines scanned at the rate of 60 fields and 30 frames per second. Dubbing the 16mm film into PAL format helped with the ruse that this sadomasochist material was foreign, exotic, and truly warped. The films were exotic and warped, but not made in Amsterdam.

6. The work was so much illusion that when a truly twisted actress wanted to actually perform masochistic stunts, her enthusiasm for self-mutilation got in the way of the production. According to Travis, it became a policy not to use individuals in the production whose pathologies too closely mirrored those of the intended audience. *Grand Guignol* refers to Le Theatre du Grand Guignol, which operated in Paris from 1897 to 1962 and was synonymous with dramas featuring grisly, bloody violence.

7. Anthony Rapp may be best known for having created the role of Mark in the Broadway production of *Rent* but has appeared in several film productions as well, including *A Beautiful Mind* (dir. Ron Howard, Universal Pictures, 2001), *Road Trip* (dir. Todd Phillips, DreamWorks, 2000), *Man of the Century* (dir. Adam Abraham, Fine Line Features, 1999), and *David Searching* (dir. Leslie L. Smith, Water Bearer Films, 1998).

8. These remarks were culled from an informal address Anthony Rapp gave to fans and students on September 6, 2001, in the Brown Theatre of the University of North Carolina at Greensboro and the next day in a personal interview in the home of Frank Donaldson in Greensboro. Notes from both interviews are in the possession of the author.

9. The idea of eternal youth and immortality through media is discussed at length in chapter 2.

10. For example, the behind-the-scenes documentary *A Passage to Middle-Earth: Making of Lord of the Rings* (prod. Todd Darling, SciFi Channel, 9 Dec. 2001) did less to reveal the secrets of production and more to impress future audiences with the Herculean task of preproduction planning, design, and special effects that went into the making of the film based on the J. R. R. Tolkien book.

11. I should comment here that "realism" can vary across time and cultures, so that films accepted as credible and convincing portraits of the world for some audiences may seem contrived and stylized to others.

12. This time-out policy might sound like it would make for an inefficient production; however, we never fell behind and on some days were actually ahead of schedule.

13. Principal photography is that period when all the primary image and sound material is acquired for a film or video project. This is when the movie is actually shot, as opposed to preproduction planning and postproduction assembly and editing.

14. Andy Cadiff directed episodes of the *Geena Davis Show* (ABC, 2000–2001), *The Norm Show* (ABC, 1999–2001), *The Hughleys* (ABC, 1998–2002), *Teen Angel* (ABC, 1997–98), *Home Improvement* (ABC, 1991–99), *Spin City* (ABC, 1996–2002), and *Quantum Leap* (NBC, 1989–93), among others, as well as the movie *Leave It to Beaver* (1997).

15. I conducted a variety of interviews with film and television producers and directors who requested that they remain anonymous. These included a diversity of types from studio-connected professionals, to independent producers, to college faculty members who teach film and video production courses as well as produce narrative and documentary projects. All the college faculty producers were members of the University Film and Video Association and were interviewed August 2–3, 2001, during the conference in Rochester, New York. Professionals were interviewed by telephone or at various special programs and conferences, such as the Academy of Television Arts and Sciences faculty seminar in Los Angeles in November 2003. Mine was not a scientific sample of producers, but it's interesting to note that college production faculty and independent producers who had smaller production budgets tended to express fewer doubts about the transformative qualities of the media production process than producers of larger-budget Hollywood or commercial productions.

16. By the late 1960s, many of these documentaries had been spliced and respliced and needed to be projected under the vigilant attention of a media specialist who could nursemaid fragile splices through a reel. Still, an announcer's droning recitation might be abruptly cut off, only to continue again midpoint in a completely new thought. Inevitably, the films lost sync, or brittle frames caught on a bent sprocket would burst into flame, to the delight of applauding preteens. I can't help but suspect that these film-viewing experiences helped to prepare a future audience for the illogical and dynamic aesthetic of music television.

4. Evil, Enchanting, Divine, and Ecstatic

1. See the following Gallup poll websites measuring belief in the occult: <http://www.gallup.com/poll/content/login.aspx?ci=4483>; belief in the Devil: <http://www.gallup.com/poll/content/login.aspx?ci=7858>; and belief in ghosts: <http://www.gallup.com/poll/content/login.aspx?ci=2380> (accessed 15 Mar. 2005). All of these suggest that though there appears to have been a decline in religiosity in the last decades of the twentieth century, belief in the supernatural and magic was on the rise.

2. See the Associated Press article "Bush Plan May Include Less-Popular Religions," *Greensboro News and Record* 7 May 2001: A3.

3. J. K. Rowling's books have been some of the fastest selling titles in history and have been highly praised among teachers and parents. However, a July 17, 2000, *Newsweek* article, "Why Harry's Hot," reported that some conservative parents and religious leaders felt the books advocated witchcraft, and they brought challenges or attempted to have the books removed in twenty-five school districts in seventeen different states (52).

4. Early Christians defended Christ from the suggestion that he was a common sorcerer. See Singer and Singer 97.

5. In *Leap of Faith* (dir. Richard Pearce, Paramount Pictures, 1992), Steve Martin portrays a fake miracle worker who may actually work miracles. In *The Apostle* (dir. Robert Duvall, October Films, 1997), Robert Duvall plays an evangelical preacher with complete confidence in the power of prayer to change events. *The Third Miracle* (dir. Agnieszka Holland, Sony Pictures Classics, 1999) deals with the nature of saints and miracles, when Father Frank Shore investigates a weeping statue and miracles attributed to a

woman whose blood the statue is supposed to weep. Father Shore explains that a saint is a "person with God in heaven. If you pray to that person and your prayers are answered it means that person has a special connection with God ... [and has] convinced God to answer your prayers." The film makes it clear that such a miracle worker is not a witch controlling his or her own magic but someone interceding on behalf of individuals. In *Household Saints* (dir. Nancy Savoca, Fine Line Features, 1993), sainthood is unofficially bestowed on a girl completely submissive to her faith.

6. The animated features *Shrek* (2001) and *Beauty and the Beast* (1996) are examples of films featuring a plot that turns on a witch's curse, but the witch is not a distinctive character.

7. The *Internet Movie Data Base* (<http://www.imdb.com>) allows keyword and genre searches of a large database of films and television programs. My student assistants and I used this database along with other sources to help us compile the filmography.

8. An *intertitle* provides narration or dialogue for a silent film by flashing the printed words full-screen between the scenes.

9. Witch hunts and McCarthyism would be allegorically linked throughout much of the 1950s. Often credited with helping to destroy McCarthy's crusade against communists, *See It Now* began the attack with an October 1953 segment, "The Case Against Mill Radulovich," which exposed the injustice dealt to a young man asked to resign from the Air Force because unnamed accusers suspected his father and sister of having subversive tendencies.

10. Gerald Gardner (1884–1964) was an avowed witch, "the Grand Old Man of Witchcraft," the founder of the Wicca movement, and the author of *Witchcraft Today* (New York: Magickal Childe, 1954). In his book, Gardner traces the origins of the craft and describes the activities of contemporary covens in England. The thesis of the book is that witchcraft is descended from harmless but eccentric fertility religions. The book carried an introduction by respected Egyptologist Margaret Murray.

11. Alexander, or Aleister, Crowley (1875–1947) was an infamous English witch who endorsed sexual excess, drug abuse, and animal and human sacrifice. In 1923, Crowley was involved in a scandal involving the death of one of his disciples. The Wiccans amended Crowley's famous quote, "Do what thou wilt shall be the whole of the law," into a decree that indicates a concern for others: "Do what thou wilt and it harm no one." Crowley referred to himself as "the Great Beast" and "the wickedest man alive." See Hutchinson; Singer and Singer 73; and Wilson.

12. A jury sentenced Damien Echols to death in 1994 for the brutal murders. Jesse Misskelly and Jason Baldwin are serving life sentences. All filed appeals. At the hearing for the appeal, the HBO filmmakers who made the original documentary returned to Jonesboro to get footage for a sequel. This time cameras and tape recorders were not allowed in the courtroom. The defense attorneys' motion claimed that the presence of cameras in the courtroom would hinder Echols and Baldwin from receiving effective counsel.

13. The *mockumentary* is a fictional story that imitates the form of a documentary with compilation-style editing, "unrehearsed" imagery, handheld or news-style camera movement, voice-over narration, and even "reporter" stand-ups. Examples of mockumentaries include the *Blair Witch Project* (1999) and *Curse of the Blair Witch* (1999).

14. Purkiss believes stories of witchcraft told about Matthew Hopkins and others during this period functioned to remind men that supposedly invincible women's magic

could be overcome. See "Desire and Its Deformities: Fantasies of Witchcraft in the English Civil War," *Journal of Medieval and Early Modern Studies* 27.1 (1997): 103–33.

15. Obeah is one of several Afro-Caribbean religions, which include voodoo, Santeria, Umbanda, and Candomblè.

16. There are some who believe the *Malleus Maleficarum* (Hammer of Witches) continues to hold philosophical power in a contemporary world. Traditional crimes of witchcraft included using or advocating the use of contraception, performing abortions, and robbing a man of his virility. These are issues that are still key to women, "who remain at the mercy of men in an overpopulated man's world" (Jane Stanton Hitchcock, "The Witch Within Me: What I Learned from a Medieval Book about 'the Evilness of Women,'" *Newsweek* 27 Mar. 1995: 16).

17. *Rosemary's Baby* was number nine in the AFI list, which included films of horror, suspense, and drama. The other two films in the top ten that included magical elements were *The Exorcist* (third) and *Raiders of the Lost Ark* (tenth). *The Exorcist* featured a girl possessed by the Devil but no witches, and *Raiders of the Lost Ark* featured the magical power of the Ark of the Covenant. See David Grossman, "Group Lists Films That Make Heart Race," *Greensboro News and Record*, 13 June 2001.

18. Not all media depictions of lesbian witches are satanic. Willow Rosenberg (Alyson Hannigan), the ingenue witch from the television series *Buffy the Vampire Slayer*, discovers her lesbian preferences and becomes involved in a deeply committed lesbian partnership over the course of the series.

19. A similar skepticism about the supernatural is a feature of the 1958 animated Disney version of *Sleepy Hollow* narrated by Bing Crosby.

20. The documentary does include one suggestion that the ancient Celtic beliefs were associated with evil, when the old Irishman sings:

When he came to this shore,
this land was strewn o'er,
by witchcraft and dark necromancy;
Deluged, you may say,
in the dark, evil way,
was pleasing to Beelzebub's fancy.

The suggestion being made is that the Celtic religion was evil and needed to be purged. Because it is a documentary, *The Celts* was classified as one representing the historical rather than the shamanic witch.

21. According to both film and novel, muggles are those unfortunate people born without magic and blind to the magical world around them. Muggles tend to be thoughtless, unfeeling, and cruel, but witches go out of their way to protect the muggles' misguided belief in logic.

22. In subsequent films, *Harry Potter and the Chamber of Secrets* (dir. Chris Columbus, Warner Brothers, 2002) and *Harry Potter and the Prisoner of Azkaban* (dir. Alfonso Cuarón, Warner Brothers, 2004), Harry is still an ingenue witch, still learning who he is and how to use his magic.

23. A similar plot thread appeared in the Fox television series *Boston Public* (prod. David E. Kelley, 20th Century Fox Television, 2000). Teachers learn about a game played by senior boys, who score points for sleeping with the most freshmen girls. Interestingly, the words *score* and *scoring* have long been slang for coitus during a reckless sexual escapade, suggesting that the game isn't one relegated to film and television characters.

24. The film might be interpreted as criticism of the misogyny of the football team and "boys' club" attitudes that foster the idea of girls as objects. However, I observed that young male audiences hooted with enjoyment at the vicious and derisive statements about women and obvious lack of political correctness of some of the film's characters.

25. The reference is to another witch film, *The Witches of Eastwick*, dir. George Miller, Warner Brothers, 1987.

26. The "Law of Threefold Return" maintains that any harm a witch causes through witchcraft will come back to that witch with an injury three times worse. To see what Pat Devin wrote about her experiences as technical supervisor for the film, see the website for the Covenant of the Goddess, <http://www.cog.org/nextgen/thecraft.html>. This website makes a point of separating the Covenant of the Goddess from film and television representations of witches.

27. Lilith is a name that gets used more than once in witchcraft films. In legend, Lilith was the first wife of Adam, and she refused to be subservient to him. According to David Pickering, *Dictionary of Witchcraft* (London: Cassell, 1996), she abandoned Adam to "indulge herself with demons, producing a hundred demon offspring every day . . . often being attracted to couples having intercourse in the hope of stealing a few drops of semen with which to create more evil spirits" (171).

5. The Divine Animal

1. This story about an ape man terrorizing residents of New Delhi originally appeared in Pamela Constable, "'Monkey Man' Lurks among New Delhi's Poor, or at Least in Their Minds" (*Washington Post* 21 May 2001: A14) and was subsequently carried by a number of American newspapers as an item of curiosity.

2. Among the several sources on the story of Peter Stubbe, see Wilson 73; Singer and Singer 125–26; and Sidky 234–38. Sidky reports that a pamphlet written in 1590 by George Bores, "The Damnable Life and Death of Stubbe Peeter," is the original source for the story. (Anyone researching this topic should be aware that Peter Stubbe's name has been spelled in various ways.) There are several popular Internet sites with discussions about Peter Stubbe, including a site developed by Shannon Powell in 1996–98, "Peter Stubb, Werewolf of Bedburg," which includes a link to a translation of the early George Bores manuscript. See <http://www.shanmonster.com/witch/werewolf/weredoc.html> (accessed 23 Mar. 2005).

3. Nazis and colonial empires would use Lombroso's theories to justify their subjugation of other peoples. More recently, members of the Ku Klux Klan and similar groups have used this line of thinking to support racial discrimination by declaring some racial groups to be less genetically advanced.

4. Fairy tales often suggest that humans and animals interact. The English folktale "Puss 'n Boots" tells how a clever cat wearing a nice pair of boots becomes the adviser to a poor miller's son, helping him to better his fortunes and marry a princess. In a more negative interaction, the wolf in the fairy tale "Little Red Riding Hood" seduces a young girl. Other animals such as dogs, birds, mice, and lions can become colleagues or enemies to humans. Similarly, in the myths of various cultures, people interact with deities who take on the form of animals.

5. The growth of pet cemeteries may also indicate a combination of too much discretionary cash and closer ties people have formed with their pets, which have been encouraged by pet supply stores, veterinarians, and pet health insurance. One anonymous critic explained that having a pet cat cremated and burying the ashes in the backyard did

not indicate a belief in the cat's soul. "I do not believe they have souls but could not throw away their bodies as if they were trash. My burying them was honoring their memory and my love for them—not an indication that I believe in an afterlife for either pets or people."

6. *Everybody Loves Raymond*, "Pet Cemetery" 23 Oct. 2000, dir. Ken Levine, CBS, 1996–2005.

7. For a collection of Native American folktales that provides several examples of spirit animals, see *The Indian Fairy Book* (Fredrick A. Stokes, 1916).

8. *Legend of the Spirit Dog*, dir. Martin Goldman and Michael Spence, Republic Pictures, 1997.

9. It's worth noting that this film was made a decade after Eastern mysticism, hallucinogenic drugs, personal questing, and Carlos Castaneda had entered the lexicon of America life. Castaneda's shaman, Don Juan, was supposed to have shared a paste made of the datura plant, or Jimsonweed, which allowed a person to fly through the air, speak to animals, and experience other amazing visions when it was rubbed on the body. See *The Teachings of Don Juan: A Yaqui Way of Knowledge* (New York: Washington Square, 1968).

10. While these legendary creatures from alternate evolutionary paths are usually depicted in media as violent, not all representations are as fierce as those listed. The television series created by Joe Ruby and Ken Spears, *Bigfoot and Wildboy* (ABC, 1977) and *Harry and the Hendersons* (developed by Lin Oliver and Alan Maskowitz, Universal TV, 1991–93) are examples of more gentle portraits of evolutionary cousins who are still depicted as elusive and endangered but also wise and docile.

11. I discuss the film *Carrie* in chapter 4.

12. Vampirism has also been likened to a sexually transmitted disease, particularly HIV/AIDS, in discussions of horror films. See Frank Rich, "Sex, Death and the New Blood Culture," *New York Times* 7 Dec. 1992: B1.

13. *Ginger Snaps* was popular enough to inspire a sequel, *Ginger Snaps 2: Unleashed* (2004), and a prequel, *Ginger Snaps Back: The Beginning* (2004).

14. Audiences' motives for watching horror movies that feature werewolves and similar creatures are parallel to the mitigation of boredom that the werewolf character seeks. Research suggests that audiences choosing media with predictable violence may be searching for thrills that will provide vicarious relief from the banal business of everyday life. Berlyne and Madsen differentiate between curiosity and "diversive exploration." Boredom motivates diversive exploration; anxiety motivates curiosity. The bored individual wants stimulation. The curious individual wants information to solve a problem or calm worries. See D. Berlyne and K. B. Madsen, *Pleasure, Reward, Preference: Their Nature, Determinants, and Role in Behavior* (New York: Academic, 1973).

15. Convicted killer Aileen Wuornos provides an example of the existential dilemma of society's equivalent of the werewolf, the serial killer. The State of Florida sentenced Wuornos in 1992 and executed her in 2002 for the serial murder of seven men in 1989 and 1990, including her own brother. News reports quote Wuornos as saying that she had no respect for life, even her own, and asked the state to dismiss all appeals and proceed with her execution: "This world doesn't mean anything to me." Interestingly, her story would be depicted in two movies, *Overkill: The Aileen Wuornos Story* (1992) and *Monster* (2003), a documentary, *Aileen Wuornos: The Selling of a Serial Killer* (1992), and an opera by Carla Lucero, *Wuornos* (2001). In 2004, Charlize Theron received an Oscar for best actress in a leading role for her portrayal of Wuornos in *Monster* (dir. Patty Jenkins, Newmarket Film Group, 2003).

16. A rare film that stands outside the media dichotomy of the divine beast and savage monster is *Mad at the Moon* (1992). Set in the old West, a young woman marries a man she doesn't love. The young husband is a successful rancher afflicted with lycanthropy, or "moon madness." The film treats the condition as a pathetic mental illness, which the townspeople and young wife learn to accept.

6. The Recycled Soul

1. While Judeo-Christian religions didn't adopt the concept of reincarnation, the spiritualist movement of the mid-nineteenth century helped to spread New Age ideas in Europe and America. Groups such as the Theosophical Society approved interest in out-of-body travel, near-death experiences, as well as reincarnation. See Kay Alexander, "Roots of the New Age," *Perspectives on the New Age*, ed. James R. Lewis and Gordon Melton (Albany: State U of New York P, 1992), 30–47.

2. Lama Khyentse Norbu served as a consultant for the film *Little Buddha*. Born in 1961 in Bhutan, Norbu was himself recognized by monks in the Tibetan exile community as the reincarnation of a spiritual leader. Upon release of the film, he explained that modern media were not a threat to Buddhism: the true threats are ego, pride, and negative emotions.

3. The Hindu Bhagavad Gita also compares the body to clothes: Just as a person puts on new garments after discarding the old ones, similarly Atman (the supreme universal self) acquires new bodies after casting away the old bodies. A translation of the text by Swami Prabhavanda and Christopher Isherwood (New York: Barnes, 1995) reads:

Worn-out garments
Are shed by the dweller
Within the Body.
New Bodies are donned
By the dweller, like garments. (2.22)

For another translation by Dr. Ramanand Prasad, see "Exploring World Cultures: Readings from Ancient India," 1988, 3 Feb. 2003 <http://eawc.evansville.edu/anthology/gita.htm>.

4. In 1994, I interviewed Dr. Erlendur Haraldsson, professor of psychology, Reykjavik, Iceland, at a Sociology of Religion conference, where he was presenting case studies of children's past-life memories. Though the interview was for the documentary *Wondrous Events: Foundations of Folk Belief* (dir. Emily D. Edwards, Penn State Media, 1994), Dr. Haraldsson did tell me about his investigations in Sri Lanka of young children who insisted they had lived previous lives. He had interviewed the children and their families and then attempted to verify elements of their stories. He seemed convinced that reincarnation was a possible explanation for the findings of his research. Among other investigations of children's memories is Ian Stevenson, *Children Who Remember Previous Lives* (Charlottesville: UP of Virginia, 1987). Stevenson has accumulated a large number of credible cases. Tom Shroder presents an intriguing account of Stevenson's work in *Old Souls* (New York: Simon, 1999).

5. The films *I Was a Teenage Werewolf* and *Face of the Screaming Werewolf* are both listed in the filmography of atavistic media in chapter 5. There are other witchcraft films that also feature reincarnation, usually when a witch who was put to death in a previous century is reborn in contemporary times. Examples include *Necropolis* (dir. Bruce Hickey, Empire Pictures, 1987), portraying a reincarnated "satanic witch" who attempts

to revive her ancient cult in modern times; and two films listed in the filmography of chapter 4: *The Devonsville Terror*, depicting a reincarnated witch exacting revenge on community leaders; and *Seduced by Evil*, in which the sorcerer is not reincarnated, but his consort from an earlier time is.

6. Edgar Cayce (1877–1945) was an American medium who put himself into trances to reveal information about his own previous lives as well as the former lives of others. Cayce was one of the founders of past-life therapy, believing that what he could reveal to a person about a previous life might help that person better cope with the present. Cayce attracted a following that still maintains an archive of his writings and trance readings at the Cayce headquarters, the Association for Research and Enlightenment, in Virginia Beach.

7. *American Idol: The Search for a Superstar* (created by Simon Fuller, Fox Network Television, 2002–), is a television program that combines features of "reality" programming with those of game shows and star searches. From thousands of contestants sorted through by a panel of celebrity judges, viewing audiences help to select one individual to become the "American Idol."

7. Conclusion

1. In both series, *Crossing Over with John Edward* (dir. Dana Calderwood, SciFi Channel, 1999–2004) and *Beyond with James Van Praagh* (dir. Tom Mcguire, Tribune Entertainment, 2002–), psychics interpret for the dead before a live audience.

2. *Primetime Live*, ABC, 31 Oct. 2002. *Channeling* is supposed to be a communication process in which the information source is not the ordinary consciousness or physical sensory perceptions of the communicator. Interestingly, *channel* is also the term for a frequency band wide enough to transport telegraph, telephone, radio, or television messages. See Suzanne Riordan, "Channeling: A New Revelation?" *Perspectives on the New Age*, ed. James R. Lewis and Gordon Melton (Albany: State U of New York P, 1992): 105–26.

3. One such guide is Robin Mead, *Haunted Hotels* (Nashville: Rutledge Hill, 1995).

4. *Rose Red* (dir. Craig R. Baxley, Warner Brothers, 2002) was a fictional story, though folklore surrounding the Winchester Mansion reportedly inspired the miniseries.

5. *Media breederism* is a common occurrence in the newsroom. When I was a working journalist, our news director might berate the assignments editor if our newscast omitted a story carried by competing news outlets. Even when reporters had purposefully decided not to pursue the item, we might be made to feel that we had "missed" an important story because it was carried by our competitors. This was particularly true when the story was a negative one.

6. Ghost walks are also available in other cities, such as New Orleans, Memphis, Leesburg, Gettysburg, San Antonio, Austin, Philadelphia, Key West, Chicago, and Savannah, among others. I should also note that some tours not publicized as "ghost tours" will frequently feature haunted sites.

7. Some people believe ghostly disruptions of electromagnetic fields will cause televisions and other electrical equipment to malfunction, a theory reinforced by some movies. For example, the presence of Coronado's ghost in *Charlie's Ghost Story* (dir. Anthony Edwards, Regency Enterprises, 1994) has odd effects on the television as well as other electrical appliances, implying that ghosts share some mysterious link to the electrical devices or the electromagnetic field.

8. As might be expected, I noticed variations in our guide's telling of the folklore and some of the written accounts that were his recognized sources. John Bennett's *Doctor*

to the Dead (Columbia: U of South Carolina P, 1945) was developed from transcriptions of Gullah stories, two of which our guide recited with considerable modifications. Another source our ghost-walk guide mentioned was Margaret Rhett Martin's *Charleston Ghosts* (Columbia: U of South Carolina P, 1963).

9. For a comprehensive filmography of these and the other ghost films referenced in this chapter, see E. Edwards, "House."

10. The hour-long program *The Ghostly Homes of Charleston* (dir. Rick Lewis, Horizon Entertainment and HGTV, 2000) first aired October 29, 2000. The restaurant's reputation is such that it would later place third in the Travel Channel's *Top Ten Ghostly Getaways* (exec. prod. Kathleen Cromley, 2002) and also be featured on the Food Channel's *Haunted Restaurants* (2002).

11. The International Ghost Hunters' Society invites visitors to explore America's most haunted places. The website (<www.ghostweb.com>) lists haunted bed-and-breakfast inns in thirty states and Australia.

12. The New Age is not alone in this type of marketing. Christian bookstores have developed similar consumer items for devout believers, including such things as WWJD (What Would Jesus Do) bracelets and T-shirts, angel dolls and necklaces, and other Christian merchandise.

13. Several of my interviewees suggested they were part of a movement that was attempting to help revive an ancient, pagan form of worship founded by Gerald Gardner. Margaret Murray, the controversial author of *The Witch Cult in Western Europe* (Oxford: Oxford UP, 1970) and *The God of the Witches* (Oxford: Oxford UP, 1970), suggests that witchcraft was a surviving pagan religion that worshipped the goddess Diana. Gardner reconstructed the religion Murray describes, creating a coven in England in 1939, which has since been imported to the United States. See Aidan A. Kelly, *Crafting the Art of Magick, Book I: A History of Gardnerian Witchcraft, 1939–64* (St. Paul: Llewellyn, 1991).

14. I should note that I may be the common denominator of "pretense" in these New Age rituals, a nosy outsider toting cameras and asking questions. However, I did not have a video camera or inform anyone that I was there with the intention of observing, participating, and reporting. Other interviews reported in this chapter were conducted for the documentaries *Wondrous Events* (1994) and *Wondrous Healing* (2002) or specifically for the purposes of this chapter.

15. The "Book of Shadows" is a handwritten record of magical rituals and herb lore or a personal journal of spells kept by an individual witch. Several movies and television shows have alluded to such a book. For example, the sisters in the television series *Charmed* frequently refer to the Book of Shadows they keep hidden in the attic of their house. The sisters inherited the oversized volume of spells, which are written in elaborate calligraphy, almost as if labored over by monks. Some movies make reference to a "Grimoire," a similar book of spells and instructions for how to perform rituals. For example, in the film *Warlock* (dir. Steve Miner, New World Pictures, 1989), an evil warlock travels forward in time to find the "Grand Grimoire," a satanic bible. This Grimoire is supposed to possess the secret name of God, which—when spoken backward—will destroy all of God's creation.

16. The *Unsolved Mysteries* episode (dir. Patrick Taulere) first aired on CBS, November 2, 1988, and was rebroadcast on Lifetime in 2002. According to two neopagan witches I interviewed, the "binding spell" is a ritual or incantation used to stop either a person or a spirit from doing or saying something harmful. To stop a person, the witch will perform a ritual that can involve the symbolic use of a doll, a photograph, or a personal

object that is tied up with string or silk threads during the ceremony. To stop a spirit, the witch will recite a spell or a "binding incantation." *The Craft* (1996) also features a binding spell, with which a good witch attempts to stop a misguided witch from harming someone.

17. One witch I interviewed expressed the surprising thought that for a witch to attempt to subjugate natural energies to conform to her individual will—something many of the witches of folklore and media consistently do—was not proper, nor did it reflect what really happens in neopagan worship, according to her. Apparently, she didn't believe in practicing magic. She preferred to honor nature with rituals that express a sense of humility and admiration rather than attempt to control natural forces, which seems to reflect more of a Christian supplication to the divine rather than the witch's desire for acquisition of supernatural power.

18. Several people complained about this film. One complaint suggested that people might confuse the *Blair Witch Project* with the "Bell Witch," a fairly well known Southern folklore about a real farmer, John Bell, who lived in Robertson County, Tennessee, in the early 1800s. Bell and his family were persecuted by an invisible force that would hit, pinch, and throw stones at them. The "poltergeist" killed Bell with a fatal blow to the head in 1820. Some accounts suggest that the evil spirit was that of Kate Batts, a neighbor and enemy of John Bell. On a Travel Channel program, *Top Ten Cursed Places* (exec. prod. Kathleen Cromley), first broadcast on October 25, 2002, an interviewee makes the distinction that the Bell Witch is "not just a movie like the *Blair Witch Project* . . . this is real history." The complaint is that neither the folklore nor the movie represent neopagan witchcraft. "The Bell Witch was not a witch, and the Blair Witch is not folklore."

19. The presence of news cameras can have a similar effect on a breaking news story, bringing a counterfeit drama to an otherwise spontaneous happening when people realize they are being videotaped. As a news reporter, I have personally witnessed wearied protest marchers become reinvigorated when a news camera appeared on the scene, causing a march that was about to disband build into a newsworthy event.

20. The concept of the "sleeper effect" originates with the research conducted by Carl Hovland and his associates on source credibility. Their findings suggest that as time passes, people tend to separate information or an opinion from its source. See Carl Hovland, Irving Janis, and Harold H. Kelley, *Communication and Persuasion* (New Haven: Yale UP, 1953).

Bibliography

Alper, Matthew. *The "God" Part of the Brain: A Scientific Interpretation of Human Spirituality and God*. New York: Rogue, 1998.

American Psychiatric Association. *Diagnostic and Statistical Manual of Mental Disorders: DSM-IV*. Washington: American Psychiatric Assoc., 1994.

Andrew, J. Dudley. *The Major Film Theories: An Introduction*. London: Oxford UP, 1976.

Arata, Stephen D. "The Sedulous Ape: Atavism, Professionalism, and Stevenson's 'Jekyll and Hyde.'" *Criticism* 37.2 (1995): 233–60.

Arnheim, Rudolf. *Art and Visual Perception*. Berkeley: U of California P, 1967.

Ashford, S., and Timms, N. *What Europe Thinks: A Study of Western European Values*. Aldershot: Dartmouth, 1992.

Ashmole, Elias. *Theatrum Chemicum Britannicum. Containing severall poeticall pieces of our famous English philosophers, who have written the hermetique mysteries in their owne ancient language. Faithfully collected into one volume with annotations thereon*. London, 1652. Introd. Allen G. Debus. New York: Johnson Reprint, 1967.

Ault, Susanne. "Every Witch Way but Up." *Broadcasting and Cable* 130.43 (2000): 26.

Baker, Robert K., and Sandra Ball, eds. *Violence and the Mass Media*. Washington: GPO, 1969.

Baker, Ronald L. *Hoosier Folk Legends*. Bloomington: Indiana UP, 1982.

Barnouw, Erik. *The Magician and the Cinema*. New York: Oxford UP, 1981.

Barstow, Anne Llewellyn. *Witchcraze: A New History of the European Witch Hunts*. San Francisco: Pandora, 1994.

Bauer, Raymond A. "The Audience." *Handbook of Communication*. Ed. Wilbur Schramm, Nathan Maccoby, and Edwin B. Parker. Chicago: McNally, 1973. 141–52.

Bazin, Andrew. *What is Cinema?* Vol. 1. Berkeley: U of California P, 1971.

Becker, Carl. *Breaking the Circle: Death and the Afterlife in Buddhism*. Carbondale: Southern Illinois UP, 1993.

Benjamin, Walter. "The Work of Art in the Age of Mechanical Production." *Film Theory and Criticism: Introductory Readings*. Ed. Leo Brady and Marshall Cohen. 5th ed. New York: Oxford UP, 1999. 731–51.

Bentley, Beth. *Phone Calls from the Dead*. Athens: Ohio UP, 1970.

Berger, Helen A. *A Community of Witches: Contemporary Neo-Paganism and Witchcraft in the United States*. Columbia: U of South Carolina P, 1999.

Bernstein, Morey. *The Search for Bridey Murphy*. Garden City: Doubleday, 1956.

Bettis, Myra, Michael Blackwell, Robert Hoffman, Patty Sonka, and Lovetta Swingle. "The Care of the East Tennessee Dead." *Glimpses of Southern Appalachian Folk Culture: Papers in Memory of Norbert F. Riedl.* Ed. Charles H. Faulkner and Carol K. Buckles. Knoxville: Tennessee Anthropological Assoc., 1978. 108–30.

Bondeson, Jan. *A Cabinet of Medical Curiosities.* Ithaca: Cornell UP, 1997.

Briggs, Katharine. Introduction. *A Dictionary of British Folk Tales in the English Language.* New York: Pantheon, 1977.

Brockett, Oscar G. *History of the Theatre.* 7th ed. Boston: Allyn, 1995.

Burch, Frank. "Blood Gags." *Morbid Curiosity* Mar. 1997: 69–71.

Burch, Noël. *Theory of Film Practice.* Trans. Helen R. Lane. Introd. by Annette Michelson. New York: Praeger, 1973.

Burke, Kenneth. *A Grammar of Motives.* New York: Prentice, 1945.

Burns, Stanley B. *Sleeping Beauty: Memorial Photography in America.* Altadena: Twelvetress, 1990.

Cadiff, Andy. Personal interview. 10 Oct. 1998.

Cameron, Julia. *The Artist's Way: A Spiritual Path to Higher Creativity.* New York: Putnam's, 1992.

Campion-Vincent, Veronique. "The Baby-Parts Story: A New Latin American Legend. *Western Folklore* 49 (1990): 9–25.

Cantor, Joanne. "Fright Reactions to Mass Media." *Media Effects: Advances in Theory and Research.* Ed. Jennings Bryant and Dolf Zillmann. Hillsdale: Erlbaum, 1994. 213–46.

Cantor, Joanne, and Glenn G. Sparks. "Children's Fear Responses to Mass Media: Testing Some Piagetian Predictions." *Journal of Communication* 34.2 (1984): 90–103.

Carey, James W. *Communication as Culture: Essays on Media and Society.* Boston: Hyman, 1989.

Carroll, Noël E. *The Philosophy of Horror, or Paradoxes of the Heart.* New York: Routledge, 1990.

Carter, Stephen L. *The Culture of Disbelief: How American Law and Politics Trivialize Religious Devotion.* New York: Basic, 1993.

Chase, Richard, Jr., and David Teasley. "Little Red Riding Hood: Werewolf and Prostitute." *Historian* 57.4 (1995): 769–76.

Clover, Carol J. *Men, Women, and Chainsaws: Gender in the Modern Horror Film.* Princeton: Princeton UP, 1992.

Coffin, Margaret M. *Death in Early America.* New York: Nelson, 1976.

Coudert, Allison. *Alchemy: The Philosopher's Stone.* Boulder: Shambhala, 1980.

Crane, Jonathan Lake. *Terror in Everyday Life: Singular Moments in the History of the Horror Film.* Thousand Oaks: Sage, 1994.

Crissman, James K. *Death and Dying in Central Appalachia: Changing Attitudes and Practices.* Chicago: U of Illinois P, 1994.

Cuneo, Michael. *American Exorcism: Expelling Demons in the Land of Plenty.* New York: Doubleday, 2001.

D'Aquile, Eugene, Charles D. Laughton, and John McManus. *The Spectrum of Ritual.* New York: Columbia UP, 1979.

Darwin, Charles. *Origin of the Species.* London: John Murray, 1859.

Davis, Phillip G. *The Goddess Unmasked: The Rise of Neopagan Feminist Spirituality.* New York: Spence, 1998.

DeFleur, Melvin L., and Sandra Ball-Rokeach. *Theories of Mass Communication.* New York: Longman, 1989.

Dewey, John. *How We Think*. Boston: Heath, 1933.

Diem, Anfrea Grace, and James R. Lewis. "Imagining India: The Influence of Hinduism on the New Age Movement." *Perspectives on the New Age*. Ed. James R. Lewis and Gordon Melton. Albany: State U of New York P, 1992. 48–58.

Dixon, J., and M. Wetherell. "On Discourse and Dirty Nappies: Gender, the Division of Household Labour and the Social Psychology of Distributive Justice." *Theory and Psychology* 14.2 (2004): 167–90.

Dobson, Dennis S. "Pray TV: A Powerful New Tool for Religious Cults." *Impact of Mass Media: Current Issues*. Ed. Ray Eldon Hiebert and Carol Reuss. New York: Longman, 1985. 457–59.

Douglas, Susan J. *Where the Girls Are: Growing Up Female with the Mass Media*. New York: Times, 1994.

Douglass, John S., and Glenn P. Harnden. *The Art of Technique: An Aesthetic Approach to Film and Video Production*. Boston: Allyn, 1996.

Drury, Nevill. *Pan's Daughter: The Magical World of Rosaleen Norton*. Oxford: Mandrake, 1993.

Duclos, Denis. *The Werewolf Complex: America's Fascination with Violence*. Trans. Amanda Pingree. New York: Berg, 1998.

Edwards, Catherine. "Wicca Casts Spell on Teen-Age Girls." *Insight on the News* 25 Oct. 1999: 22 .

Edwards, Emily. "The Ecstasy of Horrible Expectations: Morbid Curiosity, Sensation Seeking, and Interest in Horror Movies." *Current Research in Film: Audiences, Economics, and Law*. Ed. Bruce A. Austin. Vol. 5. Norwood: Ablex, 1991. 19–38.

———. "A House That Tries to Be Haunted." *Hauntings and Poltergeists: Multidisciplinary Perspectives*. Ed. James Houran and Rense Lange. Jefferson: McFarland, 2001. 82–120.

Edwards, Paul. *Reincarnation: A Critical Examination*. Amherst: Prometheus, 1996.

Eisenbud, Jule. *The World of Ted Serios: "Thoughtographic" Studies of an Extraordinary Mind*. New York: Morrow, 1967.

Eisenstein, Sergei M. *Film Form: Essays in Film Theory*. Ed. and trans. Jay Leyda. New York: Harcourt, 1949.

Eisler, Robert. *Man into Wolf: An Anthropological Interpretation of Sadism, Masochism, and Lycanthropy: A Lecture Delivered at a Meeting of the Royal Society of Medicine*. London: Routledge, 1951.

Eliade, Mircea. *The Forge and the Crucible: The Origins and Structures of Alchemy*. Chicago: U of Chicago P, 1956.

———. *The Myth of the Eternal Return, or Cosmos and History*. Trans. Williard R. Trask. New York: Princeton UP, 1954.

———. *Shamanism: Archaic Techniques of Ecstasy*. Trans. Williard R. Trask. Princeton: Princeton UP, 1974.

Eller, Cynthia. *The Myth of Matriarchal Prehistory: Why an Invented Past Won't Give Women a Future*. Boston: Beacon, 2000.

Estés, Clarissa Pinkola. *Women Who Run with the Wolves: Myths and Stories of the Wild Woman Archetype*. New York: Ballantine, 1992.

Farrell, James J. *Inventing the American Way of Death, 1830–1920*. Philadelphia: Temple UP, 1980.

Flanigan, Kathy. "Witches Spin Some of Their Magic over Young Women." *Milwaukee Journal Sentinel* 25 Oct. 1999. 18 July 2000 <http://www.jsonline.com/enter/gen/oct99/witch25102299.asp>.

Fountain, John W. "Exorcists and Exorcisms Proliferate Across U.S." *New York Times* 28 Nov. 2000: A16.

Freud, Sigmund. *Civilization and Its Discontents.* Trans. James Strachey. New York: Norton, 1961.

Gahr, Evan. "Religion on TV Doesn't Have a Prayer." *American Enterprise* Sept.–Oct. 1997: 58–60.

Gardiner, H. M., Ruth Clark Metcalf, and John G. Beebe-Center. *Feeling and Emotion: A History of Theories.* 1937. Westport: Greenwood, 1970.

Gardner, Martin. *The New Age: Notes of a Fringe Watcher.* Buffalo: Prometheus, 1988.

Garfinkel, Harold. "Conditions of Successful Degradation Ceremonies." *Drama in Life: The Uses of Communication in Society.* Ed. James E. Combs and Michael W. Mansfield. New York: Hastings House, 1976. 315–20.

Gates, David. "Odyssey of a Psychonaut—Timothy Leary's Well-Advertised Trip: 1920–1996." *Newsweek* 10 June 1996: 92.

Gates, Richard. *Production Management for Film and Video.* Boston: Focal, 1992.

Gerbner, George. "Violence in Television Drama: Trends in Symbolic Functions." *Media Content and Control.* Vol. 1 of *Television and Social Behavior.* Ed. George A. Comstock and Eli Rubinstein. Washington: GPO, 1972. 28–187.

Gerbner, George, Larry Gross, Michael Morgan, and Nancy Signorelli. "Living with Television: The Dynamics of the Cultivation Process." *Perspectives on Media Effects.* Ed. Jennings Bryant and Dolf Zillman. Hillsdale: Erlbaum, 1986. 17–40.

"Getting Ready for the Millennium." *Time* 18 Jan. 1999: 60.

Geuens, Jean Pierre. *Film Production Theory.* Albany: State U of New York P, 2000.

Gibeau, Dawn. "Poor Clares Pray in Long Shadows of History." *National Catholic Reporter* 17 Feb. 1995: 32–34.

Glaser, Barney, and Anselm L. Straus. "The Ritual Drama of Mutual Pretense." *Drama in Life: The Uses of Communication in Society.* Ed. James E. Combs and Michael W. Mansfield. New York: Hastings House, 1976. 359–68.

Goethals, Gregor T. *The TV Ritual: Worship at the Video Altar.* Boston: Beacon, 1981.

Goffman, Erving. *The Presentation of Self in Everyday Life.* Garden City: Doubleday, 1959.

Goleman, Daniel. *Emotional Intelligence.* New York: Bantam, 1995.

Gollmar, Robert H. *Edward Gein: America's Most Bizarre Murder.* New York: Pinnacle, 1981.

Gottner-Abendroth, Heide. *The Dancing Goddess: Principles of a Matriarchal Aesthetic.* Trans. Maureen T. Krause. Boston: Beacon, 1991.

Gregory, Anita. *The Strange Case of Rudi Schneider.* Metuchen: Scarecrow, 1985.

Hess, David J. *Science in the New Age: The Paranormal, Its Defenders and Debunkers, and American Culture.* Madison: U of Wisconsin P, 1993.

Hibbs, Thomas S. *Shows about Nothing: Nihilism in Popular Culture from "The Exorcist" to "Seinfeld."* New York: Spence, 1999.

Hill, Michael. "Urban Legends Spread as People Seek Solace." *Greensboro News and Record* 19 Sept. 2001: A1, 9.

Hogan, David. *Dark Romance: Sexuality in the Horror Film.* Jefferson: McFarland, 1986.

Howard, Roland. "Charm Offensive." *New Statesman and Society* 21 Apr. 1995: 18–19.

Hutchinson, Roger. *Aleister Crowley: The Beast Demystified.* Edinburgh: Mainstream, 1998.

Hutson, Scott R. "Technoshamanism: Spiritual Healing in the Rave Subculture." *Popular Music and Society* 23.3 (1999): 53–62.

Hutton, Ronald. "Paganism and Polemic: The Debate over the Origins of Modern Pagan Witchcraft." *Folklore* 111.1 (2000): 103–25.

Ingills, B. *Natural and Supernatural: A History of the Paranormal from Earliest Times to 1914*. London: Hodder, 1977.

Ingold, John. "Students 'Degraded' for 'Spells.'" *Denver Rocky Mountain News* 15 May 1999. 23 Mar. 2005 <http://cfapp.rockymountainnews.com/news/archive>.

Innis, Harold Adams. *The Bias of Communication*. Toronto: U of Toronto P, 1951.

"Is Your Computer Possessed by a Demon?" *Weekly World News* 7 Mar. 2000. 1 Oct. 2000 <http://www.weeklyworldnews.com/stories/1745.html>.

Iyer, Pico. *The Global Soul: Jet Lag, Shopping Malls, and the Search for Home*. New York: Knopf, 2000.

Jevning, R., R. K. Wallace, and M. Beidebach. "The Physiology of Meditation, a Review: A Wakeful Hypometabolic Integrated Response." *Neuroscience and Biobehavioral Reviews* 16.3 (1992): 415–24.

Jong, Erica. *Witches*. New York: Abrams, 1981.

Jung, Carl Gustav. *Psychology and Alchemy*. Trans. R. F. C. Hull. London: Routledge, 1953.

Kaminer, Wendy. "American Gothic." *American Prospect* 18 Dec. 2000: 38.

Katz, Steven D. *Film Directing Shot by Shot: Visualizing from Concept to Screen*. Studio City: Weise, 1991.

Kelly, Aidan A. "An Update on Neopagan Witchcraft in America." *Perspectives on the New Age*. Ed. James R. Lewis and Gordon Melton. Albany: State U of New York P, 1992. 136–51.

Kerlinger, Fred N. *Foundations of Behavioral Research*. New York: Holt, 1973.

Kermode, Mark. "The Exorcist." *New Statesman* 127 (1998): 43–44.

———. "Lucifer Rising." *Sight and Sound* 8.7 (1998): 6–12.

Khan, Hazrat Inayat. *The Sufi Message of Hazrat Inayat Khan: The Mysticism of Sound, Music, the Power of the Word, Cosmic Language*. Vol. 2. London: Barrie, 1960.

King, Stephen. *Danse Macabre*. New York: Berkley, 1979.

Klaits, Joseph. *Servants of Satan: The Age of the Witch Hunts*. Bloomington: Indiana UP, 1985.

Korzybski, Alfred. *Science and Sanity: An Introduction to Non-Aristotelian Systems and General Semantics*. Lancaster: Science, 1941.

Kubey, Robert. "On Not Finding Media Effects: Conceptual Problems in the Notion of an 'Active' Audience (with a Reply to Elihu Katz)." *The Audience and Its Landscape*. Ed. J. Hay, L. Grossber, and E. Wartella. New York: Westview, 1996. 187–205.

Laderman, Gary. *The Sacred Remains: American Attitudes Toward Death, 1799–1883*. New Haven: Yale UP, 1996.

La Ferla, Ruth. "Like Magic, Witchcraft Charms Teenagers." *New York Times* 13 Feb. 2000, late ed., sec. 9: 1.

Lam, Tina. "Principal Testifies on Satanic Prevention." *Detroit Free Press* 3 Mar. 1999: 3.

Lederer, Wolfgang. *The Fear of Women*. New Haven: Yale UP, 1996.

Lescarboura, Austin C. "Edison's Views on Life and Death: An Interview with the Famous Inventor Regarding His Attempt to Communicate with the Next World." *Scientific American* 30 Oct. 1920: 446, 458–60.

Lethbridge, Thomas Charles. *Ghost and Ghoul*. London: Routledge, 1961.

Lindsey, Shelley Stamp. "Horror, Femininity, and Carrie's Monstrous Puberty." *Journal of Film and Video* 43.4 (1991): 33–44.

Lippmann, Walter. *Public Opinion*. New York: Macmillan, 1921.

Littlejohn, Stephen W. *Theories of Human Communication*. 3rd ed. Columbus: Merrill, 1989.

Lombroso-Ferrero, Gina. *Criminal Man, According to the Classification of Cesare Lombroso*. Montclair: Patterson Smith, 1972.

Lowell, Ross. *Matters of Light and Depth: Creating Memorable Images for Video, Film, and Stills Through Lighting*. New York: Lowell-Light, 1999.

Lowery, S., and M. L. DeFleur. *Milestones in Mass Communication Research: Media Effects*. New York: Longman, 1983.

Maher, Michaeleen, and G. P. Hansen. "Quantitative Investigation of a Reported Haunting Using Several Detection Techniques." *Journal of the American Society for Psychical Research* 86 (1992): 347–74.

Maine, Patricia. Personal interview. 27 Jan. 1997.

Mamer, Bruce. *Film Production Technique: Creating the Accomplished Image*. Belmont: Wadsworth, 1996.

Marshall, Catherine, and Gretchen B. Rossman. *Designing Qualitative Research*. Newbury Park: Sage, 1989.

Mattelart, Michele. *Women, Media and Crisis: Femininity and Disorder*. London: Comedia, 1986.

McClenon, James M. *Wondrous Events: Foundations of Religious Belief*. Philadelphia: U of Pennsylvania P, 1994.

McIlwraith, Robert D. "'I'm Addicted to Television: The Personality, Imagination, and TV Watching Patterns of Self-Identified TV Addicts." *Journal of Broadcasting and Electronic Media* 42.3 (1998): 371–87.

McLean, Adam. *The Triple Goddess: An Exploration of the Archetypal Feminine*. Grand Rapids: Phanes, 1989.

McLuhan, Eric, and Frank Zingrone, eds. *Essential McLuhan*. New York: Basic, 1995.

McLuhan, Marshall. "A Last Look at the Tube." *New York Magazine* 3 Apr. 1978: 45.

———. *Understanding Media: The Extensions of Man*. London: Routledge, 1964.

McLuhan, Marshall, and Quentin Fiore. *The Medium Is the Massage*. New York: Bantam, 1967.

Metz, Christian. *Film Language*. New York: Oxford UP, 1974.

Mills, Charles Wright. *White Collar: The American Middle Classes*. New York: Oxford UP, 1951.

Mitry, Jean. "Remarks on the Problem of Cinematic Adaptation." Trans. Richard Dyer. *Bulletin of the Midwest Modern Language Association* 4 (1971): 1, 7–8.

Morgan, Hal, and Kerry Tucker. *More Rumors!* New York: Penguin, 1987.

Muhlen, R. "Comic Books and Other Horrors: Prep School for Totalitarian Society." *Commentary* Jan. 1949: 80–87.

Mulrine, Anna. "So You Want to Be a Teenage Witch?" *U.S. News and World Report* 1 Mar. 1999: 70.

Musello, Christopher. "Objects in Process: Material Culture and Communication." *Southern Folklore* 49 (1992): 37–59.

Nicholson, Linda J. *Gender and History: The Limits of Social Theory in the Age of the Family*. New York: Columbia UP, 1986.

Nickell, Joe. "Exorcism! Driving Out the Nonsense." *Skeptical Inquirer* 25 (2001): 20–30.

———. "Phantoms, Frauds, or Fantasies?" *Hauntings and Poltergeists: Multidisciplinary Perspectives*. Ed. James Houran and Rense Lange. Jefferson: McFarland, 2001. 214–23.

Nimmo, Dan. "The Drama, Illusion, and Reality of Political Images." *Drama in Life: The Uses of Communication in Society*. Ed. James E. Combs and Michael W. Mansfield. New York: Hastings, 1976: 258–70.

Nimmo, Dan, and James E. Combs. *Nightly Horrors: Crisis Coverage by Television Network News*. Knoxville: U of Tennessee P, 1985.

Noelle-Neumann, Elisabeth. "The Effect of Media on Media Effects Research." *Journal of Communication* 33 (1983): 157–65.

Noll, Richard, ed. *Vampires, Werewolves, and Demons: Twentieth Century Reports in the Psychiatric Literature*. New York: Brunner, 1992.

Oppenheim, Janet. *The Other World: Spiritualism and Psychical Research in England, 1850–1914*. Cambridge: Cambridge UP, 1985.

Ornstein, Robert Evan. *The Psychology of Consciousness*. San Francisco: Freeman, 1972.

Ortner, Sherry B. *Making Gender: The Politics and Erotics of Gender*. Boston: Beacon, 1996.

Otten, Charlotte F., ed. *A Lycanthropy Reader: Werewolves in Western Culture*. Syracuse: Syracuse UP, 1986.

Palmer, John. "A Mail Survey of Ouija Board Users in North America." *Journal of Parapsychology* 63.3 (1999): 217.

Palmgreen, Phillip, Lawrence A. Wenner, and Karl Erik Rosengren. "Uses and Gratifications Research: The Past Ten Years." Ed. Rosengren, Wenner, and Palmgreen. *Media Gratifications Research: Current Perspectives*. Beverly Hills: Sage, 1985. 11–37.

Paul, William. "What Rough Beasts: Confessions of a Gross-out Maven." *Film Comment* 30 (1994): 80–85.

Pekala, Ronald, J. V. K. Kumar, and James Cummings. "Types of High Hypnotically Susceptible Individuals and Reported Attitudes and Experiences on the Paranormal and Anomalous." *Journal of the American Society for Psychical Research* 86 (1992): 135–50.

Penczak, Christopher. *City Magick: Urban Rituals, Spells, and Shamanism*. New York: Weiser, 2001.

Perrine, Daniel M. *The Chemistry of Mind-Altering Drugs: History, Pharmacology and Cultural Context*. Washington: American Chemical Soc., 1996.

Perry, David K. *Theory and Research in Mass Communication: Contexts and Consequences*. Mahwah: Erlbaum, 1996.

Pipher, Mary Bray. *Reviving Ophelia: Saving the Selves of Adolescent Girls*. New York: Putnam, 1994.

Press, Andrea Lee. "Class, Gender and the Female Viewer." *Television and Women's Culture: The Politics of the Popular*. Ed. M. E. Brown. London: Sage, 1991.

Pulliam, Carol M. "We Should Turn Away from Occult Influences" [letter to the editor]. *Greensboro News and Record* 29 Feb. 2000: A12.

Ravenwolf, Silver. *Teen Witch: Wicca for a New Generation*. St. Paul: Llewellyn, 1998.

Redgrove, H. Stanley. *Alchemy: Ancient and Modern*. New York: Harper, 1973.

Reed, Thomas, and Nicole M. Slagle. "The Transforming Draught: Stevenson's Mirror of Temperance." MLA Convention. Chicago. 28 Dec. 1999.

Roeper, Richard. "Let's Separate Fact from Fiction." *Chicago Sun-Times* 18 Sept. 2001: 11. 1 Oct. 2001 <http://www.suntimes.com/terror/archives/0918.html>.

Roll, William G., and Michael A. Persinger. "Investigations of Poltergeist and Haunts: A Review and Interpretation." *Hauntings and Poltergeists: Multidisciplinary Perspectives*. Ed. James Houran and Rense Lange. Jefferson: McFarland, 2001. 123–63.

Rosaldo, Michelle Zimbalist, and Louise Lamphere, eds. *Woman, Culture, and Society*. Stanford: Stanford UP, 1975.

Rotschild, Bertram. "Exorcism Lives!" *Humanist* 61 (2001): 41.

Rousseau, Jean-Jacques. *The Social Contract, and Discourses.* New York: Dutton, 1913.

Rubin, Alan M. "Uses and Gratifications and Media Effects Research." *Perspectives on Media Effects.* Ed. Jennings Bryant and Dolf Zillman. Hillsdale: Erlbaum, 1986. 417–36.

Ruby, Jay. "Portraying the Dead." *Omega: Journal of Death and Dying* 1.19 (1989): 1–20.

Rumi. *The Essential Rumi.* Trans. Coleman Barks with John Moyne. San Francisco: Harper, 1995.

Rust, Michael, and David Wagner. "Dumbing Down God." *Insight on the News* 14.20 (1998): 8–12.

Sacks, Ethan. "September 11th Heroes Inspire New Comic Books." *Greensboro News and Record* 6 June 2002: A2.

Sagoff, Mark. "Patented Genes: An Ethical Appraisal." *Issues in Science and Technology* 14.3 (1998): 37–42.

Sardiello, Robert. "Secular Rituals in Popular Culture: A Case for Grateful Dead Concerts and Dead Head Community." *Adolescents and Their Music: If It's Too Loud, You're Too Old.* Ed. Jonathan S. Epstein. New York: Garland, 1994. 115–40.

Saxonhouse, Arlene. *Women in the History of Political Thought: Ancient Greece to Machiavelli.* New York: Praeger, 1985.

Schechner, Richard. *Between Theatre and Anthropology.* Philadelphia: U of Pennsylvania P, 1985.

Schneider, Kirk J. *Horror and the Holy: Wisdom and Teachings of the Monster Tale.* Chicago: Open Court, 1993.

Schumaker, John F. *Wings of Illusion: The Origin, Nature, and Future of Paranormal Belief.* Buffalo: Prometheus, 1990.

Schwartz, Tony. *Media: The Second God.* New York: Anchor, 1983.

Schwartz, Vanessa. "Cinematic Spectatorship Before the Apparatus: The Public Taste for Reality in *Fin-de-Siècle* Paris." *Cinema and the Invention of Modern Life.* Ed. Leo Charney and Vanessa Schwartz. Berkeley: U of California P, 1995. 297–319.

Sconce, Jeffrey. *Haunted Media: Electronic Presence from Telegraphy to Television.* Durham: Duke UP, 2000.

Severin, Werner J., and James W. Tankard. *Communication Theories: Origins, Methods, and Uses in the Mass Media.* 3rd ed. New York: Longman, 1992.

Shah, Idries. *The Exploits of the Incomparable Mulla Nasrudin.* New York: Simon, 1966.

Shelley, Mary Wollstonecraft. *Frankenstein, or the Modern Prometheus.* 1831. New York: Portland House, 1988.

Shenk, Joshua Wolf. "America's Altered States." *Harper's Magazine* May 1999: 38.

Sidky, Homayun. *Witchcraft, Lycanthropy, Drugs, and Disease: An Anthropological Study of the European Witch-Hunts.* New York: Lang, 1997.

Singer, Andre, and Lynette Singer. *Divine Magic: The World of the Supernatural.* New York: TV Books, 1995.

Singer, Ben. "Modernity, Hyperstimulus, and the Rise of Popular Sensationalism." *Cinema and the Invention of Modern Life.* Ed. Leo Charney and Vanessa R. Schwartz. Berkeley: U of California P, 1995: 72–99.

Smith, Gail. "School Warns Three Students over Peers' Fears of 'Death Spells.'" *Charlotte Observer* 21 Jan. 1999: 2B.

Soloway, Colin, Evan Thomas, Karen Breslau, and Ron Moreau. "A Long, Strange Trip to the Taliban." *Newsweek* 17 Dec. 2001: 30.

Sontag, Susan. "The Imagination of Disaster." *Against Interpretation, and Other Essays.* New York: Farrar, 1966.

Sparks, Glenn G. "Paranormal Depictions in the Media: How Do They Affect What People Believe?" *Skeptical Inquirer* 22.4 (1998): 35–40.

———. "The Relationship Between Paranormal Beliefs and Religious Beliefs." *Skeptical Inquirer* 25.5 (2001): 50.

Sparks, Glenn G., C. L. Nelson, and R. G. Campbell. "The Relationship Between Exposure in Televised Messages about Paranormal Phenomena and Paranormal Beliefs." *Journal of Broadcasting and Electronic Media* 41 (1997): 345–59.

Sparshott, F. E. "Basic Film Aesthetics." *Film Theory and Criticism: Introductory Readings.* Ed. Gerald Mast and Marshall Cohen. 3rd ed. New York: Oxford UP, 1985. 284–304.

Summers, Montague. *The Werewolf.* New Hyde Park: University Books, 1966.

Thomas, Keith. *Religion and the Decline of Magic.* New York: Scribner, 1971.

Thompson, Richard. "A Guide to Christian Metz." *Cinema* Spring 1972: 37–45.

Thrasher, F. M. "The Comics and Delinquency: Cause or Scapegoat." *Journal of Educational Sociology* 23.1 (1949): 195–205.

Viera, Dave. *Lighting for Film and Electronic Cinematography.* Belmont: Wadsworth, 1993.

Wales, Lorene M. *The People and Process of Film and Video Production: From Low Budget to High Budget.* Boston: Pearson, 2004.

Walker, Jearl. "The Amateur Scientist." *Scientific American* 2 Aug. 1991: 126–31.

Walter, Tony. "Reincarnation, Modernity, and Identity." *Sociology* 35.1 (2001): 21.

Warshow, Robert. "Paul, the Horror Comics, and Dr. Wertham." *Mass Culture: The Popular Arts in America.* Ed. Bernard Rosenberg and David Manning White. New York: Free, 1957. 199–211.

Watson, Lyall. *Beyond Supernature: A New Natural History of the Supernatural.* New York: Bantam, 1988.

Weis, Elisabeth, and John Belton Film, eds. *Film Sound: Theory and Practice.* New York: Columbia UP, 1985.

Weiss, Joanna. "Hoax, Smoke Photo Called Search for Meaning." *Boston Globe* 18 Sept. 2001: B1.

Wertham, Fredric. *Seduction of the Innocent.* New York: Rinehart, 1954.

Wessinger, Catherine. *Women's Leadership in Marginal Religions: Explorations Outside the Mainstream.* Urbana: U of Illinois P, 1993.

"Wiccan Teacher Fights Suspension." *Christian Century* 2 Feb. 2000: 114.

Williams, Raymond. *Marxism and Literature.* Oxford: Oxford UP, 1977.

Wilson, Colin. *The Occult: A History.* New York: Random, 1971.

———. *Witches.* New York: Crescent, 1981.

Wilson, Colin, and Patricia Pitman. *Encyclopedia of Murder.* New York: Putnam's, 1962.

Winn, Marie. *The Plug-in Drug.* New York: Viking, 1977.

Winston, Brian. "Showdown at Culture Gulch." *Impact of Mass Media: Current Issues.* Ed. Ray Eldon Hiebert and Carol Reuss. New York: Longman, 1985. 473–81.

"Witch." *American Heritage Illustrated Encyclopedic Dictionary.* Boston: Houghton, 1987.

"Witch." *Webster's Dictionary of the English Usage.* Springfield: Merriam-Webster, 1989.

Wright, Daniel L. "'The Prisonhouse of My Disposition': A Study of the Psychology of Addiction in 'Dr. Jekyll and Mr. Hyde.'" *Studies in the Novel* 26.3 (1994): 254–68.

Zettl, Herbert. *Sight, Sound, and Motion: Applied Media Aesthetics.* 3rd ed. Belmont: Wadsworth, 1999.

Index

abominable snowman. *See* Bigfoot
addictions: and exorcism, 3–4; and media, 44–45; and *The Strange Case of Dr. Jekyll and Mr. Hyde*, 145; street drugs, 43–44
adolescent. *See* teenager
advertising: and added value, 203; and effects of, 7–8, 49; and witches, 79. *See also* marketing; publicity
alchemist, 52, 53. *See also* witch; wizard
alchemy: and production, 63; in *The Secret World of Alex Mack*, 111; in *The Tempest*, 110; and transmutation, 52; versus illusion, 53. *See also* magic
All of Me, 185–86, 189
Alper, Matthew, 16
altar, 24–26, 25
Altered States, 148–49, 160–61, 182
American Idol, 188, 228n. 7 (chapter 6)
American Werewolf in London, An, 153, 160, 162
Andrew, J. Dudley, 59
animal spirits, 108, 144. *See also* soul, in animals
Ape Woman, The, 157, 162
apparitions. *See* ghosts
Apprentice to Murder, 92–94, 131
archaic time: and popular media, 26–29; and print, 29; and production processes, 56, 219n. 5
archetype, 28, 34, 195
Arnheim, Rudolf, 58
art: and cult value, 53–56; and production, 56–66; sacred elements of, x, 53, 64; versus business, 64–68
artist: 47, 52–56, 58, 195
Ashcroft, John, 37, 219n. 12
astral projection, 21, 24, 142. *See also* out of body
atavism: and *Cat People*, 153; explanations for, 140; and Jekyll and Hyde, 145–49; and myths

139, 140; and shape-shifting, 156; and telepathy, 142; and violence, 159–62
Attack of the Mayan Mummy, 175, 189
audience: as gullible, 6; and media dependency, 17; media effects on, 4–7, 217n. 2; as obstinate, 8–9, 11, 196; as selective, 9–10; as wizard, 8, 48–49, 195, 196
Audrey Rose, 165, 169, 171–72, 176, 188, 189
Awakening, The, 179, 189

bad aesthetics, 9, 100, 196
Bad Moon, 153, 160, 162
Bauer, Raymond, 8
Bazin, Andrew, 58
beast (animal): in myth, 139–40; and reincarnation, 169; and soul, 142–45, 179–82; and werewolf, 141, 149–56. *See also* atavism; monster
Beauty and the Beast, 159, 163
Becker, Carl, 166–67, 173
Being Human, 168–69, 189
belief: and obstinate audience, 11, 196; and occult, x; in Ouija board, 210, 212; in paranormal, x–xi; and reincarnation, 167; in ritual magic, 74, 140; in witches, 74
Bell, Book and Candle, 119, 131
Benjamin, Walter, 53–55
Bernstein, Morley, 174
Bewitched, 76, 77, 78, 117–18, 128, 131
Bigfoot, 149, 226n. 10
bin Laden, Osama, 35, 36
Black Hawk Down, 34
Black Magic, 117, 119–20, 131
Black Magic Woman, 120–21, 131
Black Robe, 105–7, 131
Blair Witch Project, The, 78, 100, 209, 223n. 13, 230n. 18
Bless the Child, 97, 129, 131

Blood from the Mummy's Tomb, 186, 189
Bondeson, Jan, 157
Book of Shadows, 207, 229n. 15
Brainstorm, 23–24
Bram Stoker's Dracula, 178–79, 189
Bride and the Beast, The, 176, 187, 189
Buddha, 169–71. *See also* Siddhartha
Buddhism, 36, 165–67, 173
Buffy the Vampire Slayer, 79, 224n. 18
bullet theory. *See* direct media effects
Bush, George, 35, 74

Cabot, Laurie, 207
Cadiff, Andy, 66, 222n. 14
Cameron, Julia, 65–66
Caporael, Linda, 88–89
Captain Kangaroo, 19, 219n. 1
Carrie, 114, 132
Castaneda, Carlos, 44, 50, 52, 226n. 9
Cat People, 153–54, 161, 163
Cayce, Edgar, 178, 228n. 6 (chapter 6)
cemetery: haunted, 199, *202*; for pets, 144, 225n. 5
Chances Are, 183, 184, 190
channeling, 196, 204, 228n. 2
Charmed, 74, 76, 77, 132, 208
Chocolat, 124, 208
Chong, Tommy, 46–47
Christianity: and *Black Robe*, 106–7; and Christ as sorcerer, 222n. 4; and faith healing, 77, 78; and fear of alternative religions, 11, 75; and fundamentalism, 5, 33, 43, 93; and marketing, 229n. 12; and miracles, 77–78; and paganism, 109; and reincarnation, 167, 168, 182; and supplication, 77, 230n. 17; and witch, 81, 94–101
Church of Satan, 85, 87
cinematographer (camera operator), 54, 60, 61–62
Circe, 116, 132
Collateral Damage, 32, 34
comic books: and influence of, 6; and real life heroes, 34; witch characters developed from, 112
communication processes, 57–58
Company of Wolves, 150–51, 162, 163
computers: and addiction, 44–45; as devil, 7; and games, 24; and technopagan, 26
Conan the Barbarian, 116, 132
Conqueror Worm, The. See Witchfinder General
Corbett, Michael, 61–62, *63*
counterculture, 39–43, 148, 167. *See also* Dead Head; music subculture

coven, 95, 100, 102, 104, 201, 207, 208
craft. *See* magic; spell; witchcraft
Craft, The, 73–74, 83, 115–16, *116*, 132, 208
Crowley, Aleister, 87, 88, 223n. 11
Crucible, The, 89, 91, 132
crystal ball, 25
Cueno, Michael, 3–4
cult: and media depiction of, 112–13; media exposure of, 10; and *Sabrina, the Teenage Witch*, 112–13; and satanic, 87
cult value: in acting, 54; and art, 53–56; defined, 53; in production processes, 56–65, 195
curse, 120, 140, 142, 151, 181, 183. *See also* magic; spell
cyber witch, 24. *See also* neopagan; technopagan

Dark Angel, 159, 162, 163
Dark Shadows, 79, 132
Dark Wind, 107–8, 132
Darwin, Charles, 16, 139, 140. *See also* evolution
Dead Again, 176–78, 190
Dead Head: and Dead TV, 42, 220n. 15; opposition to mainstream media, 42–43; and secular ritual, 39; as subculture, 38–45; and the Well, 42, 220n. 15
Dead Write, 61–64
Death Becomes Her, 117, 132
degradation ceremonies, 35–38
Déjà Vu, 177–78, 190
demon: in *Black Robe*, 106; in *Häxan*, 84; in *Witches of Eastwick*, 120. *See also* devil; Satan
devil: as alchemist, 53; in computer, 7; in dubious witch films, 91–93; and exorcism, 3–5; and have-nots, 15; and *Malleus Maleficarum*, 94–95; in media, 4–7, 17; and mental illness, 84; and *The Ninth Gate*, 95–96; reality of, 92; and self-empowerment, 96, 97; and *Sleepy Hollow*, 104; and werewolf, 150; as wizard, 53. *See also* demon; Satan
Devin, Pat, 115, 225n. 26
direct media effects, 4–7, 8, 9, 217nn. 2, 3
disbelief, 9, 196. *See also* skepticism; suspension of disbelief
docudrama, 29
Dr. Jekyll and Mr. Hyde: and Jekyll's boredom, 160–62; and popularity of, 145; story retold in films, 145–49; titles in filmography, 163; as werewolf, 151–52
Dr. Moreau: and genetic manipulation, 159; and *Island of Dr. Moreau*, 147, 164; and *Island of Lost Souls*, 146–47, 164
Down to Earth, 184–85, 187, 188, 190

Dragonslayer, 129, 133
Drawing Down the Moon, 126, 133
drugs: and altered consciousness, 43; and Dead Heads, 40; Dr. Jekyll, 145, 148; LSD, 43–44; media compared to, 44–45; as spiritual pathway, 43, 44
druid, 89, 109
dubious witch, 81, 90–94, 196
Duclos, Denis, 159

Echols, Damien, 87–88, 223n. 12
Edison, Thomas, 20–21, 219n. 3
Edwards, Paul, 182
ego, 45, 98, 145, 165, 181, 188, 196
electromagnetic-field detector (EMF), 198, 201, 203
Eliade, Mircea, 27–29, 29–30
enchantress, 81, 116–21
ergot poisoning, 88–89, 141
Everybody Loves Raymond, 144
evolution: and animal traits, 140–41, 145–49; and Dr. Moreau, 146–47; and reincarnation, 175–76; and telepathy, 142–43
Evolution's Child, 143, 163
Excalibur, 129, 133
exorcism: abolition of, 3; and psychological problems, 3–4. *See also* possession
Exorcist, The, 3–7, 4, 13, 15, 17, 211, 217nn. 1, 4, 5

fairy tale: animal and human relationships in, 225n. 4; and atavism, 144; and media appropriation of, 209; and Red Riding Hood, 149–51; and witch, 101–4. *See also* folklore; myths
fairy-tale witch: definition of, 81; media depiction of, 101–4; popularity of, 82
Fait Accompli, 108, 133
faith healing, 77, 78, 92–93
Farscape, 122, 123, 133
Faust, 98, 100, 133
feminism, 81, 85, 122
fertility rite, 97, 124, 126
film: and art, 54; and grammar, 58–60. *See also* media
Fitzpatrick, Sonja, 142
Fluke, 179–81, 190
folklore: and apocalypse, 33; and marketing, 202–3; and media appropriation of, 209–10; and media narratives, 212, 230n. 19; and werewolf, 151; and witch, 94. *See also* fairy tale; myths
formalism, 59–60
frame, 58
Freud, Sigmund, 145

Garcia, Jerry, 38, 41–42
Gardner, Gerald, 85, 223n. 10, 229n. 13
Gerbner, George, 218n. 12
ghosts: and electromagnetic-field detector, 198, 201, 203; and folklore, 198–201; and media narratives, 199–201, 229n. 11; and photography, 201–2; and technology, 22, 228n. 7 (chapter 7); and tourism, 197–203, 228nn. 6 (chapter 7), 8, 229nn. 10, 11; and witch, 78
Ghost Story, 200
ghost walk, 198–205, *199*
Gift, The, 124–25, 133
Ginger Snaps, 154–55, 160, 161, 163, 226n. 13
global village: and global city, 27; and global society, 35; and McLuhan, 26–27. *See also* tribe
gnosis, 25
Goddess Remembered, 86, 133
Goleman, Daniel, 68
Gonzalez, Elian, 30–31
Goosebumps, 102, 133
Graham, Billy, 7
Grateful Dead, 38–39. *See also* Dead Head
grimoire. *See* Book of Shadows

Halloween: and games, 212; and Samhain, 109; and terrorism, 33
Haraldsson, Erlendur, 227n. 4
Hardison, Travis, 49–52
Harry Potter: banning or boycotting of, 218n. 11; in books and movies, 11; as ingénue witch, 111, 224n. 22; as leader, 129; merchandising, *12*, 75; and muggle, 77, 224n. 21; popularity of, 75, 222n. 3
Haunting of Morella, The, 98–99, 133
have-nots, 15
Häxan, 84–85, *84*, 133
Heaven Can Wait, 184, 187, 189, 190
Hello Again, 126, 133
Here Comes Mr. Jordan, 184, 185, 187, 190
heresy, 9, 90
Hess, David, 12
hex, 93. *See also* magic; spell
Hindu, 139, 165, 166
historical witch: defined, 81; in documentary, 83–90; in narrative, 90–94
historic time. *See* linear time
hoaxes, 20, 50
Hold That Hypnotist, 174, 190
Hopkins, Matthew, 89–90, 223n. 14
horror movies: and enchantress witch, 82; and reincarnation, 171, 178–79, 182; and satanic

horror movies *(continued)*
 witch, 95–97, 100; supernatural depicted in, 12; and werewolf, 150, 156
Household Saints, 77–78, 222n. 5
Howling, The, 155–56, 163
hypertrichosis, 157
hypnosis, 173–76, 177

id, 145, 146
I Married a Witch, 116, 118–19, 134
immortality, 14, 23, 56
ingénue witch, 81, 82, 110–16
Innis, Harold, 22
Inquisition, 84, 96, 99, 140
interpersonal communication, 57, 212
intrapersonal communication, 57
Islam, 35, 77, 167
Island of Dr. Moreau, 147. *See also* Dr. Moreau
Island of Lost Souls, The, 146–47
I Was a Teenage Werewolf, 164, 175, 227n. 5

Joan of Arc, 89, 134
Jong, Erica, 75–76
Judaism, 77, 167, 187
Judeo-Christian time. *See* linear time
Jung, Carl, 55, 141–42
Jungle Goddess, 109, 134

karma: and animal reincarnation, 179–82; and Dead Heads, 41; defined, 166–67; and evolution, 175; justice in, 182, 189; misery in, 173; retribution in, 177
Katz, Steven D., 55–56, 59, 61
Kelly, Adian A., 207
Kesey, Ken, 44
Khan, Hazrat Inayat, 27
Khouri, Callie, 8
Krulwich, Robert, 28
Kull the Conqueror, 116, 134
Kundun, 169, 171, 187, 190

Larson, Bob, 87, 131
LaVey, Anton Szandor, 85
Leary, Timothy, 43–44
Legend of the Spirit Dog, The, 144, 226n. 8
lesbian, 99, 224n. 18
light, 58–59
Lilith, 121, 225n. 27
limited media effects. *See* uses and gratifications
Lindh, John Walker, 36–38
Lindsey, Shelley, 114
linear time, 27–29, 56, 219n. 5. *See also* archaic time

Lippmann, Walter, 17
Little Buddha, 169–71, 179, 187, 190
Little Red Riding Hood, 149–52
Little Witches, 96–97, 115, 134
Lombroso, Cesare, 141, 225n. 3
Lucifer. *See* Satan
lunacy. *See* mental illness
lycanthropy, 141–42, 149

magic: audience response as, 58; belief in, 16; and computer, 24; definition of, 77; and dubious witch, 94; and enchantress, 116–21; and fairy-tale witch, 102–3; as feminine attribute, 128; as illicit, 127; and illusion, 53; and ingénue witch, 110–15; and intuition 113, 116; media properties as, 58–60, 106, 213; need for, 10; as neutral, 82–83, 208; and New-Age witch, 122–26; and power, 127; proved false, 109; and satanic witch, 94; and shamanic witch, 105, 107–9; and shapeshifting, 140, 160; as weapon, 127, 214; and Wiccans, 86
magical thinking, xi, 18–21, 74, 82
magic bullet. *See* direct media effects
magician, 77. *See also* alchemist; witch; wizard
Malleus Maleficarum, 94–95, 224n. 16
Marin, Cheech, 46
marketing, 197, 198, 202–3. *See also* advertising; publicity
Matilda, 111, 134
McLuhan, Marshall, 22, 24, 26, 35, 44, 45–46
McNally, Dennis, 41
Medea, 105–6, 106, 134
media: as art, 54–55; breederism, 198, 228n. 5; as drug, 38, 43–45; effects of, 4–9, 217n. 2, 3; and grammar, 58–60; possession by, 7; and production of, 56–64; publicizing occult beliefs, x, 16, 21, 23, 202–3; as shaman, 45–47; as trickster, 46–47; uses and gratifications, of 9–13; and violence, 10, 14, 217n. 2. *See also* computers; film; technology; television
medium: defined, 23; and grammatical misuse of, 46; and hoaxes, 20; and TV ritual, 25–26. *See also* computer; film; media; television; witch
menstruation, 114–15, 154–55
mental disability, 99
mental illness: in *Apprentice to Murder*, 92; and lycanthropy, 141; and possession, 3–4, 84; and scientists, 147; in *The Wolf Man*, 152–53
Mephisto Waltz, 186, 190
Merlin, 101–2, 125, 134
mesmerism, 38. *See also* hypnosis

metaphysics: and Dead Heads, 38–43; definition of, ix; and degradation ceremonies, 36; and media technology, 22–26; and popular culture, 12

metempsychosis, 165, 184. *See also* transmigration

Midnight in the Garden of Good and Evil, 134, 200–201

millennium: and anxiety, 11, 28; and celebration of, 28–29; and Y2K, 28. *See also* linear time

Mills, C. Wright, 17

miracle ticket, 40–41

mise-en-scène, 59

misogyny, 86, 89, 90, 115, 119–20, 127, 225n. 24

Mists of Avalon, The, 125–26, 208

Mitry, Jean, 58

mockumentary, 88, 223n. 13

monster, 31, 78, 97, 141, 176, 178. *See also* beast

morbid curiosity, 219n. 6, 221n. 3

Morgan le Fey, 125

mortal: and awareness of, 16; and muggle, 77; and witch, 76

muggle, 77, 224n. 21

Mummy, The, 178, 190

Murray, Margaret, 85, 223n. 10, 229n. 13

music subculture, 41. *See also* counterculture; Dead Head; subculture

music television, 10–11

mutual pretense, 202–5, 213

My Mother the Car, 175, 187, 190

myths: and animal forms, 142–44; and classical gods, 40, 141; and disaster, 31–33; and Elian Gonzalez, 30–31; and heroes, 34–35; of media production, 66; and metamorphosis, 139–40; in narrative, 29–30; and propaganda, 34; and September 11th, 31–32; and time, 27. *See also* fairy tale; folklore

Nasrudin, Mulla, 46

neopagan, 205, 207–8, 213. *See also* pagan; technopagan

New Age: and alternative religions, 15, 88, 227n. 1; and animal soul, 142; and consumer goods, 205, 229nn. 12, 14; in *Practical Magic*, 120; and regression therapy, 173; and reincarnation, 172; self-empowerment, 76; as type of witch, 81, 82, 100, 112, 121–26; veneration of nature, 96, 121

nihilism, 160–62

Nimmo, Dan, 30, 35

Ninth Gate, The, 95–96, 135

nirvana, 166, 171, 178, 181, 189

Nostradamus, 33

numerology, 33

Obeah, 93, 224n. 15

occult: and alchemy, 53; as cliché, 21; and consumer goods, 205; definition of, x, 3, 15; and divine union, 43; and Halloween, 33; and Islam, 35; media exposure of, x, 21, 127; media lore, 210; and power, 129, 130; and production processes, 58–60, 69, 196; and social anxiety, 15–17; and supernatural, 16; and violence, 14

Offreduccio, Clare, 18

Oh, Heavenly Dog, 182, 187, 190

On a Clear Day You Can See Forever, 176, 187–88, 190

100 Deeds for Eddie McDowd, 181, 190

opinion leaders, 8

Ouija board, 6, 42, 210–12, 217n. 6

out of body: and drugs, 45–46; and media, 21–26, 44–45; and Clare Offreduccio, 18; and psychic travel, 24

pagan, 85, 86, 109, 143, 205, 207. *See also* neopagan; technopagan

Paradise Lost: The Child Murders at Robin Hood Hills, 87–88, 135

paranormal. *See* supernatural

parapsychologist, 203

passion: and media production, 68; and romanticism, 67; and stoicism, 66–67

Pastrana, Julia, 157

Peasboro, Jim, 7

Perrine, Daniel, 43

Pet Psychic, 142–43, 164

photography: and cult value, 53–54; double exposure, 22; and ghosts, 201; and mediums, 20, and Satan's-face urban legend, 32–33

Pipher, Mary, 73

Pokemon, 11, 218n. 10

Poltergeist, 198–200

pornography: and production of, 49–51; and sacred image, 52; and Wiccan, 209

possession: and demon, 94; depicted in media, 6, 13, 99; and direct media effects, 4–7; and Ouija board, 211; and *Sleepy Hollow*, 104; and transmigration, 186, 187. *See also* exorcism

Practical Magic, 120, 135

Prelude to a Kiss, 186, 190

production processes: as business, 64; cult value in, 53–60; and formalism, 59–60; and grammar, 58–59; and independent film, 60–64; as

production processes *(continued)*
  occult process, 52–53, 69; and passion, 66–
  69; and pornography, 49–51, 220n. 2
psychic abilities, 176, 207. *See also* telepathy
psychokinesis. *See* telekinesis
publicity, 197–98, 202–3. *See also* advertising;
  marketing

Quantum Leap, 187, 190
Quartier Mozart, 103, 135

Rage: Carrie 2, The, 114–15, 135
Rapp, Anthony, 55
Ravenwolf, Silver, 75
realism, 57, 221n. 11
reality TV, 13–14
reincarnation: and African beliefs, 167, 178; and
  American counterculture, 167; and Buddhism, 165–67; and Christianity, 167; definition of, 165–67; and heresy, 167; and Hindu,
  165; and incest, 183; and Judaism, 167; and
  memory, 171–72, 175–76, 180, 181; and New
  Age, 167, 227n. 1
Reincarnation of Peter Proud, 183, 190
religion: and alternative beliefs, 15, 17, 37; and
  art, 55, 64–65; and occult, x; and orthodoxy,
  x, 30, 78, 144, 160, 167, 204
Remember the Witches, 86, 135
Resurrection, 124, 135
ritual: and magic, 10, 127; and mutual pretense,
  213; and production, 56, 60, 63–64; and
  smudging, 204, 206; and TV scrying, 24–26;
  types of, 204
Roeper, Richard, 33
Romanticism, 67
Root Doctor, 64
Roseanne, 42
Rosemary's Baby, 85, 95, 96, 135, 224n. 17
Rose Red, 198, 228n. 4
Rowling, J. K., 218n. 11, 222n. 3

Sabrina, the Teenage Witch, 74, 78, 112–13, 208
Salem witch trials, 83, 85
Sasquatch. *See* Bigfoot
Satan: and documentary films, 85, 87; face in
  news photo, 32; and Satanic witch, 81–82,
  94–101; in *Sleepy Hollow*, 104. *See also* devil
satanic witch, 81, 82, 94–101, 104
Satanism, 85, 87, 96–97
Satan's Princess, 99, 135
Sawyer, Diane, 19, 30
Scariest Places on Earth, 88, 135

Scarlet Letter, The, 91, 135
Schumaker, John, x
Sconce, Jeffrey, 20
scrying, 24–26
séances, 20
Search for Bridey Murphy, The, 167, 174, 175, 187,
  190
Secrets of the Dead, 88, 136
Secrets of the Unknown, 85, 136
Secret World of Alex Mack, The, 111, 136
Seduced by Evil, 121, 130, 136, 178, 227n. 5
seeker: and Dead Heads, 44; and degradation of,
  35–38
September 11th: and mythical elements, 31–35;
  and urban legends, 32–33; and yin-yang me-
  dia, 31, 219n. 6. *See also* terrorism
serial killer, 155, 156, 159, 226n. 15
Serpent and the Rainbow, 22, 108, 129, 136
Serpent's Lair, The, 121, 136
Seventh Seal, The, 92, 93, 136
Seventh Sign, The, 182–83, 187, 190
Shadowhunter, 107, 136
shaman: and *Altered States*, 148; and artist, 53;
  and media, 47; as type of witch, 81, 105–10.
  See also alchemist; witch; wizard
shape-shifting (shape-changing): and atavism,
  156; and folklore, 139–40; and privileged class,
  160; as schizophrenia, 152; as sexual disease,
  154, 155; and *Wolfen*, 156. *See also* atavism
She, 117, 118, 136
Siddhartha, 170, 187, 191
Silver Bullet, 153, 164
Sinbad and the Eye of the Tiger, 103, 129, 136
Sixth Sense, The, 200
skepticism, 12, 85, 196
skinwalker, 107–8
Sleepy Hollow, 104, 136
smudging, 204, 206
Snow White, 102, 136, 209
Sontag, Susan, 31, 33–34
sorcerer. *See* alchemist; shaman; witch; wizard
sorceress, 76, 117, 121, 136. *See also* witch
soul: in animals, 142, 144–45, 149; and ego, 165–
  68, 188; and memory, 170–72, 188; and passion, 67–68; and reincarnation, 165–85; and
  stoicism, 67; and transmigration, 185–87
Sparks, Glenn, x, 11
Sparshott, F. E., 50
special effects, 22, 31, 49, 50
spell, 78, 89, 121, 207, 229n. 16. *See also* magic;
  ritual

spirit. *See* ghosts; soul
spirituality, 16
Star Wars: and archaic time, 29; and Jedi Knight religion, 17
Stevenson, Robert Louis, 145
stoicism: definition of, 67; and media production, 66; and passion, 67–68
Stubbe, Peter, 140, 225n. 2
subculture, 38–43. *See also* Dead Head
supernatural: and animals, 143; belief in, 16, 196; and media exposure, 11, 196, 197; and occult ritual, x, 205–7, 212; and orthodox religion, x; and publicity, 197–202; and teens, 73, 74; and tourism, 196–201, 205
suspension of disbelief, 21–22, 69, 195, 213
Suspiria, 99–100, 137
Swept from the Sea, 92, 137

taboo, 10, 95
technology: as drug, 44–45; as hoax, 20; human reliance on, 142; and McLuhan, 45–46; as miraculous, ix, 18–21, 23–24, 56; revealing the supernatural, 201; as shaman, 45–46; and special effects, 22, 49, 50
technopagan, 21, 24, 26. *See also* neopagan; pagan
teenager: and taboo, 10; and violence, 14, 100; and witchcraft, 73–75, 110–17
telekinesis, 114, 142, 159
telepathy, 142–43
television: for scrying or divination, 24–26; as drug, 44. *See also* media
Tempest, The, 110, 137
terrorism, 14, 19, 31–35
Thelma and Louise, 8
Theosophical Society, 227n. 1
Tighe, Virginia Burns, 174. *See also The Search for Bridey Murphy*
time: and hypnosis, 174; manipulation of, 25–26, 56. *See also* archaic time; linear time
tourism, 197, 203, 205
transformation, 139, 195. *See also* transmutation
transmigration, 165, 185–87, 188. *See also* reincarnation
transmutation: and audience, 48–49; definition of, 52; and destiny 60; and media production, 56–58; and spiritual regeneration, 55; versus construction, 67
tribe: and coven, 208; and Dead Heads, 39; defined by media, 13–14; and degradation ceremony, 35–38; and global community, 35, 37; and production crew, 61–64, 195
Twins of Evil, 79, 137

Undead, The, 174, 191
urban legends, 32–33
uses and gratifications, 9–10

vampire, 79, 178, 179
Viera, Dave, 59
voodoo, 26, 93, 108–9

Walter, Tony, 167
warlock. *See* witch
Warrior and the Sorceress, The, 137, 177
werewolf: in comedy, 158; existential dilemma in, 160–62; folklore origins of, 151; and Little Red Riding Hood, 149–51; medical explanations for, 141–42; and serial killer, 156, 161–62, 226n. 15; witchcraft films, 79; and witchcraft persecutions, 140
What Happened to Rosa? 167, 191
Wicca: and *Buffy the Vampire Slayer*, 79; and *Charmed*, 77; definition of, 76; as different from Satanism, 208–9; and *Drawing Down the Moon*, 126; and Gerald Gardner, 85–86; and magic, 86; and neopagan, 205–9; and New Age, 121–22; and teenagers, 75
Wicker Man, The, 109, 137
Wilderness, 155, 164
Winchester Mansion, 197–98
Winn, Marie, 44
witch: belief in, 74; definition of, 75; dubious, 81, 90–94; enchantress, 81, 116–21; fairy-tale, 81, 101–4; and feminism, 80, 85; gender of, 127; and ghost, 78; historical, 81, 83–90; ingénue, 81, 110–16; and lesbian, 99, 224n. 18; and mental disability, 84; New Age, 81, 121–26; as other, 130–31; paraphernalia of, *206*; and power, 127; satanic, 81, 94–101, 104; shamanic, 81, 105–10; teen fascination with, 73–75; types of, 80–83, *83*; and vampire, 78–79; versus saint, 222n. 5. *See also* wizard
Witchblade, 113, 114, 137
Witchboard, 210–11
Witch City, 87, 137
witchcraft, 73–75, 77, 90, 119, 126, 207. *See also* magic; spell
Witchcraft Through the Ages. See Häxan
Witches, The, 101, 102, 138
Witches of Eastwick, 120, 138, 225n. 25
Witchfinder General, 89–90, *91*, 138
Witching of Ben Wagner, 122–24, 138
wizard: and alchemy, 52–53; and ambition, 24; and audience, 48–49; and magic, 24; as media producer, 49, 57–58, 195; as pornogra-

wizard *(continued)*
    pher, 50; as technology, 47; and transmuta-
    tion, 52–53. *See also* witch
Wizard of Oz, 101, 103, 138
Wolf, 158, 162, 164
Wolfen, 156–57, 164
Wolf Girl, 157–58, 162, 164
Wolf Man, The, 152–53, 156, 160, 164
women: as other, 127–30; as witch, 77, 113, 129
Wondrous Events, 212, 229n. 14
Wondrous Healing, 229n. 14

World's Creepiest Destinations, 86, 138
Worst Witch, The, 129, 138
Wuornos, Aileen, 226n. 15

xenoglossy, 173
X-files, 187, 191

Yeti. *See* Bigfoot
yin-yang hypothesis, 31, 219n. 6
You Are There, 85, 138
You Never Can Tell, 181–82, 191

Emily D. Edwards was a media producer and journalist before receiving her doctorate from the University of Tennessee, Knoxville. The producer of many documentary and narrative films, including *Deadheads: An American Subculture, Wondrous Events: Foundations of Folk Belief,* and *Root Doctor,* she currently teaches media writing, production, and media studies at the University of North Carolina at Greensboro.